INTRODUCTION

Olympic Dreams by Melanie Panagiotopoulos
Revisit the magical moments of the first modern Olympic Games of 1896 with the American sports enthusiast and classicist, Henri Preston. When he meets the lovely Sophia, a young woman who shares his love of classical studies, sports, and, most importantly, God, he suspects that his heart is on the mend. But is his condescending and judgmental manner toward the people hosting the games going to cost him the love and respect of the lovely and highly intelligent Sophia?

Olympic Hopes by Lynn A. Coleman
Dameon's family is in desperate need of money along with many others in the grip of the Depression. Hoping for prize money, he hitchhikes from Massachusetts to Lake Placid, New York, to compete in the Olympic speed skating event. Unable to compete, he finds some temporary jobs with the aid of Jamie Preston, a volunteer on the Olympic Host Committee, who offers him a place to sleep at her family's rented farmhouse. He soon discovers this family is not farmers but wealthy business owners from Princeton, New Jersey, with a home in Athens, Greece. Can there be any hope for them when wrongful accusations fly?

Olympic Goals by Kathleen Y'Barbo
When Preston Grant could no longer run for God, he began to run from Him. Unfortunately, his running nearly cost him everything he once held dear. Can he forget his own pain and cheer the woman he loves on to victory in Rome at the 1960 summer games? All Bonnie Taggart ever wanted was to settle down with Preston Grant and raise a family. Now she must choose between her dreams of Preston and her goal of Olympic gold.

Olympic Cheers by Gail Sattler
Brian McDermot has helped build what has become the 1988 Calgary Winter Olympics. Sophie Dupuis is planning to build the 1992 Albertville, France, Winter Olympics. As the Calgary games progress, they watch the games together but with different perspectives—Brian sees the completion of his Olympic project, whereas Sophie works toward the beginning of her part in the timeless Olympic saga, one that is important to her family's past. . .but that is soon to become even more important to her future with Brian.

OLYMPIC MEMORIES

Four Stories of Inherited Athleticism and Love

LYNN A. COLEMAN
MELANIE PANAGIOTOPOULOS
GAIL SATTLER
KATHLEEN Y'BARBO

BARBOUR
PUBLISHING

OLYMPIC MEMORIES

Olympic Dreams

by Melanie Panagiotopoulos

To the Greek people—both the ancient and modern—
for giving to the world such wonderful examples
to follow in the fields of art, drama, medicine,
science, philosophy, literature, mathematics, and sports.

In loving memory of my father-in-law,
Demosthenis Panagiotopoulos (1912–1986).
Husband, father, lawyer, governor. . .but mostly,
a man of dignity who ran a good race.
We have missed you dearly.

Note: In honor of Greece being the home not only of the ancient games but also of the first modern Olympics and of the interim Olympics of 1906, I have used the Julian calendar, which was in use in Greece in 1896. It differs by twelve days from the Gregorian calendar, which is in common use around the world today. Thus, according to the Julian calendar, the games were held from March 25–April 3, 1896, whereas according to the Gregorian calendar, the dates of the first modern Olympiad were April 6–15, 1896.

Chapter 1

Athens, Greece—March 25, 1896

It seemed Sophia Papadopoulou had been waiting for the opening day of the Olympic Games her entire life. Bands played, people laughed, and church bells rang throughout the city. Flags from the thirteen nations that were participating in the games fluttered on tall masts in the breeze.

Sophia didn't think she had ever seen her countrymen happier. It was the seventy-fifth anniversary of the Hellenes shaking off more than four hundred years of occupation, the opening day of the Olympic Games, and Easter time. Easter Monday, to be exact.

Looking over the mass of joyous people filling every nook and cranny of the stadium and the hillside above, she breathed out, "Thank You, God. Thank You for the miracle of this day." She clasped her gloved hands tightly together as she always did when emotion threatened to overwhelm her.

This day's ceremonies had been achieved through the

labors of so many people—from the most powerful world leaders to the poorest of Greek villagers. Both Sophia and her dear father had dreamed about and worked toward this day for years. Coming from a village near ancient Olympia, her father, who had been a classicist like herself, had passed on to her his dream of resurrecting the Olympic Games. Today was a realization of hopes and dreams, sacrifice and hard work on their part.

Sophia looked at the vacant seat next to hers. She only wished her father had lived a few months longer in order to share the day with her. She took a deep, controlling breath as grief over her father's passing welled within her. Before he closed his eyes to earth and started his life in heaven, he had asked Sophia to promise that she wouldn't be heavy of spirit on this day. Rather, she should rejoice in these games and what they meant to the people of Greece and the rest of the world. Sad as her heart remained, she was determined to take pleasure in these events for both of them.

With more than three hundred athletes meeting in the city, the fact that Athens had been put into shape fast enough to host the games—the most extensively organized international sporting event the world had ever seen—was a feat Sophia attributed to God above. Not even two years had passed since the Paris International Congress for the Reestablishment of the Olympic Games had decided unanimously to have Athens be the site for the first modern Olympics.

Knowing the inside story, as her friendships allowed her to do, Sophia understood that no other major city in the world had been willing to take a chance on such a venture. Not only wasn't there much time or money to accomplish all that was necessary for such an expensive event, but most people thought that the Olympic Games would be a tremendous flop. Few individuals believed that sport was good not only for the body, but also for the mind and the spirit.

In spite of the opposition they faced, Baron de Coubertin and Dimítrios Vikólas, president of the International Olympic Committee, had persuaded the government and people of Greece to host these first games.

Looking around at the quickly filling stadium, Sophia smiled. Well, the Greek people certainly did believe in the idea behind the revival of the Olympic Games. The original games might have been in honor of the pagan god Zeus, but today these games had nothing to do with such a notion.

Sophia's heart thrilled with the adventure of this day, an adventure that had begun earlier in the century when the world had rediscovered ancient Olympia. That thought never ceased to bring a poignant smile to her lips. The academic world claimed it had rediscovered ancient Olympia then. But she knew, as did most from the area surrounding ancient Olympia, that it had never been lost. All the people of the area knew where it had lain, protected and hidden throughout the long years.

Feeling a shadow against her, Sophia glanced up just in time to instinctively reach out and brace a man who looked as if he were about to fall on her lap. Even though he was slender, when her gloved hands caught his jacketed arms just below his shoulders, she was glad for all the hours she had spent playing lawn tennis. Otherwise, she doubted she would have had the strength to prevent his squashing her flat as a bug.

⊗

Mortified, Henri Preston felt his neck go hot, and he was certain that his face had turned the color of a beet.

"I. . .beg. . .your pardon, madam," he stammered out, even as he endeavored to right himself.

But that proved only to put him in a more compromising position as his left leg with its ailing knee refused to bend. Except for the few times he had chastely kissed his ex-fiancée's cheek, he had never been this close to a woman.

And those times had never felt like this moment.

Not only did the young woman smell delicious—like the jasper plant that had wafted its sweet fragrance to his nose that morning as he awoke from the most restful slumber he had had in months—but she also radiated a vitality he hadn't known a woman of refinement could possess.

She was small, yet if it weren't for the strength in her arms, he was certain he would have landed in her lap. In spite of the choice location of their seats and the French styling of her clothing, to possess such strength, she must be a servant in one of the elegant neoclassical homes he had passed on the stately avenue while on his way to the stadium. He didn't want to reflect on why thinking she was below his social status disappointed him.

Henri tried again to right himself, but his right knee landed against her shin. She grunted—a sound that confirmed his belief that she was well below his social rank. His ex-fiancée, Amanda, would never have allowed such a crude sound to escape her mouth.

Regardless, his endeavors were only making the situation worse. His nose was practically touching her cheek. He had only to turn his head and his lips would brush against hers. He didn't move a muscle. He hadn't felt so helpless since the afternoon of his accident two months earlier, when he had been rendered unconscious in the street after being pushed into a carriage by a mob of workmen. He almost wished for that blessed oblivion to return.

"My apologies," he muttered again but didn't know what he could do to rectify the situation. The seats all around them were taken, and the space was too small for him to twist his way around. Ever since his mishap and the resulting injury to his knee, he had loathed crowds of any sort, but he had thought he would be able to manage the large turnout at the stadium since it was under such precise control. He just hadn't planned on meeting a woman who caused his attention to stray from the focused concentration it took for him to walk without a cane. Truth be told, the sight of so many women in brightly colored dresses had shocked Henri. They numbered as many as the men. He never would have been able to get Amanda to attend such an event. He had tried.

"Ella, ella—come, come." A deep, booming voice spoke from above and behind him. Half a moment later, Henri felt strong, capable hands grasping him under his shoulders and lifting him to his feet as if he were a small child. A hearty laugh erupted from the big man, who sported a handlebar

mustache, as he patted Henri on his shoulders in a good-natured way. "We men. We do anything to get close to pretty women, eh?" he said in heavily accented English.

"No. I. . ." Henri looked at the young woman, glad that his view was again from the vantage of standing on his feet. As a classicist, he had an advanced knowledge of ancient Greek and a working acquaintance with modern Greek, but all that knowledge seemed to escape him. He could only think in his native English. "I do beg your pardon." He flicked his hand toward his knee. "It's this leg of mine."

But he knew that his leg wasn't really the cause of his misstep. It was actually the woman. Something in her demeanor and her look had stunned him, so that his leg froze up on him.

She nodded and smiled, and he noticed that her eyes seemed to shine like honey touched by the Grecian sun. She motioned first toward the ticket he still clutched in his hand, then to the vacant seat that was between her and the big man who had come to his rescue. "Is this your place?"

"I believe it is," he replied.

"Please. Sit down." She laughed softly, a sound that wasn't unkind but rather sweet and giving and meant to assure. And friendly. Really friendly. "I think it's safer—for both of us—if you do."

Grinning unlike he could ever remember himself doing since reaching adulthood, Henri nodded and sat on the cushion. But then came the problem of how to arrange his leg. The man on his left was big, and there wasn't any room to stretch his leg out in that direction without hitting the backs of the people in front of him. He began regretting his decision to sit among the populace of the city—albeit in an expensive section—rather than with his friends down in the Princeton University area. Just then, the woman shifted her legs closer to the woman on her right, her skirt crinkling femininely upon itself. She motioned for him to use the extra space for his leg.

"I truly am sorry," he repeated, but he couldn't hide the relief he felt at stretching out his throbbing leg.

"If you apologize again, I really will get angry," she said, cutting him off with another of her smiles, which effectively eased the sting of her words. "I am quite certain, sir, that you did not fall on me purposefully."

The woman intrigued him. Not only did she speak English perfectly with the softest, most pleasing accent his ears had ever heard; but there was also an open, confident air about her that fascinated him. The fact that she was even talking to him was astounding. In this day and age, it was rare for a woman to speak to a man with whom she was un-acquainted. He was astonished when the thought whisked through his mind that he hoped she wouldn't stop. "I do hope that I didn't hurt you."

"Not at all." She lightly flexed her gloved fingers, an un-feminine movement Amanda and her friends would never have used. Somehow, Henri found the movement appealing.

"I play quite a bit of lawn tennis," she explained. "I think it has held me in good stead."

"Lawn tennis?" He couldn't believe it. He had tried for the two years of their courtship to interest Amanda in the game. But she had considered sports of any kind vulgar, especially for well-brought-up young women. He had tried to convince her that lawn tennis was a very refined sport—one even kings and queens played—but he had failed at every turn. He had regretted that. He had thought it something they could do together. Not that it mattered anymore.

She nodded. "I love it." A woman in service playing lawn tennis? That seemed strange to him. But perhaps things were done differently in Greece than in America. She probably had a very forward-thinking mistress or, better yet, a mistress who needed her to make up a pair.

"Myself as well," he finally answered.

Chapter 2

In light of the problem he seemed to have with his leg, the man's enthusiasm for lawn tennis surprised Sophia.

"You play?" she asked, but at the quick, stormy look that turned the previously friendly, if embarrassed, lines of his face into one that was as ominous as a North Aegean gale in midwinter, Sophia not only regretted her insensitive question but felt fingers of apprehension slither up her spine.

She wasn't used to people getting angry with her.

Especially when her question was, if a bit too personal, a logical one in light of his having almost sat on her because of an obvious physical limitation. She sensed, however, that not only was there something about his affliction that went much deeper than just the injury sustained to his leg, but that the limitation must be of a relatively recent nature. Overriding all her questions was the fact that he was a guest in her country, and it pained her to think that she might have offended him.

"Oh, I do believe it is my turn now to apologize to you," she said. "Other than it being none of my business, that question was an absolutely insensitive thing to ask."

Slowly, he seemed to will the muscles in his face to smooth out—a very nice face, she noticed, with a straight hairline, a fine chin, and nicely spaced brown eyes.

Motioning down to his knee, he spoke, but his voice was deep with strain, reinforcing her belief that there was more to his injury than just the obvious physical problem. "This is temporary. When it fully recovers, I'll be able to participate in sports again. I play lawn tennis, but I particularly like running."

She thought she understood his anger. Compassion filled her. Waving down toward the track, she softly ventured to ask, "You were to have competed?"

A good-natured grimace made his brown eyes light up in a self-deprecating way. "No, madam. Unfortunately, I don't have the abilities of the men of my alma mater."

"Alma mater?" She knew that the term was Latin and that it meant "fostering mother." But he obviously had to be using it in a different context.

He motioned toward the Americans sitting together farther down in the lower tiers and explained, "The College of New Jersey. Although I should start using its new name: Princeton University."

"Princeton?" Her eyes widened, and clasping her hands together, she couldn't help the excitement that coursed through her veins. She had realized immediately, of course, that he was from America, and that had thrilled her. But Princeton, New Jersey? It was just too wonderful. She had wondered if she might perhaps meet any of the Princeton team and now thought it positively providential that God had placed a man from that city next to her.

As his lashes narrowed and he regarded her with suspicion, the pleasure she had felt in discovering the name of his home city was effectively doused. "That. . .is. . .correct," he replied carefully, as if she possessed some ulterior motive for being moved by his divulging the name of his town.

What did he think she was after? Sophia wondered. She was only filled with great surprise because, after the games were over, she was going to be moving to Princeton to live with her aunt and uncle in order to further her education under the wise tutelage of her uncle—a renowned professor of the classics at the university.

But this man's distrustful attitude in turn made her own innate apprehensions about revealing her background to strangers emerge, and she decided against blurting out the news about her move. What did she know about the man anyway? He was a stranger and from a foreign land, after all. Could she trust him? Her father had raised her to be open with people, much more so than was the norm for women of her time, but he also taught her to mingle her openness with caution.

She motioned in the direction of the men she assumed to be his acquaintances. "I understand that Princeton University has sent a fine representation of men to compete in the games." Her aunt and uncle had written to her about Mr. Garrett, Mr. Tyler, Mr. Lane, and Mr. Jamison, the four men hoping to return with wreaths of olive branches and first-place medals of silver. With a history of athletic participation at their university, they were experts in their fields, had trained extensively, and thus possessed very good chances of bringing honor to themselves, their school, and their country.

He glanced over toward the team standing off in the distance. "They are fine athletes," he agreed. "The Boston Athletic Association has an excellent and well-trained team, too. Not to mention Mr. Connolly of the Suffolk Athletic Club. And despite the long, oceangoing journey, they all seem to be in the pink."

"In the pink?" she repeated, needing clarification.

He turned his face with its neat and tidy mustache that rode perfectly above his upper lip to her. She blinked when she now read admiration in his gaze. The man was an enigma. Only a moment earlier, he seemed wary of her; now he regarded her with what she could only call esteem. "You speak English so well, I just assumed that you would recognize that colloquial phrase."

She didn't know why his compliment should delight her—especially since his mood swings gave her cause for alarm. He seemed to change with the speed of lightning—one moment stormy and suspicious, the next open and warm and agreeable. But pleased she was. "Thank you."

"How did you learn to speak English with such precision?"

"From an English lady who used to live in Athens." She didn't tell him that the lady had been her nanny, then governess. And after her mother had died when Sophia was four, her nanny had become a dearly loved mother figure. When Miss Jones had had to return to England a few years earlier to look after her elderly mother, it had been a sad day for Sophia.

"I'm impressed. I think for young ladies to learn languages foreign to their native tongue is a very good way for them to train their minds."

She looked at him carefully. Another personality change? He seemed to be treating her now with a condescending air. His attitude invited a sharp retort, but she reminded herself again that he was a guest in her country. And, too, in spite of his seemingly patronizing ways, there was some elusive *something* about him that she liked immensely and that kept her from judging him too quickly or harshly. Besides, wasn't one of the main objectives of the Olympic Games to bring people of different countries together in order to break down the social stereotypes people have about those of different backgrounds? With that in mind, she only replied, "Oh, I agree."

But she couldn't help but wonder what he would say if he knew that besides her native Greek, she also spoke French, German, and Russian, as well as holding a university degree in Latin and ancient Greek. She had heard from her aunt and uncle that American men were a bit old-fashioned when it came to women being educated. She just hadn't come up against such prejudice during her studies at the University of Athens. She decided to keep her educational background to herself for the moment. "Do you speak a language foreign to your own tongue as well?"

He sat up straighter in his seat, a gesture that almost made Sophia laugh. She had to add "stuffy" to the eclectic list of attributes that described his character. "I not only read ancient Greek and Latin but have a working knowledge of modern Greek, too."

"You have trained your mind nicely then," she said, turning his own words concerning women back on him.

He looked at her sharply. She was certain that he had caught her innuendo. She was glad. It meant that he wasn't blind to his condescending manner; perhaps even that it wasn't an attitude he wore naturally. To her mind, it meant that there was hope for him. That somehow made her glad.

"A man must have a trained mind," he remarked carefully, with an edge of stubbornness to it. "Anything else makes a man less than what he can be. And a body that is trained complements the mind."

She decided to ignore the first part of his statement for now—it was true, after all. She would have said *person* rather than *man*. Instead she commented on the second point he had made. That was an area in which they both definitely agreed. Smiling into his brown eyes, she said, "That's the idea behind sports and most especially"—she waved her hand to encompass the stadium, which was alive with the movement of people—"behind the reestablishment of the Olympic Games."

He tilted his head to the side and flashed her a pleased look. Regard was back. She gladly accepted it. "You seem to know a great deal about the games."

"Umm," she agreed. "Their revival was a dream of my father's and mine for as long as I can remember. Our Olympic dream." That's what they had called it. "We worked very hard to realize it."

❧

Her statement startled Henri. He wondered how she had

worked for the revival of the games. Perhaps her father had a part in some aspect of the physical labor involved in organizing the events. Maybe her father was in construction and had helped to refurbish the ancient stadium in which they now sat.

But even though the reestablishment of the games was something Henri had always desired, he nonetheless fought an inner conflict. As a classicist, he had great respect for the civilizations that had been ancient Greece and Rome— particularly Greece. In a world where the irrational had ruled, they were the first who advocated the use of the mind, the use of reason, something that in turn enabled them to understand and interpret the gospel message. But as a Christian, he had a hard time reconciling his fear that the revised Olympic Games might not be in honor of Jesus Christ. The original games had been in honor of the mythological Zeus, after all.

"You don't believe that they are a pagan reinstitution?" he heard himself asking the young woman, something that surprised him. The way he was conversing with her was most extraordinary.

"The Olympic Games will be whatever a person makes them to be," she responded without hesitation, easily using her ancient ancestors' famous logic to the same high degree as they. "If someone is a weak Christian or a nonbeliever, then they will probably make sport their 'god' or else use the games for commercial advantage. But for those who are Christians, it is a marvelous way to bring others to God. Paul did that, after all."

He blinked. "Paul?" He had lost her somewhere along the way.

"St. Paul," she clarified. "He used the ancient Isthmian Games—which were second only to the Olympic Games—to show people how they should live the Christian life. 'Know ye not that they which run in a race run all, but one receiveth the prize? So run, that ye may obtain. And every man that striveth for the mastery is temperate in all things. Now they do it to obtain a corruptible crown; but we an incorruptible.'"

"First Corinthians 9:24–25," he said softly as he identified the reference for the words she had recited from the Bible. Taking into account his love of sports, those words were some of his favorites. It came as a shock to consider that he hadn't thought about them in a very long time—about any of his favorite Bible verses.

"That's right," she confirmed. "Paul was most likely in Corinth when those games took place. My father always held that he might have left Athens because they were to occur, and Paul wanted to be in the city at that time. He knew it would be a very good way to reach more people with the good news he was hand-delivering all over the Hellenic and Roman world. And St. Paul used those footraces in the Isthmian Games as examples of the Christian life."

"I'd never really thought about that." But even more, Henri was impressed that he was having such an intellectual conversation with this young woman. He couldn't remember ever talking to a woman like this. Not even his mother. Definitely not Amanda, who was, he suddenly realized, exactly like his mother: a beautiful social butterfly whose main concern was the womanly pursuits of running a good home—something in which she excelled—and wearing the latest fashions from Paris.

That thought brought his attention to the woman's attire. From his mother and Amanda, he had learned to recognize fine apparel. Although of a very expensive Parisian quality, the clothing she wore was in a style several years old. He suspected that her mistress probably handed down gowns to her. Amanda had done that with less fortunate cousins of hers and occasionally with her maid.

The young woman nodded. "I've always wondered how many people who attended those games became Christians after being taught about the gospel by Paul." A great commotion at the entrance of the stadium drew her attention. "Oh, look! The royal family is arriving! The games are soon to start!"

Chapter 3

*R*oyal family? Henri thought he must be dreaming. He had never been anywhere where a royal family was in attendance. Amanda would have been very impressed. He wished he had thought to tell her that royalty would be present when he had been trying to get her to arrange their wedding so that they could come to Athens—and the games—on their wedding trip. Amanda considered herself Princeton "royalty." But in lieu of the circumstances, he knew that it was better that he hadn't told her. She might have married him just for that reason.

He shook himself, wanting to get his thoughts away from Amanda and, most importantly, from what she and Percival had done to him. Wasn't that the main reason he had suddenly, in spite of the injury to his leg, decided to travel to Athens, after all? He had to be far away from Princeton on this day, the day that he was to have wed Amanda.

"Do you recognize any of the people?" He was in awe at how easy it was for him to ask questions of the woman beside him. He had never possessed good skills when talking with women, not even with Amanda. But somehow with this Grecian beauty, it just seemed natural. He considered that it was probably the situation, the import of the day. Even still, he was certain that they would never have started conversing if he hadn't practically sat on her lap. He felt his ears turning red at the remembrance.

She nodded toward the group of men who were walking toward the entrance of the stadium to greet the new arrivals. "The tall man is Crown Prince Constantine. He's the president of these games, and if not for him, the Olympic Games wouldn't be taking place today. He not only lent his moral support and that of his name and title to get others to work toward this goal, but he himself has toiled day and night to achieve it."

"The crown prince? The future king?" Henri had had no knowledge about this. He hadn't actually given much thought to what the people of Greece had had to do in order to host these games. But looking around him at the marble stadium—*marble*—and at the brightly dressed guards who had moved such a vast amount of people so successfully into such a relatively small space, he knew that a tremendous effort had to have taken place.

He noticed how she didn't take her eyes off the people walking in the center of the stadium as she answered him. "We quite simply owe the Olympic Games to the crown prince. Without his taking up the banner that had been thrust upon him by the Olympic Committee only last year and his, in turn, having formed the necessary committees in order to organize these games, we wouldn't be sitting here.

None of us would." Her lips curved into a poignant smile. Giving a little nod, she finished with, "He's a good man."

From the soft tone in her voice, it seemed to Henri as if she knew the man personally. But how could that be possible, particularly for one of her social class?

"Walking beside him are his brothers, Prince George and Prince Nicolas, as well as the rest of the cabinet." He looked at the men she indicated. "The three brothers are about to greet their father, the king. King George I, king of the Hellenes."

Henri turned back to her. "Pardon me, but don't you mean king of Greece?"

"No," she insisted. "King George is king of all Hellenes, whether those living in the small bit of land the modern country has managed through God's gracious provision to recapture or those still living in the Greek lands that are under the strong arm of foreign domination."

Looking around him, Henri could better understand that Hellenic nationalistic pride than when reading about it from the comfort of his study in Princeton. The city of Athens—and even more, her gracious, welcoming people— hadn't disappointed him. He had to agree with numerous other historians and classicists of his day that the only thing separating these people from their ancient ancestors was time. The staging of this event in such a short period proved it. He doubted that any other country would have been sufficiently motivated to expend the energy necessary to host such a vast international event. Even more, no other nation in the world had the history—the foundation—upon which to build.

He took his eyes off the royal retinue for just a moment to glance up at the jewel of the city, the Acropolis, which reflected golden light about a quarter of a kilometer away. Below it were the reaching heights of St. Dionysius, the Cathedral of Athens. Its bells had just finished sounding the hour of three. The columns of the temple of Olympian Zeus—the place where lawn tennis was to take place in two days' time—were even closer. And rising from its Doric columns in a beautiful garden on the other side of the Ilyssos River stood the Zappeion, the hall that had been built using Evangelis Zappass's bequeathed money. Henri recalled how Zappass was the moving force behind the Olympian Games, those athletic competitions staged in Athens four times from 1859 to 1889.

Henri had read how Athens had been neglected and left in squalor by its Turkish overlords. When made the capital of the new modern Greece in 1834, it had held only a few houses that were livable. Yet after a little more than sixty years, Athens was once again a gem of a city.

As the band started playing the royal anthem, all the people in the stadium rose as one from their seats, and a giant cheer resounded all over Pindar's violet-crowned city. The Greek people were greeting their royal family, greeting these Olympic Games. The woman beside him clapped her hands and looked over at him with a face flushed with pleasure. "Isn't it glorious!" she exclaimed.

It *was* glorious, the entire feeling of the moment: the royal family walking toward their seats, the men resplendent in their uniforms, the ladies, in their gowns; the band playing;

the ovation of the people. But more than anything, the day was glorious because Henri was next to this woman whose exuberance and intelligence made him feel alive and content in a way only his participation in sports and study had ever made him feel before.

He could hardly comprehend his own joy, an emotion that had been missing from his life for such a long time. With sudden insight, he realized that his joy had left him as his courtship with Amanda had progressed. Could it be that he had done the same thing to Amanda? Was that why she had found love elsewhere, in the arms of his best friend?

He watched as the people continued to wave their hats and shout out in delight while the king and queen seated themselves on the royal thrones with the porphyry-colored coverings. They greeted everyone around them: to their right, the members of the cabinet and the members of the Christian clergy, both Greek and foreign; and to their left, the members of the diplomatic corps and foreign representatives.

Then Henri watched as the crown prince, obviously full of esteem for his father, advanced toward the king and delivered a speech.

A hush fell over the people sitting in the stadium and over those on the two hillocks above as all strained to hear. Because of the proximity of his seat and the acoustics, Henri could follow almost all of the historic speech. Never was he happier to be able to understand the modern Greek language.

"O King!" The crown prince's deep voice rang out as he addressed his father with respect. "The fulfillment of the decision of the International Congress of the Olympic

Games, which was convened in Paris, that these be held for the first time in Athens, was one which imposed itself on the country in which these games have their birth and prospered.

"In order to carry out this decision, whatever was possible was done in a short time. I am persuaded that the imperfections of the undertaking will be judged with just indulgence as due to the natural difficulties and the lack of instruction which only acquired experience can teach. . . .

"May it be, O King, that the revival of the Olympic Games binds closer the links of mutual affection of the Greek and of other peoples, whose representative for the Olympic Games we consider ourselves happy to welcome here. . . .

"With these hopes, I pray, O King, that you graciously agree to declare the opening of the first International Olympic Games."

Crown Prince Constantine finished, and all eyes watched as the king stood. He was a man with the dignified appearance one would expect of a sovereign.

"He's standing! The king is standing!" the woman beside Henri sang out.

Looking over at her, Henri wasn't surprised to see unshed tears making her eyes sparkle with the brilliance of pebbles on a beach bathed by gentle waves. She smiled over at him but nodded back toward the king. "Look! He is about to officially open the games! Don't miss it. It's one of the happiest and most historic moments of our time."

As the king, with a sonorous voice that didn't disappoint, answered the man who was both his son and crown prince, Henri knew that the woman was right. It was not only one of the most historic moments of their lives, but, even more unusual, one of extreme goodwill. Nations were meeting together not in a battlefield or for a political conference, but rather in order to play together, to have fun on equal terms. Henri breathed out deeply. It was a freeing sound.

For the first time, he was almost glad that Amanda and his best friend, Percival, had deceived him. He was glad to be here in this stadium filled with people of such noble and farsighted spirit. But mostly, he thought as his gaze settled on the soft but strong profile of the beauty beside him, he was glad to be standing next to the young woman whom the Fates had placed next to him. He wouldn't want to be anywhere else in the world.

Pulling his silver pocket watch—an heirloom from Switzerland that had belonged to his grandfather—from the fob pocket of his vest, he glanced at it. Three and a half hours past noon.

If he had been in New Jersey, he would have just been awakening to his wedding day. He gave a slight shudder. Yes, even though he was still bitter over the humiliation of having been discarded by his fiancée, he was definitely thankful to be here.

The sound of the king's voice brought Henri's attention back to the events in front of him. King George's voice was full, possessing a deep, rich quality that Henri was certain was capable of reaching every person in the marble stadium. "I declare the opening of the first International Olympic Games in Athens," the king proclaimed. "Long live the nation! Long live the Greek people!"

Goose bumps prickled across Henri's arms as the king's welcoming words vibrated through the air, resounding from hill to hill. When the sovereign lifted his right arm, thunderous cheers arose from every mouth, from every nation represented, including Henri's own. Happiness itself seemed to vibrate in the air.

"Isn't it wonderful!" the woman beside him exclaimed, touching her lace handkerchief to the corners of her eyes, where moisture had gathered.

"Wonderful," Henri agreed and swallowed as emotion clogged his throat. But "wonderful" didn't begin to describe what Henri was feeling. The word *freedom* did.

Freedom to start again.

Freedom to live again.

Freedom to maybe, just maybe, forget the pain and humiliation of having been deceived by the two people he had thought himself closest to. And freedom to move on with his life. It was the seventy-fifth anniversary of Independence Day for the modern country of Greece. Henri was beginning to feel that it might be independence day for him, too.

He glanced over at the young woman again. His eyes lingered on the golden strands of honey-colored hair that were shining out from beneath her straw hat. What was it she had said? To run the Christian life?

Maybe he would rediscover at these games how to let go of the anger, the bitterness, and the suspicious nature that had befallen him.

Maybe—he glanced around at the stadium—maybe the wonder of these games would help him to do even that.

Chapter 4

The starter's pistol cracked. The runners took off, streaking down the track. In just twelve and one-fifth seconds, Francis Lane of Princeton won the first heat for the 100-meter race. Henri shot to his feet along with every other person in the stadium.

The games were on, and Lane was the first man to cross the finish line. The fact that it was only the first trial race of three didn't make a difference to Henri or to anyone else in the stadium or on the hillsides above.

All felt the thrill of Lane breaking the tape as if they had done it themselves.

All knew what it meant.

It was the start, the actual start of the games. After a 1,503-year intermission, the Olympics and all the good they represented were on again. The Olympic Games of the modern era had begun.

Henri found the Greek people to be exceptional spectators, cheering the men from all thirteen represented countries with an enthusiasm that was as encouraging as it was infectious and strong. But when their own Mr. Chalko-kondylis, a member of the Athens Athletic Club, came in second after Curtis of the Boston Athletic Club in the second heat of the 100-meter race, the stadium quite understandably went wild. One of their own athletes—a descendant perhaps of one of the ancient competitors—would be competing in the finals of the 100-meter dash on the fifth day of the games.

And Henri's heart matched the excitement when the young woman's hand, in her extreme joy, landed on his forearm. Even through the wool of his jacket and her kid gloves, the feel of her slender fingers resting against his arm became the highlight of the moment, more so even than the historic events going on all around him. And when she lightly squeezed his arm, Henri's mouth went dry while the skin on the back of his neck went hot.

"Oh," she exclaimed when her eyes registered what she had done. As if discovering her hand too close to a lit stove, she immediately lifted it. He wished she hadn't. It had felt so right. "I'm so sorry. I'm used to having my father with me and—"

"No apology necessary," he cut in, glad for the noise that hid the gruff quality in his voice. "But I would count us even if you would honor me by the relinquishment of your name." Didn't her touching him justify that?

Her lips turned up in that sweet way that he was coming to expect of her—that way that made her eyes sparkle with fun while a little pinpoint dimple appeared on her left cheek. He could feel his own lips replying in kind. "I'm Sophia Papadopoulou."

Sophia. What a pretty name. He wanted so badly to use it,

to feel it as it rolled off his lips. But he knew that that would have to wait until he was invited to address her thusly. Even though she was most likely only a lady's maid, to use her first name without her permission would be too forward, a social blunder. He nodded and, slightly doffing his bowler with his right hand, replied, "Henri Preston at your service, Miss Papadopoulou."

She laughed, a sound that was like a soft summer breeze ruffling the leaves of a poplar tree; then glancing at the place on his arm that she had just touched, she responded, "Well, Mr. Preston, I'm afraid that I have already used your services, so thank you."

"My pleasure." After a moment, Henri added, "This is the third time you've mentioned your father." But when sadness washed the smile away from her face, he wished he had refrained from pointing out her having done so before. But he was curious about the man.

"He passed away several months ago. I miss him so."

Since she wasn't wearing black, he hadn't expected to hear of the man's death. He hated seeing her bright eyes dull with pain. He had only thought that her father was out of town or indisposed. "I am so sorry." He truly was.

She nodded, but taking a deep, settling breath—one that probably required strength far in excess to that needed by the athletes who competed in the games—she looked out over the stadium and replied, "I am, too, but. . .today is not a day for sorrow. My father did not want that, and he made me promise him that I would be out of mourning clothes for Easter and for these games. Today is Easter Monday, and one of the most extraordinary days Athens has seen in a very long time. Look!" She pointed down toward the sandpit. "They are preparing for the second event."

"The hop, step, and jump," he agreed as he watched the ten men ready themselves. Even though the men possessed well-built bodies, he knew that if they could exhibit in their triple jumping just a fraction of the strength that he suspected it took for Sophia—he might not be able to call her by her given name, but that couldn't keep him from *thinking* of her in that way—to sit in the stadium without the father she had obviously loved, they would win.

They watched with one hundred thousand other spectators as Connolly of the United States won first place; the Frenchman Tufferi, who had been raised in Athens, second place; and the Greek Persakis, third.

For the first time in the modern Olympics, a winning flag was hoisted at the entrance of the stadium on a mast that had been erected for that purpose. Men of the Greek Royal Navy had the honor of performing that duty.

As Henri watched the Stars and Stripes going up, with the symbol of the cornerstone of Western civilization—the Acropolis of Athens—shining in the background, moisture touched his eyes. Glancing around him at the wildly cheering people, Henri wasn't sure whether he was most moved about one of his countrymen being the first winner in the modern Olympics or about the way the freedom-loving, democratic Greek people were so grandly applauding a flag that wasn't their own.

It was an amazing occurrence.

Had a city full of people from one nation ever cheered another country's flag so enthusiastically? At that moment, Henri knew that this was what the Olympics were all about. This was the idea behind the peaceful games—humanity coming together in a show of brotherhood just as God desired of His people.

While surrounded by more people of Greek ancestry than he'd ever seen before in his life, Henri realized that, for the moment, all political and social barriers had been dismantled. It was by far one of the most astonishing occurrences Henri had ever seen, and he wondered if the modern world had experienced such a thing before or if it would ever again.

Then the Boston contingent, forgetting they were in a country where college and club cheering were unknown, shouted out in unison across the field: "Rah, rah, rah! Rah, rah, rah! Rah, rah, rah! Connolly!!" The people in the stands stared at the performance with a certain dazed surprise. But in the hospitable if inquisitive fashion Henri had come to expect from the people of Hellas, they did not show disdain. Instead, they heartily joined in.

"A most extraordinary sound," Sophia said of the unusual cadence of his countrymen's cheers. "I've heard about club cheering. I just never had the. . ." It seemed to him that she was searching for the correct word. "The *pleasure* of experiencing it before."

He couldn't help the laughter that burst forth from him. She was so endearingly diplomatic; truthfully, the unison-rooting cry could sound like a barbaric battle shout to a stranger's ears.

"Do you like it?"

She added her laughter to his. "Why ever not? It's what makes these Olympic Games so special: people coming together with all their strange and wonderful ways. These ways will soon, however, become familiar in a manner in which they never could hope to do otherwise. Familiarity is—after the love of Christ—the best breeding ground in the world for friendship, for peace." She laughed. The American group cheered heartily once more, and when many of the Greek people joined in, she put her hand out to the side in a "see what I mean" gesture.

As the day progressed, Henri couldn't have agreed with her more. Friendship—something he had never really shared with a woman—was developing between Sophia and him at the Olympics in a way that never would have been allowed to happen under normal circumstances.

When the last event of the day was completed and the royal party had departed amid more enthusiastic hoopla, Henri and Sophia talked and laughed together as they left the stadium. They walked down the brightly lit streets toward *Platia Syntagma*—Constitution Square. About a hundred thousand people in the crowd around them acted as chaperones.

The city was floating in lights while the festive sounds of people chatting, bands playing, and happy children everywhere permeated the air. The feeling seemed to seep into Henri's very being, and even though there was a great crowd of people, he hardly noticed them and certainly didn't feel the usual discomfort he'd experienced in such conditions since his accident. Christian brotherhood abounded in this city of chiming church bells and freely flowing goodwill.

Even more, the feelings that Sophia inspired in him left Henri nearly spellbound. He didn't know whether it was because of the historic day or because of her. The only thing he was certain of as he bade her good night in front of one of the aristocratic avenue's more stately homes was that he was looking forward to the morrow and the opportunity to see her again. To look forward to a future event was something Henri hadn't experienced in a very long time.

"You promise to attend tomorrow afternoon and to sit in the same seats?" He would have liked to offer to buy them for her, but he knew that, in spite of their growing friendship, that would have been totally inappropriate.

"I do."

Tapping his hand to the brim of his bowler, he said, "Then I shall see you tomorrow afternoon."

"Tomorrow," she agreed, and with graceful steps, she bypassed the wrought-iron gate that led to the front entrance of the mansion and, with a feminine rustle of her skirt, glided toward the side entrance of the home.

Henri frowned. By doing so, she confirmed his suspicions of her being just a servant and probably not even a lady's maid. The mistress would have breezed up the marble steps to the massive front portal of the home. That's what Amanda would have done even though—his gaze took in the elegant edifice—Amanda's home was not nearly so grand as this one.

Turning away, his shoulders slumped at the blatant reminder of the differences in their backgrounds. Not only did they come from different countries—itself an imposing obstacle in Henri's opinion—but a major social barrier stood between them, too. During their free-flowing conversation that day, he had quite forgotten his suppositions about her social standing. He walked toward the Grande Bretagne, his hotel, mindful that his leg was suddenly starting to pain him. Funny how he hadn't felt his knee while in Sophia's company.

He slapped his hand against his thigh.

How could she possibly be a servant? She certainly didn't speak like any servant in his parents' home or in the homes of any of his acquaintances. Maybe servants were different in Greece, or maybe she was a less fortunate relative of the mistress of that stately, neoclassical mansion.

That thought filled him with hope.

Yes, that had to be it. Her father *had* recently died, after all. But how could he find out for certain? And find out he must, before he allowed their relationship to progress any further.

Chapter 5

Henri spied Sophia from a distance, sitting in the same seat she had held the previous day. All thoughts about her background fled. The only thing that was important was that she was there, waiting for him, and that she hadn't been a figment of his imagination as he had feared when he had awakened in the Hotel Grande Bretagne that morning.

Seeming to sense him, she turned. The bright, unaffected smile that shone out from her face almost made him lose his balance again. But this time he had come prepared. He had brought his umbrella, which could be used as a cane and was able to support his weak leg. When her eyes twinkled up at him in a mischievous way, as if to say, "Remember yesterday?" he knew that she had caught his faltering step.

"Do you want me, perhaps, to catch you again?" she asked with a wry twist of her head.

Actually, he wouldn't have minded a repeat at all, and for a moment, he wished he hadn't brought his umbrella. To feel her hands on his arms, to have the excuse to get so close to her that her breath mingled with his, to drink in the sweet scent of her. . .

He put an abrupt halt to his thoughts.

What was he thinking? He had to get control of himself. Relying on the proper way for a man to greet a woman, particularly one he had known for only a short time, he tapped the brim of his bowler and very formally replied, *"Kali mera*—Good day, Miss Papadopoulou."

Her back stiffened. Her smile disappeared and the twinkle in her eyes with it. He knew that he had embarrassed her by ignoring her good-natured banter, by not continuing to use the easy manner in which they had been speaking yesterday.

His conscience pricked him.

He wasn't being fair either to her or to himself. He didn't want formal small talk. He wanted—no, needed—a continuation of the informal yet meaningful conversations they had shared the previous day.

When she returned with a generic and colorless, "Good day, Mr. Preston," he knew that he had to do something to rectify the situation. He didn't want prim and proper responses from her. He wanted—no, desired above all else—the excitement and warmth they had shared since first meeting.

Sitting down, he asked, "Did you hear?" In a bid to make up for the discomfort he had caused her, he put as much enthusiasm into his voice as he could muster. "Your countryman, Mr. Pyrgos, won the fencing match this morning. The first Greek to win an olive crown."

When she clasped her hands together, he breathed a sigh of relief. Once again, she seemed to have forgiven him for his unpredictable moods. She had done that several times the previous day with just a look to show that she was aware. But he knew that he had to get control of the dark moods that came upon him with the speed of a serpent's strike. How many times could a person forgive another, after all?

"I know!" she exclaimed. "The news is being spread around the streets like the Easter light." He recognized her reference to the lighted candle the priest presented to the congregation on Easter. Upon the words *Christos Anesti*—Christ is risen—the candle was passed from the priest to the congregation. Symbolizing Jesus, it was passed throughout the previously dark sanctuary. Jesus' redemptive act brought light to the entire world just as that little flicker of a single candle brought its light to the entire congregation at the Easter service.

It was a beautiful analogy. Having arrived in Athens on the previous Saturday, he had felt so blessed to have witnessed the moving and thought-provoking service during the first minutes of Easter morning.

"People are so excited." Sophia's eyes widened in question. "But were you there? Did you go to the Zappeion this morning to watch the fencing contest?"

"I did."

"Oh, I wish I had known." A pout, however sweet, puckered her lips. "I would have gone, too."

She would have gone. He could have kicked himself for not asking her. It hadn't even occurred to him that she would be interested or, even more, that she would be able to be away from her work in the morning as well as during the afternoon hours. But it made the question he had been contemplating that much easier to ask. "In that case, would you honor me by accompanying me to the lawn tennis competition tomorrow? You did say that you play." He still found that amazing, even if she was just an unfortunate relative and not a domestic.

She nodded. "I was planning on going, actually. Mr. Boland of Great Britain is supposed to have marvelous technique."

She knew about Boland? That proved she was a serious player. "So I've heard. And your own Mr. Casdaglis is supposed to be very good as well. Shall we go together then?"

"I. . ." She looked down at her hands before looking back at him. "I would prefer to meet at the ticket-seller booth."

Of course. They were very newly acquainted, and even though they could talk to one another unlike he had ever been able to converse with anyone else, they possessed no common friends and hadn't been introduced in the normal way. Her reputation was at stake. He admired her for her care. It only served to raise her further yet in his esteem.

"You are correct, of course," he replied. "That would be best." He was rewarded when a relieved smile crossed her face, a smile that made him feel good in a way he couldn't remember feeling before. Silly as it sounded, it felt that to please her was the reason he had been born.

With their plans for day three of the games thus decided, the afternoon became a repeat of the previous day—one of the more wonderful of Henri's life. From the animated way in which Sophia acted as they cheered a variety of events, he thought that it had to be a fine day for her, too. And when that evening the Acropolis was lit, Henri was delighted to have Sophia by his side as they walked the city streets, studying the world-famous buildings upon the "high city" from different angles. The Erectheion and the Parthenon both seemed to float above them with a dignified, timeless quality.

They were ambling down a narrow street, gazing up and admiring the way the multicolored torches lit up the huge blocks of stones that provided the foundation to the ancient walls when Sophia tripped over a dog sleeping in her path. Her feet seemed to go flying out from beneath her.

"Agh!" she screamed, while the terrified dog jumped to its feet and moved out of the way with a yelp, followed by a deep, guttural growl.

Time seemed almost to freeze as Henri saw his arms reaching out for Sophia in an excruciatingly slow manner. He willed them to move faster. He had to prevent her body from connecting with the ground; he had to spare her that pain, as none had been able to do for him several months earlier.

"Sophia!" He felt more than heard the cry come from him. Using every ounce of power he possessed, he lunged forward. He managed to get his right arm around her waist and to somehow pull her back against him, saving her from falling upon the hard road.

Her breathing was labored, and she was trembling. "I've got you, Sophia. I've got you," he cooed as his other arm went around her and he held her steady.

"Henri." Her breath fanned against his hot neck. "Thank God you were with me."

His own breath caught in his throat. Yes, thank *God*. Numerous times Henri had contemplated why God hadn't protected him better the afternoon of his accident, but now it was as if he knew the answer. As extraordinary as it might seem, Henri wondered if it could have been for this moment—so that he would be with this woman in this far-off city and be walking next to her in her time of need.

"A man's heart deviseth his way: but the Lord directeth his steps."

Is that what he had been doing by courting Amanda? Devising Henri Preston's own way and neglecting his Christian walk while doing so? Was his accident only the instrument God had used to direct Henri's steps in the way He meant for them to travel? Perhaps God intended for Henri's steps to cross paths with Sophia Papadopoulou. If he didn't know better, Henri would say Sophia was the one meant for him in the same way that Eve had been meant for Adam. He shook his head. So many new and astonishing emotions had assailed him since coming to Athens, since meeting Sophia.

And one of them came from the closeness with which he again held this woman. But as he realized that he was even nearer to Sophia now than when he had almost landed in her lap the first day of the games, the thumping in his heart changed from that brought about by fear to that brought about by holding in his arms the woman who had so quickly come to mean more to him than any other.

His cheek rested against the top of her uncovered head. He wanted to brush his lips against the softness of her hair, which smelled of jasmine and everything clean and feminine. He settled for lightly running his hand over her back. It could be considered a caring gesture in light of her near fall.

But when she pushed back from him, he suspected that she understood the truth. Smoothing her wool coat down and accepting with a smile her hat and purse from a young boy who had retrieved them for her, she said, "I'm fine now, thank you." She looked around her. "But where is that poor dog?"

The "poor" dog chose that moment to let out a deep, long, warning growl from where it stood ten feet off by the corner of the nearest house. It looked at Sophia with narrowed, suspicious eyes. Sophia took a step toward the animal.

Henri reached out for her. "Sophia, he's scared." He spoke with the low, soft tones meant to reassure the nervous dog. "Scared dogs are dangerous dogs."

"But I'm not frightened of him, Henri." She minutely jutted her chin toward the now-silent but ever-watchful dog. "He knows it."

Looking at the canine, Henri could tell Sophia was right. Using its instincts, the dog obviously sensed her lack of fear. Henri also suspected that the dog knew that she hadn't meant to hurt it.

"*Ella etho*—come here," she said in Greek to the dog, while, with a soft motion like a cloud gently rolling across a summer sky, she put her hand out toward it. "*Ella etho, skilaki.*"

She was right to use the word *skilaki*. It was just a young dog. Probably no more than nine months old. Henri watched, mesmerized, as she took another step closer, then another, toward the dog. "*Min fovase, skilaki*—don't be afraid, doggie."

When the dog lowered its head and its tail started moving softly from side to side, Henri knew that she had won the *skilaki* over. But when the dog sidled up to her in a happy, lop-sided way, and Sophia, heedless of her gloves and skirt, bent over to rub him, to coo to him with the reassuring tones that no creature alive could mistake for anything but care, Henri was the one won over by Sophia Papadopoulou. The woman was unlike any he had ever known. Amanda couldn't abide four-legged creatures, something that had always made Henri sad. He sometimes liked dogs more than he did people.

Henri joined Sophia and knelt down to pat the *skilaki*'s soft and silky golden head. "You love dogs, don't you?"

He watched as, with a smile, she let the dog lick her hand. "One has only to look into their eyes to see all the love they have to give. All that a dog asks for in return is to be loved."

Isn't that all he had wanted of Amanda? To be loved in return. But had he ever really loved Amanda? Compared to the feelings this woman was bringing out in him in such a short period of time, he was beginning to think he had never experienced true love.

Henri was just wondering what they were going to do with the dog when the door of the nearest home opened. A woman, who was short as a child but broad as a tree, emerged.

"There you are, Jack," she said in Greek to the dog, and the animal turned to her with a happy, puppy-dog leap. "I wondered where you had gotten off to, boy."

"I'm sorry, but I tripped over him and startled him," Sophia offered.

"Was he by any chance lying in the middle of the road?" the woman asked while rubbing the dog under his golden-haired chin in a familiar way.

Sophia nodded.

"His favorite place." She gave the dog a loving pat on his head. "Maybe by the time he grows up, he'll find a safer place to sleep. Until then, I'd better keep him fenced in." The woman looked at Sophia with the sharp inquisitive eyes of a matron. "I hope you didn't get hurt falling over him."

"No." Sophia waved her hand negatively. "I'm fine."

The woman answered with a nod and a relieved smile. *"Christos Anesti,"* she said in parting.

"Alithos Anesti," Sophia replied, smiling after the wagging tail of the dog as it followed the woman into the house.

Their leave-taking words captured Henri's attention. "I'm amazed at how the people of this land use that greeting at Easter time." He had heard it spoken all over the streets, in the hotel, at the stadium, and in cabs since arriving.

Her eyes narrowed in question. *"Christos Anesti*—Christ is risen—and the answering reply of *Alithos Anesti*—truly He is risen?"

He nodded.

"But," she tilted her head in question, "what else would one say during *Pascha*—Easter?"

He shrugged. "Happy Easter?" Even to his ears, the greeting sounded like a generic one compared to the Greek manner of referring specifically to the *reason* for Easter.

"Umm." She nodded. "Kind of like *Merry Christmas.* In Greek, it's *Kala Christouyenna,* the literal translation being *Happy Christ's Birth.*" She gave that light laugh of hers that always seemed to make him smile. "I guess we Greeks just like to be specific. Perhaps it's a way to keep the meaning behind the celebration from being defused through the centuries."

He nodded. "And probably one of the reasons God entrusted Greeks and their language to the writing and safe-guarding of His Word."

Her eyes widened in pleasure. "Henri, what a lovely thought."

It felt good to make her happy. "Shall we, Sophia?" he asked and held out his arm to her. He hoped she would take it. When she smiled up at him as she tucked her arm around his own and they started walking in the direction of her residence, he felt like they were the perfect couple.

He considered it a bit strange as they ambled along the festive road that she didn't have a beau to escort her on these special days. But that was only an unwelcome reminder of the gulf that stood between them. He understood that, without a dowry, it was very hard for young women in Greece to marry. And she was probably too smart for most men of her class. He suspected that when her father had seen how quick of mind his daughter was that he had taught her himself. Henri really didn't know where their friendship might take them. The only thing he was certain of was that he enjoyed her company. And for now—for the days of the games and while he was in Athens—that was enough.

A smile touched his lips as he realized that, since the incident with the dog, they had been calling one another by their first names.

It just fit, was natural and right.

Just like their amazing friendship.

Chapter 6

As planned, Sophia met Henri at the ticket-seller's booth the next day, and they watched lawn tennis together that day as well as the next. Although Sophia found Henri—for that was how she called him since her near fall—to be a gentleman and of an enlightened spirit, she sensed that something about him wasn't quite in line with her own spirit.

He had moments of moodiness—as if he were fighting some inner battle. From little things he had said, but even more from those things left unspoken, he seemed to place an inordinate amount of emphasis on temporal qualities. Social background, wealth, and education seemed of utmost importance to him—almost to a degree that she found unbecoming. She was friend to both servant and royalty; she had a feeling that, upon being offered a choice, Henri's preference would be the latter.

That concerned her and prevented her from being totally open with him about her background and her upcoming move to the city of his birth. She didn't want to chance him finding those worldly qualities in her life more intriguing than the person she actually was, and she suspected that her social trappings would impress him.

And, too, there were those inner conflicts that seemed to seethe within him like a pot ready to boil over. For him to reconcile those contradictory forces was the key to their having a future together. She was certain that only through the grace of God could that be accomplished.

But in spite of those shadowy moments, she enjoyed Henri's company immensely. She welcomed the chance to become acquainted with an American—and one she found special in so many ways—before moving to his country. As the days wore on and they spent more time together, Sophia decided to trust her judgment in people, something that had never failed her before. She was almost certain that something had hurt Henri in the past to bring out those dour moments.

Patience, she knew, was the key.

Patience, but even more, her faith in God. She felt that God had brought Henri to the seat next to hers on that first day for a reason. Just the fact that Henri hadn't stayed cemented to his own group, as most of the foreigners did, but rather chose to sit among the populace spoke positively to her.

He was living up to one of the main reasons for the Olympic Games: that of being an avenue through which cultures could get to know one another.

And getting to know Henri better was something Sophia liked. A lot.

There were still five days of competition remaining. They had time.

And if she decided that they might have a future together, they would have plenty of time to get to know one another more completely when she moved to Princeton. But the knowledge of her planned move would remain her own until she made absolutely certain that Henri liked her for herself and that her wealth—about which she would eventually have to tell him—would have no effect upon his feelings for her.

Sophia knew that he thought her quite low on the social ladder and that it bothered him. It was quite a remarkable situation in which to find herself, one that was rather exhilarating because it was so different not to have to fear that a man's interest in her stemmed mainly from her social status and wealth. Even though Henri seemed to have a bit of a problem with thinking her beneath him on the social scale, she preferred that to the alternative—a situation in which she had found herself on more than one occasion.

Day five of the games opened with much more serene weather than the previous day. That was something for which Sophia—along with everyone else—was grateful. It had been an unusually cold and rainy Easter period. But all agreed that cool weather was better than unseasonably warm weather. Staying in a marble stadium baking in early summer heat would have felt like sitting in a furnace.

When Sophia exited the side entrance of her home that morning, she caught the scowl that crossed Henri's face. But she pretended not to. She would let him believe what he wanted to. It suited her purpose. He had never asked her about her background. He'd just assumed. She only used the side entrance of the house because she had given all the servants time off for the games, and she found it easier to manage than the colossal front door.

"Can you believe all these masses of people?" she exclaimed upon reaching his side and taking his offered arm. "Isn't it exciting?"

A slight shudder was not the answer she expected. "I don't much like large multitudes of people." The dour mask was in place, and he sounded like a sour, eighty-year-old man.

"Why ever not? I find the people thronging toward the stadium in such a lively mood enlivening."

"I find it annoying." He leaned toward her as a group passed close by them. "I don't like people pushing up against me or touching me."

"Oh." She removed her hand from his arm. That brought back the witty man she enjoyed as, with a smile that curved his mustache slightly upward, he reached for her gloved hand and placed it back on his arm.

"I don't mean you."

She slanted her gaze over to his. "Ahh, just everyone else in the world?"

"No, I—" He breathed out deeply. "I'll tell you about it sometime, okay?"

Her heart seemed to do a little leap within her chest. That was one of the things she had been waiting for—for him to trust her enough to tell her the cause of his black moods. *Thank You, God.* But when would he tell her?

"For now, can we just walk to the stadium?" Henri asked, then smiled. "Both the final of the 100-meter dash as well as the marathon run are being held today." He pulled his watch out of his pocket. "The marathon runners should have already started from the village of Marathon."

She nodded, although it was on the tip of her tongue to say, "That's why so many people are out today," but she refrained. She didn't want to draw attention to the size of the crowd again.

Yet she knew that the marathon and the drastically lowered price of tickets accounted for the huge crowd. Even though there hadn't been a race longer than twenty-four laps in the ancient Olympic Games, when Michel Brial, a linguist and student of Greek mythology, suggested including a "marathon race" at the first modern Olympic Games, the idea had been greeted enthusiastically.

The race grew directly out of ancient Greek history and commemorated the feat of the Greek runner Phidippides. The ancient Greeks used foot couriers to communicate between their city-states. Phidippides became the most famous when the Persians landed an army on the plain of Marathon north of Athens, threatening the city. Phidippides was asked to run to Sparta, a distance of 140 rugged, mountainous miles, for help. He did this in forty-eight hours. Then he ran back to Athens, donned his armor, marched with the Athenian army twenty-five miles to the plain of Marathon, and spent a day fighting the Persians. After the battle, he ran back to Athens with the news of the outcome. But this was too much running even for Phidippides, and with his dying breath, he gave out the news of the Athenian victory.

"I hope a Greek wins the marathon race," Henri said, pleasing her immensely. She was certain there was at least one American participating in the race. It would have been natural for him to want one of his countrymen to win. "It would mean so much to these people, to the country," Henri continued. "After all your countrymen have suffered over the centuries, they deserve it."

"What a nice thing to say, Henri." Especially after having just been upset by so many of "these" people all around him. When he said little things like this, golden words of sweet encouragement flavored by an extensive knowledge of history and truth, he captured her heart just a bit more. It showed the goodness and warmth and reasoning ability that were in his soul and encouraged her belief that they might have a future together.

They watched preparations for the final of the 100-meter dash with tense excitement. Almost before the race started, the winner crossed the finish line, Mr. Burke of the Boston Athletic Association. The crowd stood respectfully as the strains of the "Star Spangled Banner" played in honor of the American's accomplishment.

As they returned to their seats amid the happy cheers, Henri said, "I am so glad to be sharing this moment of triumph with you, Sophia. I am so thankful to the Fates for bringing us to the same seats."

Her heart seemed to plummet to her stomach in dismay. *The Fates?* She knew that many people used the term loosely when describing an act of destiny. But she had a feeling that

Henri didn't mean it that way. And that concerned her. Before she made an issue of this, she had to make sure of his meaning.

"You mean the Fates in terms of God, don't you?"

He turned to her, and the look of pain that washed across his face confirmed her worst fears. "To be honest, Sophia, I'm not so sure about God's care in my life anymore."

Yes, he had been hurt in the past. Hurt very badly. She sent up a prayer that the correct words with which to guide him might come forth from her mouth. She knew that trite words would not suffice. Sophia had learned through their days together that Henri was a very intelligent man who possessed a great deal of book learning. As her gaze scanned out and over the people in the stadium, she sensed direction about the way in which to respond.

"Henri, look around you," she urged and waved her arm to encompass the thousands who were still cheering the raising of the winner's flag, the American flag. "If ever a people had reason to doubt God's care, His provision, it's these people. But they haven't. Not ever. Not even when they were made slaves in their own homes, made to hold worship services in hiding for more than four hundred years, and made to give up their children in tribute payments to the Turkish sultan. Greek life for most of the past nineteen hundred years, from the moment of birth to the moment of death, has revolved around Jesus Christ. Even when in chains."

She watched as Henri's gaze traveled over the thousands of happy, cheering people—people who had suffered so much tribulation throughout history because of their faith in Jesus

Christ. Sophia knew that he was listening.

She continued to speak. "It is because of Him that they had the faith to believe that they would someday be free again. Their land was a battleground for centuries, their works of art either stolen or blown up by invading powers." She pointed over to the Acropolis, which had been terribly damaged during the Middle Ages.

"And you know what, Henri? I think the Greeks went through all that pain because, even though it was a culture that was one of the greatest the world had ever seen—the Western world, most definitely—they took the revelation of Jesus Christ and literally ran with it." She pointed down to the runners who had competed in the final of the 100-meter race. "Just as those runners ran their race."

" 'Know ye not,' " he softly recited words from 1 Corinthians, " 'that they which run in a race run all, but one receiveth the prize? So run, that ye may obtain. And every man that striveth for the mastery is temperate in all things. Now they do it to obtain a corruptible crown; but we an incorruptible.' "

She thrilled to hear him repeat the words she had quoted on the first day of the Olympics. His brown eyes stared deeply into hers for a moment, and as emotion gathered in her throat, she could only nod. But she had more to say, and since Henri was listening, she spoke. "I believe, Henri, that these people, the givers of the first Christian church, have been on the devil's personal agenda because of it. They have been persecuted for their faith more than any other—both by Christians and unbelievers. And with so many Greeks still living under the strong arm of an invader's rule, I don't think it's over yet."

She paused and leveled her gaze on him as she challenged, "I seriously doubt, Henri, that anything you have gone through in your life comes close to equaling that amount of suffering."

&

She was right. For the first time, Henri saw the immaturity of his thinking. He had never been in chains for the gospel, nor had an invading force taken his home; nor did he have to worry about a foreign ruler stealing any children he might have in the future. He had suffered the duplicity of his fiancée and his best friend and, in consequence, suffered in an accident.

He scowled. He didn't like how immature that made him seem. His faith—his Christian race—had faltered at the very first test placed upon him. How could he actually question God's care for his life? And to this woman, this very special woman? Embarrassment made his neck burn.

"I stand corrected, Sophia. Thank you for pointing out the error of my thinking."

&

Sophia knew that she was right when, in spite of his moods, she felt that there was something very special about this man. How many men would so quickly agree to erroneous thinking? Not even her father had been able to do so with such speed. There was hope for Henri. Much hope. She would just trust that God had indeed brought them together for a reason. Maybe even for that most superb purpose that could come to pass between a man and a woman: so that they might journey down the path of life together.

Reaching out, she took his hand in her own and gently squeezed it. Words were unable to convey the joy she felt.

When he wrapped his fingers around hers and smiled, she knew that they were communicating on a level that was touched by love. And she hoped—hoped so much—that Henri might become the man with whom she could travel through life. They still had barriers to cross, things to confess to one another, but "with God all things are possible."

She didn't realize she had spoken her thoughts aloud until Henry nodded and repeated her words. "Yes, Sophia. I am beginning to believe once again that with God all things truly *are* possible."

&

A little while later, when the young Greek runner Spyros Louis entered the stadium covered in dust and drenched in sweat, it was obvious that all the people in the stadium felt the way Sophia and Henri did, too. The cheers and whistles of more than one hundred and twenty thousand people clapping and shouting rang out across the ancient land. Bands played the national anthem; white doves were let loose into the sky; and the blue and white Greek flag with its Christian cross was hoisted upon the victor's mast while people waved thousands of little flags from their seats. Handkerchiefs and hats went flying into the air, and Sophia threw herself into Henri's arms over the joy of the moment.

"Isn't it wonderful!"

But as on the first day of the games, Sophia's use of the word *wonderful* didn't begin to describe what Henri was feeling as he held Sophia in his arms. As on the night when she had tripped over the dog, that feeling, that sense of *completion* did.

It felt so right to have Sophia close to him both physically and as a companion, a partner walking through these days of their lives. And as his arms held her tightly, he knew that, in spite of their differences, he wanted this woman with him always. She was smart and beautiful and, most important of all, a woman of faith.

She actually had much more faith than he. He frowned. Something seemed wrong with that.

"Oh, look!" She stepped back from him and pointed down to the right side of the track as Crown Prince Constantine and Prince George ran with Spyros Louis as he covered the final meters toward the king.

Henri could hardly believe his eyes when the man who had just run for—he pulled out his pocket watch to calculate the time—two hours and nearly fifty-nine minutes bowed to the king. The king stood, regarded Mr. Louis with deep emotion, and waved his nautical cap in honor of the glory the runner had brought to the land. But when Henri saw the two princes, who were joined by their brother, Prince Nicolas, lift the sweaty, dirty, purple-faced runner high upon their shoulders, he knew that social barriers were being dropped in a manner the world seldom beheld.

He looked over at the Christian clergy—the Greek Orthodox priests dressed like their predecessors of the early Christian period in their flowing robes; the Protestant clergy with their dark suits and starched white collars; and the Catholic priests in their black garb—and he felt certain that they noticed it, too. Even from a distance, he could tell that their eyes shone a bit too much to still be dry.

Who ever heard of princes—one of them a future king—holding a peasant, a poor shepherd, upon their shoulders?

But then, had the world forgotten that a simple carpenter from a remote part of the mighty Roman Empire had been and always would be God incarnate?

Had he forgotten?

No. Henri knew that he had never forgotten that, for which he was thankful. But what he had forgotten was to live by faith—to run the Christian race the verses in 1 Corinthians described even when under attack. To persevere as the people of this country had throughout the centuries and as the young shepherd from the village of Maroussi, a few kilometers north of Athens, had done in order to win this grueling race.

He glanced over at Sophia. She was waving a little blue and white flag in one hand and a lacy handkerchief in the other. He so wanted to tell her everything about him now. And even more, he knew that he was ready to learn everything about her. If princes could carry a peasant upon their shoulders, couldn't he forgo social status and love the woman God, not the Fates, had brought to his side?

Yes. Where Sophia was concerned, most definitely yes.

Somehow he knew that she would fit in anywhere: in the halls of kings and in those of servants, too. But more than any other place on earth, she would perfectly fill the rooms of his home—the home he fervently hoped to one day make theirs together.

Chapter 7

"M in me sproxete—don't push me! Don't push me!" Henri shouted to the throngs of people who surrounded them as he and Sophia walked in the direction of the train station that evening.

Sophia looked at him. His face was flushed, and she saw fear in his eyes. His attitude alarmed her. She knew he disliked crowds, but this bordered on the irrational. "Henri, no one means you harm."

Henri didn't seem to hear. He not only scowled at a young man who bumped up against him, but he also gave the young man a little shove in return.

"Henri!" Sophia had never seen a grown man push another.

"I don't like people rubbing up against me! I don't like mobs!"

"Henri, this isn't a mob. All these people are happy and good-natured. They're celebrating as they make their way to the festivals being hosted in Piraeus tonight." They had planned on going to Athens's port city, too, but Sophia realized she had to get Henri away from the crowd as quickly as possible. She was thankful that her home was close by. "No one means you any harm. Everyone is celebrating Spyros Louis's victory."

"I don't like being around so many people," he repeated, making Sophia determined to get to the bottom of this fear tonight. He said he would tell her about it sometime. She had decided. Now was the time.

She was relieved when they arrived at her home without additional incident and was even more gratified when she saw that her butler, *Kyrios* Nicholas, not only was at home but also had the front door open as if he had been waiting for her arrival.

"Come, Henri." Holding tightly to his arm, Sophia guided him toward the massive portal. Henri—in his own world of misery—didn't seem to notice that they entered through the front door or even the deference with which Nicholas treated Sophia. She was glad of that as she led Henri to the informal parlor at the back of the house, the one where her father and she used to spend the majority of their time.

Not wanting Henri to determine that she was the mistress of the home, she motioned to Nicholas that she wished to be alone and seated Henri on her father's favorite chair, the one closest to the fireplace.

"Stay here and calm yourself. I'll go for tea," she said, and sliding the pocket doors behind her, she asked Nicholas, who was hovering in his unobtrusive professional way, to prepare a tea tray. Until Nicholas's return, she leaned against the door, praying for the right words and the strength with which to deal correctly with Henri.

"Madam," Nicholas said a few minutes later as he placed the laden tray on the hall table, "a note from the palace arrived shortly before you returned." He proffered the silver tray that held the envelope with the official stamp on it.

"Thank you, Nicholas." She broke the seal and read the note. It was an invitation to the breakfast banquet being held at the palace on Sunday after church service. It brought a smile to her lips. Even with her father gone, his good friend, who was one and the same as the king, had not forgotten her. The gracious man and his sons had never forgotten all the help—both financial and scholarly—her father had proffered toward the games. Replacing the invitation within its envelope, she pushed it into her pocket, and with a nod for Nicholas to open the doors, she carried the tray into the cozy parlor.

Henri looked up only after she had placed the tray upon the end table. Even though the contrite expression he wore softened her heart, it did nothing for her mind. She was determined to learn the reason for his black moods this evening. She had to. The letter in her pocket demanded that she tell Henri all about herself as well. And soon.

⊗

As Henri sat looking at the warring emotions that played across Sophia's face, he realized he had never been more disgusted with himself than at that moment. Shame filled him. Never had he raised his voice at people before, much less pushed a fellow human. What had prompted him to do so and in front of Sophia, of all people?

Holding his hands out, he simply said, "Please believe me when I say how sorry I am. I panicked."

"I know that, Henri." Her skirts rustled as she moved to sit on the chair opposite from him. "You were like Jack, the dog that I nearly trampled the other day. You were growling and showing your teeth out of fear."

He grimaced at the analogy but had to admit to himself that it was sound.

"But I don't know why," Sophia continued. "What has happened in your past to cause you to behave in such an abominable manner?" Her glance went to his injured leg before returning to his face. "Whatever it is, I think it must have something to do with your leg."

Was it that she was so intuitive, or did she actually care for him enough to notice when things weren't right with him? It was an amazing thought. Amanda had hardly even noticed when he caught a chill. Henri knew then that if he hoped for a future with Sophia—and in spite of the social and geographic barriers that stood between them, he knew he wanted that above all else—then he had to be honest with her.

"Henri, if you don't tell me, I will have no choice but to terminate our friendship. I cannot keep company with a man whose attitude so alarms me."

He had frightened her! *Dear Lord, no!* She was the last person in the world he wished to alarm, the last person he wanted to hurt. But looking at her—at the lines of worry around her eyes, the tightness with which she held herself

67

erect on the edge of her chair—he knew he had done exactly that.

So he told her.

Everything.

He told her about the evening two months earlier when he had walked in on his fiancée and his best friend and found them locked in one another's arms. And he told about his mad flight away from Amanda's home and about the mob of striking workmen who had pushed him into a charging carriage, thus giving him his fear of crowds. He told her everything, and as he did, he could see the lines of tension release their hold on her face, her body. Hope—a living, breathing emotion—filled him.

"My faith in people was severely shaken by their duplicity," he said. Even though he knew now that for Amanda to call off their wedding was the best thing that could have happened, it was the act itself seemingly coming from nowhere—the surprise of it—that affected him still.

"Henri, God is the only One who will never disappoint us. Never have we been told to put our complete faith in people. Only in God."

"But why did He allow it to happen?" He pointed down to his knee. "And with such terrible ramifications." Although he felt almost certain that the accident had happened so his feet would walk the path God had laid out for him since the beginning of time—a path that would merge with Sophia's—he wanted to hear her answer. He *needed* to hear her answer. And he didn't care if he sounded like a little boy. His faith had become like an immature child's. He was beginning to wonder if it had ever been anything more.

" 'God moves in a mysterious way, His wonders to perform,' " she finally said, and he couldn't disagree.

"That's a beautiful Bible verse."

Sophia smiled. "I think William Cowper, the English poet who lived in the last century, would be very flattered to hear you say that."

"English poet?"

She nodded. There was no judgment in her look, only that sweet, giving countenance he was coming to love.

Love?

That stopped his thoughts cold.

Did he *love* Sophia?

Looking at her, he knew that other than God, his love for her was the only thing of which he was certain. His thoughts started moving smoothly again, gently, perfectly. He loved her—loved her—and wanted to spend his life with her. Any differences in their backgrounds could be overcome with love and overcome even more by having God in their lives.

He shook his head, trying to keep his thoughts on their discussion. "I think I have to study the Bible more."

"I think it might just help you more than anger or distrust will."

"I truly do apologize for my behavior." She probably wouldn't want him to court her now, much less spend her life with him.

"Because you are holding yourself accountable and because you have explained the situation to me, I accept your apology. This time," she qualified with a smile. "But please don't ever behave in such a fashion again."

"I never have before, Sophia. I don't see why I ever should again."

"Good." She reached for the porcelain teapot. "Would you like a cup of tea?"

"Actually"—he reached for her hands and stilled them in the action of pouring—"what I would like, Sophia, is to ask. . ." He paused and licked his lips before continuing. "Is there anyone. . .of whom I might ask permission. . .to court you?"

The teapot plunked back down onto the silver tray. "You want to court me?"

He nodded and, reaching out, gently cupped her smooth cheek with his right hand. "Dearest Sophia, don't you know I love you? My fondest wish is that someday you might find me worthy to be your husband."

❧

"Henri!" She couldn't have prevented the gasp that came from her had her life depended upon it.

He loved her!

Even thinking she was a servant or a less fortunate relative, he loved her.

Loved her!

But she had to make sure. "We come from such vastly different backgrounds."

"I don't care, Sophia. If you don't want to leave Greece to live in America, I will move here." She saw discomfort fill his eyes, and she knew that he was uneasy with the subject. "And I don't need a dowry, my dear. I'll admit that I always thought I did. But since meeting you, I have come to learn that riches of spirit and mind are so much greater than those of the pocket. You don't have to worry about not having a dowry, my dear," he repeated. "I love you for who you are, a woman of faith, integrity, and knowledge, who has very quickly come to be my very best friend. On the contrary, I am the one who comes to you with empty hands. Oh, I don't mean mammon—I have more than enough of that to last us a lifetime—but where faith is concerned, I am very poor. I have a great deal of learning to do in order to catch up with the woman I love. And I will do anything—*anything*—to prove to you that I love you."

"Anything?"

"Anything," he affirmed.

"Even to trusting me when you might have reason to do otherwise or possess innumerable questions?"

"Even then," he affirmed.

"Then, yes, Henri. There is someone of whom you can ask permission to court me." She fingered the letter in her pocket. The king had promised her father that he would act in that role should she require it.

"Who, my dear?"

She smiled broadly. "Why, one of my father's best friends, of course."

Chapter 8

She didn't tell him who that might be. Only that they were invited to that man's place of residence after church on Sunday at 11:30 A.M. sharp.

They spent the next day just like any other young couple in love. Well, not exactly. No other young couples until that day had ever been spectators at the final match of the Olympic lawn tennis competition. In the singles, Mr. Boland of Great Britain took first place with Mr. Casdaglis of Greece coming in second. And that evening the fairy-tale feeling of the day was only compounded when a special performance of Sophocles' play *Antigone* was presented in its original text at the Great Theater.

Henri was moved almost to tears by it. To be in the city where that playwright had watched his own plays being performed was to experience a timeless quality that was similar to the revival of the games. This play wasn't from a hundred years ago or two hundred. It was more than two thousand years old. To watch it performed in its original ancient Greek with Sophia by his side made it magical, an experience he didn't think could be topped.

But that was his thought only until the next day, when the carriage he had ordered as a special treat for Sophia pulled up in front of the residence of the man from whom he was to ask permission to court her.

"Sophia." Henri looked from her to the massive neo-classical building—the largest in Athens—and its marble porch enclosed by ten huge columns of Pendelic marble. "We're at the palace."

"That's right," she said, but from the pinpoint dimple that had appeared in her left cheek, he knew that she was enjoying herself. She removed an envelope from her satin purse and handed it to him. "Within, you will find our invitation to the breakfast banquet hosted by King George."

Although his hand accepted the fine stationery from her, his mind was still trying to understand what was going on. *"Our* invitation?"

"Well, mine, actually. You are my guest. But don't worry. I have made certain that you are welcome and that a place will be set for you," she assured. Then, to the sound of her gathering her taffeta skirt—a new one, he noticed, and one of the latest of Parisian fashions—she asked, "Would you please help me alight from the carriage, Henri?"

But Henri couldn't. Not yet. "Sophia, please tell me what's going on."

She looked at him with eyes that couldn't hide the merriment she found in the situation. "What do you mean?"

"I mean, how is it that you have an invitation to this banquet?" Henri knew that those invitations were the most coveted pieces of paper in Athens, probably in all the world, that day. He had wished he could attend but knew only a select few were invited. "And what has this got to do with my asking your father's friend permission to court you?"

Sweetly waving the liveryman away, she sat back and, taking his hands gently within her own, spoke. "You really have no idea, do you, Henri? And yet still you love me?"

He shook his head. "No idea about what? And love you? That is like asking me to breathe. To love you is natural for me. I'll always love you. No matter what."

She moved her fingers against his hand. Henri wished their hands were ungloved. He needed the security of her skin touching his own right now. The world—his world that had become so perfect since meeting Sophia—seemed to have gone topsy-turvy again. But unlike when Amanda had "surprised" him, this time he would trust God to make everything right again. *Dear Lord,* he breathed within his soul, *help me to continue to trust You. Help me to run my Christian race and to win.*

"You don't know how much that means to me, Henri," she whispered, and he had the feeling that happy tears weren't far from falling. But with the fortitude he had admired in her so many times, she blinked them back. "I asked you the other night if you would trust me always. Will you?"

"Yes." It was a pledge. He would trust her—God and her both.

"Then let's go into the palace. I promise you will learn everything there."

Swallowing, he could only nod. Nod and trust.

The great hall was filled with people, winners of the Olympic competitions, foreign athletes, and representatives of the foreign and domestic press, among many others. The table was in the shape of the Greek letter *Pi*—π—with two arms extending from each side of the main section. Henri and Sophia were directed to a lavishly set place in the middle of the left table.

Henri would have asked questions of Sophia, but as they walked to their seats, she spent most of the time greeting others. She seemed to know half of the people there. For the first time in Henri's life, he felt truly humbled by his surroundings. He had been invited to breakfast with a king. He—Henri Preston of Princeton, New Jersey. Speech at that moment—even to Sophia—would have been nearly impossible.

He was also beginning to realize that there was a great deal more to the woman he loved than what he had assumed. And he knew that *assumed* was the key word.

He stood convicted by his assumptions. For the first time, Henri realized that he had let preconceived ideas about finding a woman sitting alone in the stadium form his opinion of her. Now, not only did he hear her speak French, Russian, and German as they made their way to their seats, but he could tell that she was as at home in this setting as if she had been born to it.

That thought startled him. *Had she been born to it?* he wondered. Was Sophia a baroness, a marchioness, a duchess, or even. . .a princess? The only thing Henri was sure of as he watched her was that she was a *lady*. Maybe not a lady in the noble sense of the word but a woman of good taste and quality. He felt proud to have her on his arm, with all the pride men through the ages have felt when escorting the women they love.

When they sat at the table, Sophia turned to him with a smile that was so different from the one she had given to all the others. The smile she gave to him was flavored with a love he couldn't doubt. And he wondered what he had done to deserve this woman, this very special woman. Why should she love him?

"Are you well?"

He chuckled. "I am speechless. How do you know all these people? And even more, who are you, Sophia?"

"I am the woman you have known throughout the days of the games, Henri. No different."

"Yes, there is a difference, my dear. A very big difference." At the look of alarm that crossed her face, he hastily continued. "But I am the one who stands guilty for not seeing that there was more to you than your just being a. . .a. . ." He faltered in his speech. He couldn't say it. It seemed absurd to him now. How could he have thought her to be anything less than the lady she obviously was?

"Just being a servant or perhaps a less fortunate relative in someone's home?" She completed the question for him.

"You knew that's what I thought?"

She nodded. "But more importantly, even with your thinking that, you loved me. You, a man for whom riches and fame seemed so important when first we met, loved me, a woman who you thought was without a dowry."

Henri's neck burned at the remembrance of their conversation the evening he declared his love.

"No." She shook her head. "Do not be embarrassed. That was one of the nicest gifts you could have given to me. I will never wonder if you love me for my wealth rather than for who I am. I've been hurt in the past because of it. From when I was just a young girl, men sought me because of my father's wealth."

He had to be honest with her. "I might have, too, Sophia. Before."

She tilted her head to the side. "Before?"

"Before I came here and learned that a woman with honey-colored hair and matching eyes was more important to me than anyone else in the world. And before finding out that to run my Christian race, just as the athletes ran their footraces, was a way of living I had, without realizing it, stopped living. I am a changed man, Sophia. These games, these days with you, and, most of all, God using it all to work a miracle in my heart have changed me."

She tilted her head. "I knew even before you told me about Amanda that there was something in your past that had marked you adversely. But you know. . ." She smiled that smile that warmed his heart. "I liked you from the very beginning. There was something special about you. Something about you made my heart beat in a way it has never done before, and when you told me you loved me, I knew that I loved you, too."

"Dearest Sophia." He wished so much that he could draw her into his arms and hold her tightly against him. But he knew that such embraces would have to wait. "Please tell me." He cast his gaze around the crowd. "Who of all these men must I speak to about courting you?"

A commotion sounded at the front of the hall, and when the Corfu Philharmonic struck up the chords of the national anthem, both Sophia and Henri turned to regard the king as he entered the room.

When the monarch, resplendent in his admiral's uniform, had seated himself, Sophia leaned toward Henri and whispered into his ear, "Darling, that's the man you must speak to."

❧

After the brunch, after the speeches—and the resulting cheers that seemed to reach heaven—all the guests were invited to repair to the neighboring room where both coffee and personal conversation with the king were offered.

The king turned to Sophia after talking to the Americans from Boston and, forgoing ceremony, offered her a kiss on both cheeks. "Ah, my dear, your father would have been so proud of you for carrying on his Olympic dream."

"Sire, through the years it became my dream, too."

"I know, dear Sophia. I know." He noted her attire, and a smile lit his face. "The queen will be very happy to hear me report that you are, at long last, once again purchasing new gowns."

Sophia smiled. "Giving my clothing allowance toward the games and buying tickets to attend them were just two small ways in which I could *feel* the giving in a personal way. So many people sacrificed so much; so many gave when they had little to give. I felt that I had to do this in addition to what my father had offered."

"Your father's contribution is one of the reasons the games were successful. He would have been very proud of you for carrying on his work and for your personal contribution, as I am proud of you."

Sophia minutely bowed her head. "Thank you, sire."

"And who is this young man?" The king suddenly turned to Henri, making Henri's heart leap in his chest. As the monarch fastened his wise gaze upon him, Henri felt his mouth go dry.

Sophia placed her hand upon Henri's arm. He suspected the gesture was meant to calm him. It succeeded in doing so. "May I present Mr. Henri Preston of Princeton, New Jersey, sire. He traveled all the way from America to root for his alma mater, the Princeton University team of athletes."

The king put out his hand. With a feeling of awe, Henri took it and shook it. "Welcome, son. And thank you for your support."

"Sire, your city, your country, and your people have welcomed me most grandly. I thank you, sire, for hosting the Olympic Games in such an outstanding manner."

The king practically clicked his heels together in thanks. But then his gaze went from Sophia to Henri and back again, with a look that was more that of a father's interest than a monarch's. Henri knew that the moment had come in which he was to ask permission to court Sophia.

"Sire?"

"Yes?"

Henri licked his lips. He had never been more nervous in

his life. He had no idea about royal protocol, but since the king didn't seem to mind, he plowed on. "Miss Papadopoulou—Sophia—has come to mean a great deal to me. She has told me that you are the one I must speak to in seeking permission to court her."

"Are you asking, son?"

"Yes, sire. May I have your permission to court Sophia?"

"You are from Princeton? I think in that case that it will be possible since Sophia will soon be going to live with her aunt and uncle there."

Henri frowned. *Sophia living in Princeton? Her aunt and uncle?* The only thing that was clear to him as the king continued to speak was that there was yet more about Sophia that he had to learn. But he didn't say anything as the king continued.

"You have my permission, son, with the understanding that you will also ask Sophia's uncle upon her arrival there." He turned to Sophia. "Sophia is very dear to my family." He turned his gaze, which Henri doubted ever missed much, back to Henri. "For her to choose you, Henri Preston of New Jersey, I know that you must be a special man."

"Thank you, sire."

"Godspeed." Then, to Sophia, he added, "Please call on the queen and the princesses before you leave Hellas. I know they will want to wish you a safe journey."

With Sophia's curtsy, the king turned to the next group of people, who were eagerly awaiting his attention.

Henri turned to Sophia.

"Princeton? You're going to be moving to Princeton?"

She nodded. "That's why I was so excited on the first day of the games when you told me you were from there. I would have told you of my move then but. . ."

Henri remembered what he had thought that day. He had been wary of her exuberance, thinking she might have been planning on latching onto him with the idea of moving to America with him. He couldn't help grimacing over the irony. "But I was less than welcoming in my response. In fact, I was suspicious of you."

She nodded again. He hated the wary look on her face.

"Sophia," he was quick to assure her, "I understand. These were more of my preconceived notions about you. Only," he smiled and said, "is there perhaps anything else I should learn about you?"

She sidled up to him, and with that special smile that filled his heart and with a feminine mystery that made his blood heat up, she said, "Darling Henri, there is *so* much more. It's going to take you just about a lifetime to learn everything."

As they ambled out of the palace, across the portico, and down the marble steps toward their waiting carriage, Henri looked up into the ethereal Grecian sky and knew that learning about Sophia was an adventure he would look forward to.

Epilogue

Ancient Olympia, Greece—Summer, 1912

Sophia and Henri sat on an ancient piece of stone masonry, which they had made into their bench, while they watched their little daughter, Jamie, playing at being a butterfly among the ruins of the early Christian church. The church had been built upon the workshop of Phidias—the place where the master craftsman had fashioned the gold and ivory statue of Zeus, one of the seven wonders of the ancient world. After fifteen years of marriage and thirteen years after their son had been born, Jamie came as a surprise straight from God.

"I don't believe that we are actually here," Henri said as he gazed out over the valley of Olympia and breathed in deeply of the fragrant summer air.

Sophia laughed, that sweet laughter that had only gotten nicer through the sixteen years since they had met. "You say that every time we visit," she lovingly reminded him. Although they had made their home in Princeton, they had made regular trips to Greece throughout the years. Ancient Olympia, via the port of Katakolon, was often one of their stops.

The Olympic Games, however, were the main reason for their trips. Until now, they hadn't missed a single Olympiad. They had attended the disappointing Paris games in 1900; the unsuccessful St. Louis games in 1904; the Athens interim games of 1906, highly acclaimed games that had saved the Olympics from extinction; the successful London games of 1908; and in July, they were going to be in Stockholm for the 1912 games. They would be meeting their son there.

Henri motioned to the little two-year-old girl who not only most resembled him in appearance but was the apple of his eye. "I'm glad we've brought Jamie here."

Sophia nodded. They had brought their son here a few years earlier. "She won't remember this trip, but I am glad, too. The world is changing. I don't know when, if ever, we will be able to get back here."

Taking a deep breath, Henri turned his head to the right and looked out over what had been the Altis—the sacred precinct of Olympia—and the columns of the ancient temples. Sophia was certain that he wasn't seeing the home of the ancient Olympic Games but rather reliving the Olympics of 1896 and the day they had met. When he spoke, her thoughts were confirmed.

"I will forever thank God for the Olympics and His using them to redirect the course of my life. God took events that could have been so adverse to a young man's character—

Amanda and Percival's betrayal and my accident—and used them to bring about the greatest blessing in my life."

She knew that he had long since put all that bitterness behind him. But the miracle of their meeting and falling in love at those first games still astounded both of them. Putting her arms around his neck, she asked, knowing full well the answer, "Am I the greatest blessing in your life?"

Turning away from the romantic ruins that offered a small glimpse of what had been a place of classical beauty beyond description, he buried his face against her neck and whispered hoarsely, in that manner that always made her blood sing through her veins, "You know you are. I love you more today, darling Sophia, than I did even yesterday. You are my friend and companion, who so wisely but lovingly helps me in my Christian race." His voice lowered to a deep, gravelly sound filled with emotion, and he added, "My lover and the mother of my children."

He sat back and smiled that goofy smile that warned her of what was to come. "And on top of it all, you're almost as good a classicist as I am." She knew learning that she was a university graduate and a classicist and that her uncle had been his favorite professor at Princeton University had been the hardest thing for him to discover about her all those years ago.

"Ha! I'm better!" she retorted as she knew he expected her to do. "And I'm better at lawn tennis than you, as well!"

"You are not!"

"Am, too!"

The giggle of their daughter stopped their good-natured

banter. They both turned to her. She was running toward them across the ancient stones with her arms outstretched, her dark curls bouncing around her little shoulders, and with a smile as big as the moon spread across her face.

" 'Amie want play! 'Amie want play, too!"

Henri caught her as she jumped into his arms and squeezed her close against him. "Jamie can play, too," he assured his wiggling, giggling daughter. But when after a moment she suddenly stopped squirming, finding the comfort of her father's arm and that of her thumb to hold more appeal, Henri asked his wife, "I wonder if God might have an Olympic dream in mind for this little daughter of ours, Sophia, or other of our descendants?"

Sophia wondered, too. It seemed almost inevitable since their lives were so tied up with the Olympic Games. "That can be one of our hopes for Jamie, Henri," she said and ran her hand across her little daughter's forehead. "That something to do with the Olympic Games will touch our Jamie's life in the wonderful way in which the Olympics of 1896 did ours."

"Our Olympic hope for Jamie," he returned. And to the sound of swallows playing in the sky and the poplar trees above their heads singing like wind instruments in the gentle breeze, Henri added, "I like that, Sophia. I like it a lot."

Resting her head against her beloved's shoulder in the comfortable way she had done for sixteen years, Sophia whispered back, "Me, too, Henri. Me, too."

MELANIE PANAGIOTOPOULOS

Melanie Panagiotopoulos was born and raised in the United States (Virginia, California, Washington, New Jersey, Florida, and Alabama), but she now resides in Athens, Greece, with her physician husband and two children. She loves to read, write, study, watch documentaries and good movies on TV (yes, she admits it!), explore early Christian sites, Byzantine churches, medieval castles, and of course, the Acropolis of Athens. To arise before dawn and watch the sun as its golden rays wash down upon the historic city she now calls home is one of her greatest delights.

Olympic Hopes

by Lynn A. Coleman

This book is dedicated to my grandson, Jeremiah,
full of joy and energy.
My prayer is that he will grow
to be an honorable man
grounded in the Word of God.

Chapter 1

Lake Placid, New York—1932

Jamie scanned the long line in front of her and shivered. She'd been working the registration booths for hours. Athletes from all over the world were lining up, looking for anything and everything, and trying desperately to speak English. She had boned up on her French for the past three months, but few spoke that language much better than English.

She looked behind her for someone to take her place. A short break and a warming pit stop in front of the grand fireplace were in order. She noticed Dr. Dewey prancing about in his full-length fur coat. The man was a genuine marvel.

Her mother came through the hall with her arms loaded.

"Mother, can you relieve me for a moment?"

"Sure, I'll be back in a couple minutes."

Jamie turned back to the line in front of her and asked, "May I help you?"

"Is this the line for the speed skating competition?" a man inquired.

She smiled, hearing English. "Yes. What's your name, and which country do you represent?"

His long, thin body seemed like it would fit his chosen sport.

"Dameon Grant, U.S.A."

She reached for the list of American athletes and scanned its length. "I'm sorry, what did you say your name was?"

"Dameon Grant."

"I don't understand. You're not on the list."

"What list?"

"The list of athletes, of course. When did you qualify?"

"Qualify?"

Oh dear, she had another one of those. "Yes, the pretrial competition for the Olympics. Did you participate, and did you win a place on the team?"

He pulled the knit cap off his head. His matted, sandy blond hair practically stuck to his skull. She reached out and placed her hand upon his. "You didn't know, did you?"

He shook his head no.

Jamie's heart went out to the young man. The Depression was hitting everyone. "You thought if you won, you'd earn some prize money for you or your family, right?"

He nodded yes. He had a large backpack and a pair of racing skates slung over his shoulder.

"How long have you been walking?"

"One week. I take it there's nothing here for me."

"I'm sorry. The athletes competed in the qualifying heats

long ago. Are you hungry? I'm certain I can get you a hot meal."

He wrung his knit cap tightly in his hands. *He's a proud man and won't beg for food,* she assessed. "Let me ask around; perhaps there are some odd jobs you could help with."

"Really?" A glimmer of hope flickered through his hazel eyes.

"Yeah." It ought to be worth something that her parents were on the official Olympic Committee. They'd been working for the past three months, living in the area to help these games get under way.

"Sit over there and warm up by the fire. I'll be free in a few minutes and will see what I can do."

"Thank you. I appreciate this."

"You're welcome."

He slid off his pack and walked over toward the fire.

Jamie glanced over her shoulder as Dameon Grant left the table. She turned back to the line when the volunteer next to her leaned closer. "I bet you feed stray cats, too?" Martha Kingston purred.

"It's the least we can do. You do realize he's not the first person to have traveled here hoping to compete and win."

"Yes, yes, but that doesn't mean we have to take care of them. Oh, I don't mind giving them a meal or two, but you've decided to find him a job. How are you going to manage that? We're all volunteering."

Martha had a point.

"It's only for a day. Just something to give him pocket money for his trip home. Did you hear he'd been on the road for one week? Where do you suppose he came from?"

"I don't know, and I really don't care. I'm going crazy with all these foreigners. Didn't anyone teach them English?"

"You were supposed to learn French," Jamie countered.

"Who had the time?"

"I did." Not that she had to learn French, since she had been speaking it since she was three.

"Well, I wasn't stuck up in these mountains for three months like you and your family. I have a life."

Ouch. The truth did hurt. Was it painfully obvious to everyone that her family had been hit by the Depression? "You know my parents—ever since the unsuccessful 1904 Olympics held in St. Louis, they've been working to make this one successful."

"Did your parents learn Greek?"

Jamie noticed her mother within earshot of Martha's last question. "Some," her mother answered, not revealing that she had been born and raised in Greece.

Sophia Preston's elegant pose warned others not to speak rudely to her. Jamie's parents were in their fifties now and still had a passion for the Olympics, where they'd met and fallen in love. She turned toward Jamie and winked. "I take it that gentleman over there isn't a competing athlete?"

"Afraid so."

"Feed him a good, hot meal, and I'll take care of this line."

"Thanks, Mother." Jamie kissed her mother on the cheek and headed toward Dameon Grant.

"Hi, my name is Jamie, and I'll set you up with a hot meal. The job will be a harder problem, but I'll work on it."

"Thank you. I don't know what to say." His shoulders sagged. "I thought by coming here, I might earn the prize money."

"There is no prize money. The athletes get a gold, silver, or bronze medal and world recognition. That's why it's for amateur athletes."

"Oh. I thought when it said amateurs, anyone could compete."

"You're not the only one. Come on, there's a hot meal waiting to warm your belly." Jamie led him to the main dining hall. "Set your stuff over there and pick up a tray; then pick out whatever you'd like. I'm afraid it's cafeteria-style dining tonight. There will be a sit-down meal tomorrow night."

"This is fine. I've been eating out of a can for the past week."

Jamie prayed her family's misfortunes wouldn't have them eating out of cans someday. An image of hoboes sitting in the train yards, cooking over an open campfire, flashed through her mind. "You'll have to excuse me for a few minutes. I'll be back in a while. Just stay put." Jamie started to walk away, then turned back and said, "After you get your meal, of course."

She tracked down Dr. Dewey, who told her to track down Mr. Hammond, who told her to track down Mr. Samuels, who told her to track down John Talbot. Whom she never did find. So she decided to stop back in the kitchen to have a talk with Mr. Daschel, the head cook.

❦

Dameon's stomach rumbled from the warmth of the hot meal. Somewhere around his third helping of soup, he began

93

to feel his toes again. He'd have to be careful going home. Frostbite could be a real problem.

His petite rescuer hadn't returned yet. He didn't know how long he should wait. But walking back to Massachusetts wasn't high on his priority list. What would his parents say? All this time gone and nothing to show for it. If he had competed and lost, that would be one thing. At least he would have tried. But to come and discover he had no opportunity at all—that would be hard to excuse.

Dameon watched other athletes come in, pick up a tray of food, and sit down in groups. He'd never seen this many people in one place before. And so many different languages. How could a person understand what was going on?

The dark, short-haired head of his rescuer popped around the corner. Her smile lit up the room—or was it his heart? Either way, it was the prettiest smile he had ever seen.

Jamie sat down beside him. "I've got some good news and some bad news. I found you a day's worth of work."

That can't be the bad news, he mused.

"Unfortunately, it's washing dishes."

Ah, that's the bad news.

"I'm sorry; it's the best I could do on short notice."

"It's fine, honestly. I don't mind washing dishes."

"You will when you see the mountains of them back there." She winked.

"Oh, well, I guess I'd better start." He glanced over at his backpack. "Is it all right to leave my pack there?"

"Sure."

Dameon extended his hand. "Thank you, Miss Jamie. I

appreciate all you've done for me."

Her cheeks glowed with a delicate blush. "You're welcome. If you look for John Talbot, you might find some additional work. I wasn't able to locate him, and I have to go back to the registration desk."

"Thanks again." Dameon headed for the kitchen. A huge pile of dishes towered over the sink. The dumbwaiter was full. Dameon rolled up his sleeves and went to work.

Four hours later, the last dish and piece of silverware were washed and restacked for tomorrow's breakfast.

"Great job, Dameon. Thanks." The head cook peeled a five-dollar bill off a wad in his pocket.

"Thank you." Five dollars wouldn't get him all the way home, but it would help.

"If you stick around for a few days and haven't found anything else, come on back and I'll see what I can do for you," the cook offered.

It was nearing midnight, and he didn't have a place to stay. The dining room was dark, with shards of moonlight cutting through at an eerie angle. He found his pack leaning against the wall where he had left it. On top of it lay a folded piece of paper. He opened it. "Dameon, the guys on the U.S. team said you could bunk with them tonight." There were brief directions to the cabin. He folded the note and put it in his pocket. *Thanks, Lord. You've provided before I had time to ask.*

Making his way through the quiet Olympic village gave him a feeling of hope and anticipation. Finding the cottage, he knocked lightly on what he prayed was the door of the appropriate room. "Dameon Grant?" a male voice whispered.

"Yes," he whispered in response.

The door opened and someone pulled him inside. "Shh, the coach would have a fit if he knew what we're doing. Jack's staying at home tonight, so you can bunk in his bed."

"Thanks."

"You're welcome. Name's Herbert Taylor. I'll introduce you to the rest of the guys in the morning. Jamie Preston said you came all the way to compete. Any good?"

"I think so."

Herbert turned and looked at the blade of his skate. "If you're fast on these, you're not too bad."

"Lights out," a voice bellowed from the hallway.

"Bunk's there." Herbert slipped under the covers of his bed.

Dameon stripped down to his long underwear and slid into the softest bed he'd ever experienced. After a week on the road, sleeping in a small tent and sleeping bag, he was in heaven. *Thank You, Lord.*

❧

"Jamie, Mrs. Dewey needs your help with the tea tonight. I told her you'd love to give her a hand. It's a formal tea party with silver teapots and fine china."

"That'll be a switch," Jamie quipped.

"Honey, I know it's been difficult the past few months, but living here and helping the Deweys has been a blessing."

"I'm sorry, Mother. I didn't mean to snap. The room was bitter cold this morning."

"I know. Your father forgot to stock the woodstoves before bed."

Jamie took the warm teakettle off the top of the stove and poured herself a cup. "Has Daddy found a way to recover some of his losses?"

"I'm afraid not. We've decided not to think about it again until after the games. We'll deal with it then."

Her mother placed her hands in her lap and looked down at them. "It's a difficult time, a real testing of our faith."

"Are we going to have to move to Greece?" Jamie reached for a breakfast pastry on the plate in the center of the table.

"Most likely."

If one has to be poor, the Greek Isles is the place to be poor. Jamie pondered the implications. Go back to Princeton and have nothing, or go back to Greece and enjoy life. "It'll be nice to see everyone," she said in Greek.

Her mother chuckled and dropped the paper she'd been reading. "What was Martha's problem yesterday?"

"American arrogance. All the world should speak as they."

"Ah, and she doesn't know I'm Greek?"

"Apparently not. But let's face it, Mother, Martha is one of those flappers."

"Oh, really? And your haircut isn't?"

Jamie smiled. They'd had this conversation before. The twenties had been a wonderful time for women. Quite liberating. But Jamie had decided she could never be a true flapper. They were huge risk takers—they smoke, drank, danced, and voted. Oh, she would vote any chance she got, and she wore her hair short, and she wouldn't mind tapping her foot to a tune or two; but the drinking and smoking were something she'd decided long ago wouldn't please her Lord.

"I like it short. I like wearing makeup. Is that so wrong?"

"No, dear. Just be careful how you label people."

"You're right. I'm sorry. I guess I made the same mistake with that poor man who walked for a week to come here, only to discover he couldn't even enter the competition."

"I saw you place a note on his belongings last night. What was that about?" Her mother sipped from her teacup with the grace and fluid movements that showed years of training.

"The guys on the speed skating team said he could bunk with them last night. Jack Shea was going to spend the night with his parents."

Sophia Preston nodded. If Jamie lived to a hundred, she'd never have the poise and refinement that her mother demonstrated just sitting in her bathrobe. What kind of gene had her mother been given that simply skipped over her daughter? Jamie felt like such an ugly duckling when sitting next to her.

"Is he cute?" Her mother wiggled her eyebrows.

"I hadn't noticed." Jamie felt her cheeks burn.

"That handsome, huh? Be careful. You know what happened to me at the first Olympic games."

Jamie smiled. "Hey, you brought home the gold."

Her mother took the newspaper and swatted her, then turned serious. "Be careful, dear. All the excitement and energy of the games can turn a girl's head. Remember, he's walked for a week."

"But we barely made it here."

"That was different. Your father nearly lost everything

in the stock market crash. If it weren't for a few diverse savings and interests abroad, we would have lost the house."

"I know, but, Mother, are we any different than a poor man or a man with no home?"

"No. In God's eyes, we're no different. But some folks have problems with the different classes. Some folks in our class, for example, wouldn't have anything to do with you if you were to marry a man with fewer means. And then people from less fortunate classes often won't want to have anything to do with someone like you because they'll assume you think you're more important than they are. I know it isn't true, but it is the way people operate. It isn't right, but it is the way of the world. And we do have to make our peace in this world."

Jamie sipped the last of her tea. "I have no intentions of marrying anyone. He simply needed a helping hand, and all I did was show God's love and grace."

"And you went the extra mile. I'm proud of you." Her mother kissed her cheek, then tapped her on the shoulder. "I need to get dressed. There's a lot to do today."

Jamie jumped up and put her plate and cup in the sink. She would do the dishes later. She, too, was running late.

An hour later she pulled up to the country club and found Mrs. Dewey in a tizzy. "I'm so glad you're here. I need you to oversee the decorations. I'm scheduled to appear with my husband at some other functions this morning."

"I'll take care of it."

"Thank you. You're such a sweetheart, just like your mother." Mrs. Dewey plopped a cardboard box in her arms.

"Ramon will get whatever you need." She waved and ran off toward the Olympic stadium.

Jamie looked down at the discarded box and saw pieces of glittering fabric, some candles and holders, some wire, and, she suspected, not a whole lot more. She glanced up at the clock. Eight hours to create the decorations for a large tea party. *Why did I get out of bed this morning?* she wondered.

"Hi," a male voice boomed from behind her.

She turned and saw that bright smile of Dameon's. Her stomach did a flip. "Hi. Did you sleep well?"

"Wonderfully, thank you. I found John Talbot, and he's put me to work for the day, possibly two."

"Great. I'd love to stand and chat, but I've got a party to decorate."

He held his cap in his hands and looked down at his feet. "I just wanted to thank you, again."

"You're welcome."

She watched him slip his cap back over his head and walk off toward the ski jump area. Her mother was right; she'd need to guard her heart from the handsome stranger whose smile alone affected her.

Carrying the box of useless decorations to the back room, Jamie rummaged through it. She made a few quick trips to various places and picked up a few odds and ends. She spoke briefly with Ramon and set the menu for the tea, then went back to the farmhouse and removed all the thin white curtains, cut a few sprigs of evergreens, and grabbed a small container of bleach. Back at the country club, she went to work.

100

Thirty minutes before the tea, she ran back to the farm-house and changed into her evening gown, then froze all the way back to the country club. *Dr. Dewey's long fur coat would be wonderful right about now,* she thought, shivering.

"Marjorie, this is beautiful," Mrs. Kincaid purred.

"Thank you," Mrs. Dewey accepted the compliment.

Jamie counted to ten—slowly, very slowly—and stepped closer to the hostess.

"How positively imaginative, Marjorie." Another compliment flew through the air as the room filled with more ladies. Jamie's anger reached a boiling point, so rather than create a scene, she walked to the back room, where she'd spent the better part of the day, and sulked.

"Jamie, are you in here?" The familiar voice of Dameon melted away her anger. "Jamie?" he called again.

Chapter 2

Dameon slipped behind the curtain. "Jamie," he called again.

"Where are you?" Jamie asked.

"Behind the curtain near the front windows. Don't turn on the light, please."

"What?"

"I'm sorry. I thought it would be safe to change in here. The men's room was full and. . ."

The lilt of her laughter filled the room. "Sorry, I know it's not funny, but. . ."

"If they caught me in here and you in here at the same time in my present state of dress, I wouldn't be worrying about where I'd be changing my clothes or spending the night."

"True. Your secret is safe with me. Do you need me to find you another place to sleep?"

"No, no, I'm fine. I tore my trousers working on the ski jump and needed to put on another pair. Would you mind handing me a pair of woolen slacks? My bag is by the corner of the table."

"Sure. Dameon, why did you come all this way?"

He wrapped the curtain around himself tighter. "My father took a loan out on a tractor just before the market crashed. There's a huge balloon payment due soon. Fortunately, the bank that held the loan has defaulted itself, so we have a bit more time before someone picks up the debt and wants their money."

"I'm sorry." She handed him the woolen slacks. "Here."

"Thanks."

"You're welcome. You're a farmer?"

"Yup, from Windsor, Massachusetts."

She sat down on a chair and faced the wall away from him. There was something more than her kindness that attracted him to her, but those he worked with on the crew today had told him to keep his distance from her. She ran with those in high-society circles.

"What do you farm?"

"Dairy mostly, but we harvest enough wheat to feed the livestock, and we plant a few acres for vegetables. There's not much cash on hand, but I must say, we always have food on our plates."

"Do you like the simple life of a farm?"

Dameon's defenses went up. Perhaps she wasn't as sweet as he'd taken her to be. "Are you implying—?"

She cut him off. "No. I'm sorry. I'm thinking in terms of less stress, fewer worries. But I suppose any job has its own worries."

A sigh of relief passed through his lips. He buckled his belt and stepped out from behind the curtain. "My father runs the farm, but I keep abreast of its earnings and expenses. Father has always tried to keep me informed in case of an accident. Mother, on the other hand, she's quite a woman. I've seen her can enough food for an army. Of course, we do eat a lot."

"Doesn't show." She covered her mouth with her hand.

Dameon chuckled and sat down beside her, plopping his boots on the floor. "I've been blessed with a thin body. I eat more than most but don't gain any weight, which is quite an advantage when you love food as much as I do."

"Now that's just bragging," Jamie teased.

"True." He reached down and put one of his boots on. "Thanks for letting me stay in Jack Shea's bed last night. I haven't slept in a bed in a week. It felt wonderful."

"I figured you'd have something in common with those guys."

"Hard to say. I got there after lights were out. Thankfully, the coach didn't catch wind of it. I can't put anyone in jeopardy again, so I'll set up my tent down the road a piece and make my way back early in the morning."

"That's just silly. My parents and I are staying in this large farmhouse. We've got plenty of spare rooms. I bet I could get them to let you stay in one of them."

"How much?"

"Huh? Oh, you mean rent? Nothing. It's done all the time. No one charges their friends."

"But I'm not a friend. I'm a stranger."

"Oh, right. Hmm, let me think on it for a bit. I'll see what I can do. Head east out of town, and you'll be heading toward the farm we rented. I'll check with Mother before the tea is over."

"Speaking of which, why aren't you out there enjoying it?"

"Oh, it's silly, really."

"And?"

"I was just a little put out with Mrs. Dewey. Everyone was complimenting her for the job I did, and she didn't once let them know who had decorated the room for her."

"Ah, slight problem with pride, huh?"

She jumped up. "And who are you to tell me that?"

He raised his hands in surrender. "No one, absolutely no one. Sorry I mentioned it."

"Sorry." She plopped back down on the seat. "You're right. I–I. . ."

"Never mind, you don't have to apologize to me. Look, I appreciate all you've done, but perhaps it wouldn't be wise for me to stay at your place."

"Why?" She cocked her head to the right. "Because I have a temper?"

He couldn't help himself and chuckled. "No, because it wouldn't appear right—me being a single man, living in your house."

"Aren't we getting ahead of ourselves? Don't I need to check with my parents first?"

"Fair enough. Well, I best get going if I'm going to find a good spot for the night."

"All right. I'll look for you."

"Thank you, Jamie. By the way, what is your last name?"

"Preston, Jamie Preston."

Of the Prestons who are of the same social class as the Deweys? He should have listened to Herb this morning. He'd said something about the Prestons, come to think of it. He even mentioned her last name last night. Any thoughts of getting to know this woman froze with a cold blast of winter air. She lived in a world he could never enter. He was clothed in a world of flannel and denim, not one where wonderfully crafted evening gowns were donned at night. It was best if he didn't talk with her again. She was too easy to talk with, and if he talked any longer, he'd want to talk more. Not to mention, he was a man of few words. At least, he had been prior to meeting Miss Jamie Preston.

"Well, good night, Miss Preston. Enjoy the tea, and know that all the compliments are for you, and you're graciously giving them as a gift to Mrs. Dewey." He bowed and slipped out the back door. There was no sense creating a scandal. Jamie Preston had enough trouble. Although, at the moment, he couldn't think of a thing that was wrong with her.

❦

Jamie watched in the darkened room as Dameon headed out of town with his pack on his back. *Sleeping in the snow in a tent.* She shivered just thinking about it. It didn't seem right. He'd accepted the fact that he couldn't compete with graciousness. He didn't argue, blame anyone—just simply accepted it. His lean frame continued down the moonlit, snow-packed street.

Light flooded the room. Jamie blinked several times, helping her eyes adjust.

"Jamie?" her mother called.

"Sorry, Mom. I'll be right there."

"What have you been doing in here? Mrs. Dewey has been complimenting all your hard work, and everyone wanted to thank you."

Jamie closed her eyes and let her shoulders slump. "Sorry."

"Well, come along now, and stand up straight. That's it, wonderful. Where's that smile? That's my girl," her mother praised.

She didn't deserve Mrs. Dewey's praise. Dameon was right; she was proud and had wanted human compliments over the satisfaction of people enjoying her handiwork. Now if she could only find a hole to crawl in and hide for the rest of these games.

The attention given, Jamie sat at her mother's table with a few of her mother's closest friends.

"You really did a marvelous job, Jamie," Mrs. Thatcher commented.

"Thank you."

Jean Chesterfield asked, "Where'd you ever find all this fabric on such short notice?"

A warmth spread across her cheeks. "Well, the farmhouse we're staying in is presently missing all its sheer curtains."

Everyone giggled.

"Will they be able to go back up on the windows, or do I need to purchase new ones?" her mother asked, taking a sip of tea.

"All but one. It fell apart when I bleached them."

"Not a bad deal, Sophia. Your daughter bleaches all the

curtains, and your window dressings look like new." Mrs. Thatcher bit off a tiny piece of the Scottish shortbread that had been served with the tea.

"Not a bad deal at all." Her mother winked.

Jamie smiled as her mother's right eyebrow rose slightly. She took hold of Jamie's knee under the table and gently squeezed it. Her mother had a way of getting to the root of problems, and for some reason, Jamie had a problem hiding anything from her mother.

When the conversation hit a lull, her mother excused herself to go to the powder room. Jamie followed.

"What's on your mind?" she asked Jamie in Greek.

Jamie responded in Greek and told her about Dameon and his sleeping in a tent.

"That simply won't do. Your father and I can open a room for him." She reapplied her lipstick in the mirror. "That is what you wanted, isn't it?" Her mother narrowed her gaze.

"Yes, but I was going to ask. You just beat me to the punch."

"Very well. Tell the young man to wait by our automobile."

They had now slipped back into English. "He already left."

Her mother straightened and adjusted her clothing with an efficiency that most would not notice. But Jamie did. All her shortcomings seemed magnified when compared to her mother.

"The evening's nearly over. We'll make our excuses and find him before he freezes to death."

Her mother was on a mission, and nothing would stop

her, including some butterflies taking flight in Jamie's stomach. *How can he affect me so?*

✥

Henri Preston was a formidable man. Thankfully, most of Dameon's pride had vanished on the fourth day of his trek toward Lake Placid. Taking rides from strangers and accepting warm meals and a place to lay his head were becoming routine. But having a man upend his tent the night before and insist on Damon following him home was daunting, to say the least.

Dameon thanked the Lord for His provision once again. If nothing else, God had been showing him tremendous acts of grace on his journey. Today was opening day of the games. The air buzzed with excitement. It was hard not to get caught up in it. There was some scuttlebutt about one speed skater pulling out because they were playing by North American rules instead of the traditional two-man heats. But everything else was positive.

Dameon lifted the ax once again and forced it down on the log needing to be split. He'd noticed several chores left untended around the old farmhouse this morning, and he planned on doing as many of them as possible before heading into work with John Talbot.

Down came the thud of the ax against the solid oak log. *Crack!* It ripped open easily; the wood was so dry. He gathered the bundle of freshly chopped wood and headed into the house. He lit the woodstove and fed it fuel while fixing some eggs and bacon. It was the least he could do for the family who had given him a roof over his head and some protection from the bitter cold outside.

"Good morning, sir," Dameon welcomed Mr. Preston as he walked into the kitchen.

"Smells great. Who cooked?"

"I did."

"You?" The man looked from the plate back to him. "Any other hidden talents I should know about?"

"Don't think so. Living on a farm, you're taught to wake up early and get several chores done before breakfast."

The older man forked some bacon and placed it on his plate, then some eggs. "Jamie said you came here wanting to compete. Any good?"

"I thought so, but just listening to the guys and all their hard work, I probably would have been left at the starting line by the time they crossed the finish line."

Mr. Preston chuckled. "Probably not, but they do take their sports seriously. Didn't Jack Shea skip the semester at Dartmouth to compete in these games?"

"That's what he said." The team seemed to be counting on Jack, but each man hoped to win his own Olympic gold. Dameon had learned more about the Olympics, amateur athletics, and the competition in two days than he'd learned in a lifetime in Windsor. Dameon sat down across from Mr. Preston.

"I understand you're unable to get home."

"No, sir."

Henri Preston stopped eating and examined him more closely.

"I can go home," he clarified. "But there are a few jobs

for the asking around here, and I figured any income was better than no income."

Henri nodded.

Obviously, Mr. Henri Preston didn't know what it was to do without. Dameon looked down at his plate and proceeded to eat. No sense inflaming a situation, defending his own state in society. In the few days he'd been in Lake Placid, he'd heard more about—and from—wealthy people than he'd ever known. There were advantages to growing up on a farm. He had no idea what society expected of him. He simply grew up and enjoyed life. Some of the athletes came from well-to-do families, and they had little understanding of why buying new clothing or equipment was difficult for some of the other members of the team or how to work and save to earn the money to get to the competitions. It seemed people with money knew people with money who would sponsor and support their affluent friends or their affluent friends' children.

But how does Jamie fit into this picture? he wondered. She didn't seem anything like the others. She treated him with respect.

A mumbled sound passed his ears. "Excuse me?" he asked.

"I said, what's on your agenda today?"

"Sorry. John Talbot has some work for me. Might be my last day, though."

"Will you head home then?"

"Yes, sir. No work, no reason to stay."

Henri nodded his head and finished his breakfast.

"Daddy," Jamie called from the hallway, "what's all the—?"

Jamie screamed and slipped behind the corner wall to the kitchen.

Dameon held down a smirk. Her hair was rumpled from sleep and stuck straight out in the back. Her bathrobe hung loosely on her body, and she hadn't bothered to tie the sash. Its sleeves went past her hands so that only the tips of her fingers were exposed. She looked adorable.

"Excuse me." Dameon lifted his dish from the table and dumped it in the sink, giving Jamie freedom to enter her own kitchen.

Chapter 3

Three hours later, Jamie still felt embarrassed about having walked into the kitchen looking like something the cat might have dragged in. It was one thing for family to see her having just rolled out of bed and quite another to have been seen that way by a perfect stranger.

"Jamie," Martha said, waving her down. Martha stood in a small group of women all around Jamie's age, most of whom she knew from social gatherings.

Plastering a smile across her face, Jamie walked over. The dry snow crunched under her boots. "Hi, what are you up to today?"

"We're ducking out of the ticket sales; the line is huge. Wanna come?"

Admittedly, working huge lines was more appealing than gossiping with Martha and her friends. "I promised my mother I would relieve her." Which was true, but Jamie wasn't due to start work for another hour.

"Suit yourself. Personally, I find the job tedious."

Two of the girls huddled together and giggled. *Are they*

113

talking about me? Jamie wondered.

"Deborah says your mother is Greek," Martha stated. It wasn't really posed as a question.

Jamie nodded.

"She really does speak Greek, huh?"

"Yes." Jamie held back a chuckle.

"I can't believe she didn't say something."

Why would she bother? "It's just her way."

Martha narrowed her gaze at Jamie. "Is that some sort of Greek custom? I mean, she could have corrected me rather than have me make a fool of myself."

You're doing a good job all by yourself. "I'll let her know."

"No hard feelings?"

"None."

"Great. We're off. Have fun meeting the locals."

Why Martha even bothered to come to the games was beyond Jamie. The girl couldn't care less about the kind of work that went into putting on one of these events or the personal sacrifice. And to put down everyone who did work so hard was. . .

Jamie closed her eyes and counted. Her temper would get the better of her yet. People like Martha were a dime a dozen, and she'd probably have a grand time. Jamie, on the other hand, would have a good time *and* work hard to help others enjoy themselves.

She made her way up to the country club, where the tickets were on sale. "If only more people would catch on to the true meaning of the games," she mumbled.

"Such as?" Dameon stepped up beside her.

Jamie jumped. "Where'd you come from?"

"I was working only ten feet from you. You didn't notice the guy shoveling the entrance to the stadium?"

"No, sorry."

"Wasn't important."

Jamie pondered his response. *What did that mean?*

"Do you think it'll be a problem if I spend the night at your place tonight? I'll be leaving in the morning. There's no more work."

"Ask Father, but I don't see why not."

"Thank you. I'll look for him."

Was Dameon equally unconcerned about the games? "Don't you want to see the events?"

"Love to—but I don't have money for a ticket. I'd love to see the guys on the speed skating team compete."

Maybe he wasn't like Martha and her friends.

"You didn't answer my question," he prompted.

"What question?" Jamie played back their brief conversation, recalling that she'd told him to find her father.

"The one about the games. What's the true meaning of the games?"

"Unity, building a better world through peaceful competition, understanding others—those kinds of things."

"Sort of like the Golden Rule?" Dameon asked.

"Yeah, but on a grander scale."

"Ah, I think God's plan is a little grander. No disrespect to the Olympics, but—"

"You're so right. Sorry. I say things without thinking sometimes. Of course, nothing is more important than doing what God wants us to do, but isn't showing charity at events like this to people who may not know God important, too?"

"I wasn't arguing with that. I merely stated that God's purpose was a little larger than the Olympics."

"True, sorry. I stand corrected." She bowed to accentuate her submission to his observation.

"I'll see you later. I get off just before opening ceremonies. If it's all right, I'll simply go back to the farmhouse."

"Of course." She didn't dare say another word to this man. Why was it that she so easily stirred up difficulties in talking with him? He seemed so easy to talk with, and yet there were times when the conversation just rubbed one or the other of them the wrong way. *Why?*

❦

The last of the tickets sold, Jamie joined her parents and sat down to watch the opening ceremonies.

"Who's sitting here?" Jamie pointed to the empty seat.

"No one; that was your brother's seat."

Her brother had decided to stay back in Princeton and work rather than come to this year's Olympic Games.

"Mom, Dad, would it be okay if I invited Dameon to join us?"

Her mother's eyes blazed a trail to her soul. Then she looked over to her husband. "All right, princess," her father answered for the two of them. "But hurry; you've only got thirty minutes."

❦

Dameon worked his stiff back under the warm water. A long, hot shower was just what the doctor ordered—Dr. Dameon, of course. He closed his eyes and let the heated spray cascade over his head.

"Dameon?"

He pulled his head out of the water.

"Dameon?"

The voice seemed closer.

"Dameon? Are you in there?"

"Jamie?" He turned the faucets off.

"Hurry up!"

"What?"

"Hurry up and get dressed. Opening ceremonies are about to begin."

He stepped out of the shower and wrapped himself in a towel. "I know, but I thought I told you I couldn't afford a ticket." He walked closer to the closed door.

"You don't have to. My father has an extra one. My brother didn't come."

"Huh?"

"My brother, you know, as in another sibling from the same parents."

"I know what a brother is; it's just. . ." He reached for the doorknob, then thought better of it.

"Hurry up."

"Do you always get your way?"

"Most of the time." Jamie giggled.

Dameon groaned. *Women.* What was it about the opposite sex that they always had a way of getting what they wanted? His own mother could get his father to do just about anything she wanted. Of course, she always seemed reasonable in her requests. Except for that silly pond in the back of the house. He still didn't see the need for that. Dameon rinsed his head and briskly dried himself off.

Thankfully, he'd set out some clean clothes and a fresh pair of long underwear. He'd been planning on doing some laundry tonight if the Prestons didn't mind. Fresh clothes for his trip home would feel mighty nice. Not to mention, it would get him a few extra lifts, he hoped.

Dressed, he exited the bathroom and discovered Jamie pacing the front room.

"Do you know you dress slower than a woman?"

"I do not. Besides, I had to rinse the soap out of my hair," he defended.

"Excuses, excuses. Come on, the delegates will be marching in any second. You don't want to miss that part." She led them out of the house and to her automobile. It did seem strange seeing a woman behind the wheel, but he'd seen her driving more than once over the past couple of days.

She really was an intriguing sort. A man could get dazed just watching her run around. If he noticed one thing, it was how quickly she moved. Always busy, always on the go.

Her eyes stayed focused on the road ahead. "How many times have you seen the opening ceremonies?" he asked.

"Father and Mother have a real passion for the games. I don't know how many times, actually. I was so little the first time or two. We did miss a year here and there. But this one has been the most draining. Not that I've minded all the work," she amended.

As they drove up to the stadium parking, Dameon noticed

streams of people moving slowly to get in. The white canvas that encircled the arena exposed the upper half of the viewing stands, which were nearly full with people.

Inside the stadium, Jamie led them to her family's spot. People lined the area, several layers thick. Dameon could feel the excitement. People talked and cheered. Officials sat at the stands. Everything captivated him. He sat on the edge of the bench in anticipation.

Dr. Dewey and the governor of the state of New York spoke. "He's our president-elect." Jamie pointed toward the governor.

"I'm aware of that." Dameon bit down his frustration. Why did the rich assume everyone below them economically didn't know what was going on in the world?

"Sorry, I. . ." Her words trailed to silence.

"The question is, will his New Deal be what we need?" Dameon whispered.

"I only pray that the man who goes to the White House will be the man God can use to bring an end to this Depression."

"Amen," Dameon agreed.

Jamie shivered.

He surrendered his wool car blanket and gave it to her. "I'm fine."

"Nonsense. You're freezing, and I'd feel horrible if you caught a cold watching the opening ceremonies."

"Thank you." She wrapped the second blanket around her shoulders.

Dameon felt the cool breeze coming up through the

bleachers. He stuffed his bare hands deeper into his wool jacket and inched closer to Jamie.

◈

Guilt raked Jamie's body as the warmth of the wool blanket helped her endure the long opening presentation. Roosevelt's words were short and to the point, which probably endeared him to everyone who attended the opening ceremonies. No, no one had come to hear him; they had come for the games, for the athletes, for the excitement. Politicians were necessary but not why these people had come.

She glimpsed Dameon wiggling. "Cold?" she asked.

"I'm fine."

"Come on, let's share the two blankets."

Jamie's father turned and raised an eyebrow at his daughter.

Dameon must have seen her father's admonition. "Thank you, but I'm fine."

Men. She let out a small huff. *Dameon is too proud and Father is overprotective. I was just offering the man some warmth. . . .* Her thoughts trailed off. *Perhaps Father wasn't being so overprotective, after all.*

A dozen or so athletes from Switzerland passed by.

Pleasure oozed from Dameon's pores. The man was absolutely radiant. His hazel eyes danced across the crowd, capturing every movement.

"I told you you'd have a good time."

"It's wonderful."

They sat silently for the remainder of the ceremonies. When the music stopped and the people had cheered, it

120

was time to go home.

"Thank you, Jamie, Mr. and Mrs. Preston. I had a marvelous time."

"You're welcome, son." Her mother turned toward Jamie. "Honey, your father and I are scheduled to have dinner with Dr. Dewey and the others on the committee. We'll probably be up late solving any last-minute details."

"Need a hand?" Jamie asked.

"Thank you, but I believe we can handle it. Everything has gone rather smoothly to this point." Her parents stepped down from the bleachers and headed back up to the country club.

Jamie led Dameon down to the arena. "The ice track for the speed skating is over here."

"Yeah, the guys showed me around the other day."

"Oh, sorry." He seemed rigid, defensive almost. "Did I do something to offend you?"

"It's the second time today you've assumed I didn't know anything." He paused. "Perhaps I'm just defensive."

"Perhaps, but I didn't *assume* you didn't know anything. I was merely trying to make conversation. How was I supposed to know you knew who FDR was? I couldn't know if you've seen pictures of him. I guess you probably have if you knew he was running for president."

"Even things like presidential elections make their way to small farm towns." His words bit back.

"Oh, I get it. You've decided because my family has money, I'm a rich snob."

Dameon raised his hands in surrender. "No, not exactly. I—"

"You what? You think a rich snob would open their home to you? You think a rich snob would bend over backwards to find you work and a place to stay? I can't believe you." Jamie stomped off. *Of all the ungrateful people I've ever met.*

"Jamie," Dameon called from behind. "Jamie, I'm sorry. You're right. I'm overly sensitive."

Jamie stopped walking. The stadium was nearly empty of people. She turned to look at him. He held out his hand. "Truce?" he offered.

"Truce." She captured his hand and shook it. She shivered.

He reached for her and pulled her toward himself and wrapped her in one of the wool blankets he was carrying. She quivered and stepped back. Distance was much better.

Dameon coughed. "Jamie, I was wondering if I could wash some clothing at your place before I leave in the morning."

"Sure. We have a washing machine. I hear they're making dryers to tumble clothes dry now. I can't imagine it."

"Now that is something I never heard about. I'm not sure whether Mother would like one of those or not."

"There's something about fresh linens off the line. Of course, in the winter they freeze and you have to hang them around the radiators and stoves."

Jamie drove them back to the farmhouse.

"How long have you been driving?"

Is he criticizing my driving now? "For a couple years. Why?"

"Just wondering. There aren't too many women in my area who drive."

"I see."

"Perhaps we ought not to try and make conversation.

122

We seem to step on each other's toes."

She thought about how to respond. It wasn't that she didn't want to make conversation with the man. It was more that she was on edge being next to him. An edge she'd never experienced before with another man. "I'm just wondering why we could talk so easily the other night and tonight we find it extremely difficult."

Dameon leaned back against the front seat. "Maybe because I was—"

A deer jumped out in front of her vehicle. Jamie slammed on the brakes. The car swerved to the right, then fishtailed to the left. Jamie pulled the wheel hard to the right and pumped the brakes.

Crash!

Chapter 4

Dameon groaned. Cold and pain enveloped him. *Where am I?* He blinked, trying to focus. The bark of a large oak tree stared him in the face. *Accident. Jamie.*

"Jamie." He twisted to his left and found her lying across the steering wheel. "Jamie, wake up." He reached over and gently moved her bangs from her eyes. His heart caught for a moment when he saw the lump on her forehead. Rolling down his window, he reached out for some snow and compressed it into a small ice pack for her forehead.

He placed her in a protective embrace and leaned her body against his. With his right hand, he applied the cold snow to her forehead.

Her eyes blinked.

Water dripped from the snow down the sides of her face. Dameon scanned the compartment for something to sop up the trails of water. Seeing nothing, he used the sleeves of his wool coat.

Her delicate pink lips parted. A gentle moan passed

through them. Her eyes fluttered once again.

"Jamie, wake up, please."

She opened her eyes—the pupils were wide open. *Concussion,* he worried.

"You hit a tree to avoid the deer."

She started to bolt up. He held her down.

"Shh, relax for a minute; get your equilibrium first." He liked the feel of her in his arms. *Where did that come from?* He looked back down at the incredible woman. Her beauty went beyond her physical appearance. *Admit it; you've been attracted to her since you first laid eyes on her,* he reminded himself.

"What happened?"

"You hit a tree," he patiently repeated. "Trying to avoid a deer."

"Oh, no. How bad is the damage?"

"To you or the car?"

"The car."

"I don't know; I haven't gotten out. I was knocked out for a minute, too."

"Are you okay?" She tried to lean her head back.

"Stay still. You've got quite an egg on your forehead."

"It feels cold and wet."

"I have an ice pack made from snow on it."

"Oh." Jamie blinked. "I feel a little dizzy."

Should he lay her down on the seat and go outside to check on the damage? He should probably get her to one of the doctors at the Olympic village. There had to be a few available somewhere. "Let me put you down. I'm going to check on the car."

She nodded her head. "Ouch."

Dameon paused. "You okay?"

"I'll live. I just can't move my head without it hurting some."

"Hang on. Let me check."

With all the care he could muster, he placed her gently on the seat, then pushed at his door. It didn't budge. He rolled down the window and wiggled his body out. The impact had left them pushed sideways in a hard bluff of snow. Huge mounds from the snowplows lined the edge of the street.

Jamie sat up in the cab. She grasped the steering wheel. "How bad is it?"

"You're supposed to be lying down," he scolded. "I don't know yet. I'm going to have to dig around the car to check it out."

"Want a hand?"

"No. You are a stubborn one, aren't you?"

Jamie giggled. "I've been called worse. I'm coming out." The driver's door creaked open.

Dameon rolled his eyes heavenward. "Can You get through to her?"

"Probably not," Jamie answered with a smile.

"You're unsteady on your feet. Why can't you just relax and let me help you?"

"Oh, all right. Why do you men always feel like you have to rescue the woman?"

"Because some women need rescuing from themselves." He led her back to the cab. "Jamie, you may have a concussion. There's no need pushing yourself too hard. I'm going to see if I can drive the car back to the country club. I'm sure someone there will be able to fetch a doctor. If I can't drive the car, I'll carry you back."

"You'll do nothing of the kind. I'll walk," she protested.

"I thought debutantes liked men waiting on them hand and foot."

She crossed her arms. "Not this one."

Dameon chuckled. "That's obvious. Please take this in the best possible way. You need to sit down and relax. I'm certain you're fine, but there's no need risking that pretty little head of yours."

Her eyes widened.

What had he said? He rehearsed the lines he'd spoken. *Pretty.* "You are pretty; is that such a shock? Don't those men who attend those debutante balls know how to compliment a woman? Back on the farm, a man has no trouble telling a woman she's beautiful."

A smile spread from ear to ear. "Thank you."

"You're welcome." He formed a new snow pack for her forehead. "Now put this on your forehead and lean back."

She obeyed without a further word. Had he simply needed to tell her how beautiful she was to get her to cooperate?

❧

Jamie lay in her bed. Dameon had managed to get the car out of the tree and embankment, then to her parents and a doctor. An hour later, she wore clean clothes and was resting in her bed. Dameon had been correct in his assumption of a mild concussion. Her head throbbed from the pounding headache. The doctor had given her something for the pain but told her to wait as long as possible before taking it. Being awake was more important than sleeping or being pain free.

A gentle knock sounded on her door.

"Come in," she called out.

"How are you feeling?" Dameon's smile sent a shiver down her spine. His words about how beautiful she was floated back to the surface of her throbbing brain.

"Apart from feeling like my head hit a tree, all right." She grinned, then grimaced from the pain.

He limped closer to her bed. "Doc said you'll be fine in the morning. A bit stiff but fine."

"Were you hurt? You're limping."

"I'm fine—just banged my knee on the dashboard."

"Did you have the doctor take a look?"

"No, I'm fine."

Jamie chuckled. "Do I need to tell you you're handsome so you'll stop long enough and have the doctor look at you?"

Dameon let out a half chuckle. "Doesn't work the same with a guy."

"Oh, so you're not at all impressed when I say I love your hazel eyes."

He stepped back.

"Gotcha," Jamie teased.

He sat down in the chair next to her bed. "The cook at the club asked if I could work as his head dishwasher through the games. It'll give me nine more days of work."

"That's wonderful. Did my parents say you could stay?"

"Your parents think I'm sliced bread. They're very down-to-earth people. Your father is a little closed on his emotions, but he's so touched by how I took care of you."

"What did you tell him?"

"Jamie, I didn't do anything anyone else wouldn't have done. Don't get me wrong—I appreciate a place to stay. But I'm not special."

She reached out her hand. Dameon hesitated, then took her hand into his own. "Dameon, you are special."

"Jamie, let's be honest here for a moment. I'm attracted to you. Is it really wise for me to stay here? We come from such different worlds. I don't want to hurt you."

Jamie's heart leapt. "The attraction is mutual, but what could be the harm in becoming friends? If you're working every day, we'll barely see one another."

"True."

"Take my parents up on the offer. There's plenty of room, and we're both adults. We can be friends, right?"

Dameon released her hand and laced his hands together. "Can a man and woman become *only* friends when attraction is there?"

"I don't know, but we could try, couldn't we?" She didn't want him out of her life. There were things about him that fascinated her. She wanted to get to know him. At the same time, she'd never met a person so straightforward about himself. It was refreshing. In her social circles, all the men appeared to have the same agenda: Pick the right wife who will help you climb the social ladder. Jamie had determined long ago she wouldn't do that. Her parents were an example of people who had wealth but who also genuinely loved one another. She wanted that, and she met precious few men who were after love.

Dameon took in a deep sigh and let it out slowly. "We can try. Why is it that we find it so easy to talk with one another, then so easily find ourselves arguing and talking past one another?"

"I don't know, but just the thought of it is giving me a headache."

"I'm sorry." He got up. "I'll leave you to your rest. Would you like me to send your mother in with your pain medication?"

"Yes, please." Discussing personal feelings with her head pounding wouldn't do. On the other hand, discussing these same feelings with her heart beating rapidly from his touch, his voice, his masculine scent probably wouldn't do, either. Dameon was right: They did live in entirely different worlds. Would they ever be able to cross that void and simply overlook their heritages?

"Sleep tight, beautiful." He blushed. "I'm sorry. I'll try to remember not to tell you how beautiful you are."

Jamie chuckled with pain. *Please, don't stop.*

&

Three days later, Dameon decided his fears were unwarranted. Jamie and he had said very little besides an occasional "hello" and "how are you?" The hours working in the kitchen had been very demanding. He woke up an hour earlier every morning then the others and did some chores around the house. Chopping wood and keeping the woodstove stocked were the least he could do for free room and board. He'd shovel the walkways after the snow fell and gather the eggs and feed the chickens each morning. Shoveling out the hen-house hadn't been done for quite a while. One thing became painfully obvious: These folks were not farmers. And they hadn't hired the staff to attend to the few farming matters that were necessary.

The Prestons weren't what he would describe as typical rich folks. Not that he had ever really met anyone who was rich. He learned they owned property in Greece and took a yearly trip there. The most interesting thing he'd observed was that they were real people with ordinary, everyday issues that even his parents had to deal with.

Jamie seemed always in the thick of things, working with the other volunteers. Tonight she had made arrangements for them to spend some time with one another at the house.

Dameon looked up at the wall clock and back at the mound of dishes. His helper had snuck out an hour earlier, leaving him with all the cleanup after the dinner meal. He'd be lucky to get out before eleven. How could he get word to Jamie?

He penned a note on a brown paper towel with a grease pen. "Jamie, sorry I have to work late. Dameon."

He left the kitchen and scanned the few remaining souls in the club, looking for someone to deliver his message. Seeing Dr. Dewey, he slowly approached him. "Excuse me, sir."

"Yes, may I help you?"

"I hope so. I need to get this message to Jamie Preston. Is it possible you might find someone to pass it on to her or her parents?"

He reached out and took the note. "I'll find someone." He knitted his eyebrows together. "Are you the young man who came here hoping to compete?"

"Yes, sir."

"Ah, well, sorry about that, but I heard the cook is very impressed with your work. Keep it up, son. Everyone doing their part is making these Olympics quite a success. Wasn't it exciting to see Jack Shea win?"

"I managed to see that heat on my break. Good race, very good." Dameon's heart had pounded with each breath Jack Shea took as he skated to victory that day.

Dr. Dewey slapped him on the back and pushed the note into the pocket of his full-length fur coat. "Glad to see you saw some of the action. I must be off. I'll deliver your message."

"Thank you, sir." Dameon headed back to the kitchen. The memory of Jack Shea flying across the ice flooded back into his mind. It truly had been quite an occasion. Dameon felt blessed having been able to see the race in person.

Around midnight, Dameon arrived at the Prestons'. He didn't want to wake the family, but he needed a shower. He didn't relish going to sleep while smelling like stale grease and old garbage. As quietly as possible, he slipped into the heated shower and lathered up his body. A simple rinse and a quick wash of his hair ended in an all-time speed record of three minutes. Hopefully he hadn't awakened the Prestons.

Changed and ready for bed, he gathered his soiled clothes and made his way downstairs, walking in his stocking feet to keep the noise to a minimum.

"Hello," Jamie's sweet voice purred from the kitchen table. She had a cup of hot cocoa in her hand. "Want a cup?"

"Love one, thanks. Let me get rid of these clothes."

She nodded her agreement.

Jamie's presence engaged all of his senses. How could it be possible to desire to spend more time with someone who he knew he'd never be able to live his life with? A story from the Bible captured his imagination. Hadn't Ruth become Boaz's wife? Social class was something man created, not God.

Is she the one for me, Lord? A part of me desires her more than any other woman. Yet I can't get past the differences. She's led a life in which servants take care of her every wish. How could she settle for life on a farm? His mother worked from sunup to sundown. Jamie couldn't do that. Could she?

He made his way back to the kitchen. She smiled as he entered the room. "How are you?" he asked.

"Fine. Nasty bruise," she added, lifting her bangs to reveal the greens and purples of a healing contusion.

"Definitely prettier with the bangs down," he agreed. She handed him a warm mug of hot chocolate. "Thanks."

"You're welcome." She sat back down and placed her hands around her mug. "I have a confession." She looked up with tears in her eyes.

Chapter 5

Jamie swallowed. "I've been avoiding you."

"Oh?" Dameon sipped his hot cocoa.

"You know what you said in my room the other night? You know, about the attraction?"

He nodded his head and held on to his mug.

"I find myself thinking about you all the time. I want to talk with you, but I'm afraid. I—"

He placed his hand upon hers and caressed it with his thumb. "Avoiding me is probably making you think about me more than you would if you hadn't been trying to avoid me. But I haven't been around much, either. I've been working pretty long hours."

"Yes, and that's why I feel we need to talk. You shouldn't be putting in so many hours. Are you trying to avoid me?"

"No, I was looking forward to spending some time with you, but Wilson left work early this evening, so I had to do his job as well as my own. Trust me, I'm not working longer than I have to in that kitchen. Don't get me wrong; I'm grateful for the work. It will help my parents with their payment on the farm. But I'm not fond of washing dishes. I'd much rather be up to my arms in manure than in greasy dishwater."

"Eww, yuck." She pulled her hand free.

Dameon chuckled. "I'm clean now."

Jamie giggled.

"I did something else you probably won't be pleased with."

He sat up straight. Jamie thought for a moment before she continued. Would he see this as an invasion of his personal life? "I spoke with Mr. Daschel and asked if you could have tomorrow morning off."

"What? What on earth for?"

"I thought you might enjoy watching the speed skating competition." She crossed her arms. *Why does he have such a problem with someone giving him a gift?*

"Jamie, it's a generous offer, but don't you think you should have spoken with me first? Wouldn't it have been wiser to ask me rather than to assume I'd agree to it?"

"But. . ." She paused. She'd done it again—stepped over those boundaries that always seemed to get her in trouble. Her giving heart mixed with her take-charge personality had landed her in this position more times than she cared to remember. "I'm sorry. I didn't mean any harm by it."

She stood up and placed her cup in the sink. Drinking hot chocolate didn't appeal to her quite as much as it had a few moments earlier. "Good night."

"Jamie." He captured her hand as she passed by him.

The tiny hairs on her arm stood at attention. A longing to be closer to Dameon caused her to capture a glimpse of his wonderful hazel eyes.

"Jamie," he whispered. His voice tickled the edges of her ears like a feather and traveled down her neck to her spine. She closed her eyes and tried to break the connection.

Dameon stood. He slid his hand up her arm and held on to her shoulder. Placing his other hand on her other shoulder, he turned her toward him. "My sweet sweetheart, I'm sorry. I know you meant well."

Unable to move, she stood there, mesmerized by his words, his touch. A desire to be wrapped in his arms and held for all eternity overcame her. She stepped forward. His long arms pulled her toward him the rest of the way.

He kissed the top of her head. "Oh, Jamie, what are we going to do about us?"

She snuggled her head into his chest. "I don't know."

"I want to kiss you, Jamie." He stroked her hair with a feather touch.

I want to kiss you, too, but I'm afraid.

"I suggest you don't." Her father's harsh voice resounded through the room. Jamie jumped back out of Dameon's embrace. Her father's rigid stance in the doorway showed his anger at what he'd just encountered.

"I'm sorry, sir. I take full responsibility here," Dameon said. "I'll get my things and leave."

"That's a wise decision, Mr. Grant." Her father narrowed his gaze on Dameon.

"Daddy, don't be ridiculous. Nothing happened. Besides, I'm just as responsible for. . .for. . ."

"Henri, what's all the commotion?" Her mother came into the kitchen, cinching the tie of her bathrobe. "Jamie?

136

Dameon? What's going on?"

"I'm sorry, Mrs. Preston. I've taken advantage of your daughter. I'll be leaving immediately."

"Advantage?" Jamie felt like a microorganism under a microscope as she felt her mother's intense scrutiny. "Dameon, you didn't take advantage of me. We were only going to kiss. Is that a crime?" she huffed.

Her mother started to giggle, then stopped herself. "Dameon, you may spend the rest of the night. We'll talk in the morning. Jamie, go to bed. Now," her mother added with a bit more sternness. "Henri." She took him by the hand. "We'll discuss this in the morning."

Jamie knew better than to push her mother when she took on this tone. "Good night, Dameon. Don't leave before we get a chance to talk."

Her father glared at her.

Jamie ran out of the room.

"I should go," Dameon protested.

Jamie stopped in the hallway and listened.

"Mr. Grant," her mother addressed him in her proper tone. "It's well past midnight. There's no place for you to go, and I won't hear of you sleeping in a tent in this weather. Now go to your room, and we'll discuss this matter in the morning."

"Yes, Mrs. Preston. I'm sorry."

Jamie snuck down the hall before Dameon would see her. He walked past her with his shoulders slumped, rubbing the back of his neck.

She ran to the back stairway to avoid her parents. In her room, she paced. She had wanted to kiss Dameon, and he had wanted to kiss her. *Why is love so complicated?*

❧

Dameon packed his clothing and few personal items when he returned to his room. For an hour he castigated himself over his foolish outburst of desire. Hadn't he been reminding himself daily that there was no place for him in Jamie's life? Or for her in his life? He was a dairy farmer. Milking cows, mucking out the stalls, and watching over the livestock didn't fit her vocabulary. In her mind, milk came from a glass bottle from the store, and butter came wrapped in waxed paper.

During the second hour, he pondered his desires. Why did he want to kiss Jamie? Why did he want to get to know her better, to spend some real time talking with her? Was it so wrong to want a woman who didn't fit his social standing?

By the third hour, he was on his knees, praying and asking the Lord to guide him with his decision about Jamie and about a possible relationship with her and her parents. How could he bring honor back into the house where he had so disappointed Mr. and Mrs. Preston?

Around four o'clock, he fell fast asleep on the floor, where he'd been on his knees in prayer. When the cock crowed at five, somewhere in the back of his mind the sound registered, but he made no effort to get up. Instead, he rolled into a fetal position and continued to sleep.

"Mr. Grant." The words flooded into his foggy brain.

"Mr. Grant," the voice demanded.

Dameon stretched.

"Mr. Grant." Dameon's clouded brain finally registered it as Henri Preston.

Dameon jumped up. "I'm sorry, sir. I must have overslept." Dameon straightened the clothing he'd slept in.

Henri Preston leaned against the doorframe. "You slept on the floor?"

Dameon looked down at his feet. His Bible lay open, its pages crinkled from where he'd rubbed up against them during his sleep. "I was praying, and I must have fallen asleep."

"Do you study the Scriptures?" Henri Preston narrowed his gaze. He had the same shade of brown eyes as Jamie's, Dameon noted.

"I read and do my devotions. I'm not a theologian, but I do like to compare what the Bible says about a subject from as many references as possible."

"Interesting." Mr. Preston stood up straight. "Come into the parlor after you've cleaned up and had something to eat. My wife and I would like to have a few words with you."

"Yes, sir."

Dameon knew what the few words were, but the Prestons were too proper to simply come out with it. *Pack your bags and be gone.* Six words were all it would take.

A short time later, Dameon found himself walking down the hallway to the front parlor. His feet felt like lead. Muffled conversation emanated from the front room. Taking in a deep breath, he walked in to face the firing squad. He deserved whatever they dished out, and being a man who would take responsibility for his actions, he'd face their accusations.

"Mr. Preston, Mrs. Preston." He nodded to each of them as he entered the room.

Jamie's eyes were swollen and red. His heart skipped a

beat. He wanted to cradle her in his arms and tell her everything would be all right. He needed to make everything all right.

"Have a seat, Mr. Grant."

"Yes, sir."

"As you're well aware, I caught you and my daughter in a very compromising position last night."

"Yes, sir." What else could he say? He glanced over to Jamie, who sat across from him in a straight-backed Windsor chair.

"And you apologized for your behavior and took full responsibility for it, correct?"

"Yes, sir."

"But, Daddy. . ."

Henri Preston raised his hand, and Jamie's protest stopped.

"I've packed my belongings and will be on my way. I'll even leave Lake Placid, if you wish."

Henri Preston sat down in the corner of the room. "That is what concerns me the most. That you would take such liberties with my daughter and could leave just as easily. Are you in the habit of using women for your own pleasure, Mr. Grant?"

Dameon felt the heat rise on his face. "No, sir. I. . ." He turned and looked at Jamie and gave her a brief smile. "I like your daughter very much. But I would never intentionally do anything to dishonor her or you, her parents. I respect her too much."

Henri coughed.

Mrs. Preston stepped in. "Then may I suggest you stay but give your word that you won't dishonor Jamie again."

How could he give his word? Right now, he wanted to sweep Jamie into his arms and kiss away all her hurts. How could he stay in the house and promise not to kiss her? "No, Mrs. Preston, I can't promise that."

"What?" Henri Preston jumped up.

"Sir, let me explain. I like Jamie; I like her a lot. I want to get to know her. My heritage, my upbringing as a Yank, means if you give your word, it's a promise that you'll not go back on. I can't promise that I won't kiss your daughter. I can promise I won't compromise her or take advantage of her."

"Did you hear that, Sophia?" Henri Preston turned to his wife.

Jamie got up and joined Dameon on the sofa. She slipped her hand into his.

"Yes, Henri, I heard it. Did you?" Sophia winked at her husband, then turned to Dameon and Jamie. "Do you give me your word you will treat our daughter honorably?"

"Yes, Mrs. Preston, I give you my word." Dameon held on to Jamie's hand.

"Go. Go now and enjoy your morning off. Henri and I will speak with you two later."

Dameon didn't dare wait a moment longer. He jumped up and left the room with Jamie right beside him.

"I'm sorry," she whispered.

"I'm sorry, too." He wrapped a protective arm around her. "Get your coat. We'll go see the morning games."

"Wonderful." She leaned up and kissed him on the cheek.

Then she ran up the stairs, and he headed back toward his room. He heard a few words between Mr. and Mrs. Preston before entering his room.

"She's growing up, dear," Sophia commented.

"I know, but it doesn't mean I have to like it," Mr. Preston huffed.

"True, but I think we can trust the two of them."

"Maybe."

If nothing else, Dameon knew one thing: Sophia Preston had a way of making her husband see past his fears. Not that they weren't founded fears. He didn't know Dameon. How could a father trust a man, a stranger, with his only daughter? Dameon thought about what it would be like to have a daughter of his own one day. *Nope, sons would be better. I definitely want sons.*

⚘

Jamie wrapped her arm around Dameon's waist as they made their way to the stadium. "Did you really mean what you said about liking me?"

Dameon stopped. "Of course. Why would you ask such a silly question?"

She shrugged. He had no idea what it was like growing up with such a beautiful and graceful mother.

"Jamie." He lifted her chin with his finger so she was looking up at him. "I do like you."

"I like you, too." She gave him a weak smile. Tears threatened once again. She'd been a basket case all night long. She'd felt horrible at the prospect that he might be kicked out, especially in this frigid weather.

"I want to kiss you." He pulled her tighter into his embrace. "But not now. Not here."

"Just kiss me and get it over with. This waiting is killing me," she teased.

Dameon chuckled, then wiggled his eyebrows. "Not right now, sweetheart. The right time and the right place, but not out here where everyone can see us and quickly report back to your parents."

"I think they know you're going to kiss me. How could you be so bold with them?"

Dameon snickered. "It wasn't boldness; it was sheer fear. I can't imagine not telling your parents the truth. You and I both know what we're feeling for one another will lead to a kiss. At least once."

"Yeah, but to say no, that you couldn't give your word."

"I couldn't. I would have kissed you if I stayed with you. I know that. You know that, and I think your mother knows that. Your father, on the other hand, would rather have my hide nailed to the woodshed for safekeeping."

They continued to walk to the stadium. Jamie showed her pass, and they entered. "Daddy's never behaved that way before."

"Has he ever caught you about to kiss a man when you were in your bathrobe?"

"No. I guess I see your point."

"Trust me, men know what other men think. If I had a daughter, I wouldn't let her near a guy."

"Oh, really. And why is that?"

"Trust me, you don't want to know."

She poked him in the ribs. "Yes, I do."

"Let's just say, when a boy is growing into a man, he has quite a few thoughts that he needs to repent from regarding the opposite sex."

She'd never had thoughts about a boy she needed to repent from, had she? The flicker of a memory concerning Randolph Evans filtered through. Her cheeks flamed. "You're right. I don't want to know."

Dameon smiled. She loved the set of his jaw, so masculine and yet so personal.

They took their seats next to the speed skating rink. Jamie leaned into his shoulder. He wrapped his left arm around her once again. Peace washed over her. The late night and morning had been horrible. Now she felt calm and rested.

"Go!" Dameon jumped up. "Go, go!" he shouted, cheering on the skaters.

Chapter 6

Dameon placed the last stack of dishes back on the shelves. He glanced up at the clock and sighed. The day had dragged after coming to work. It paled in comparison to the time he'd shared with Jamie. They had talked for an hour or so after the heats; then it was time for him to go to work. He never should have taken the time off. Work would have been a lot more tolerable not knowing the thrills being experienced at the various playing fields. He suspected that his excitement with the games had more to do with Jamie and being next to her than with the actual sports. He loved to watch the competitions, but he loved the feel of her in his arms even more.

He closed his eyes, removed his apron, and replaced it with his wool coat.

"Good night, Dameon," Mr. Daschel called out.

"Good night and thank you."

"You're welcome. See you in the morning."

"Yes, sir."

The chill of the night air woke him up. He raised his

collar over his neck and pushed his hands deep in his pockets. A car horn honked.

"Jamie?"

She leaned out the window and waved. "Going my way?"

Dameon looked around before proceeding toward her. "How long have you been waiting? You should be in bed."

"Couldn't sleep," she admitted. Jamie slid over to the passenger seat. "You can drive."

"Are you nervous?" he asked, slipping into the driver's seat.

"A little. I'll get over it."

"I'm confident you will." Dameon paused for a moment behind the wheel. He turned toward her. "I've missed you."

A sigh of relief escaped her perfect lips. "I've missed you, too." She slid over a bit closer. "Dameon, I crave spending time with you. I don't understand it. I mean, it's not a bad thing that I want to be with you. It's just that, well, this has never happened to me before. I can't stop thinking about you."

Dameon held the steering wheel rather than pull the precious woman into his arms. "I know exactly how you feel. But we have to be careful. We don't really know one another yet."

"I know. Is it possible to fall in. . . ?"

Love, he wanted to finish the sentence for her but knew it was wiser not to.

"I mean. . ." She paused. "Oh, I don't know what I mean. Do you?"

He knew exactly what she meant. He'd been going over the same thoughts all night. "I'll stop working twelve hours a day and work only eight. We should be able to spend some time with one another then. How's that sound?"

"Better, but. . ." She clasped her hands over her mouth.

But she wanted to spend all her time with him. Just as he wanted to spend all his time with her. How could they know one another so well and not know one another at all?

"We'd better get home. I promised your parents."

She leaned her head back. "You're right, I suppose. But when are you going to kiss me?"

Dameon chuckled. "Is that why you picked me up? Were you hoping we could drive to someplace remote and steal a kiss?"

"A girl can hope."

"So can a guy." He slipped the car into gear. Considering it had hit a tree, it still ran fairly well. He had pulled out the right front fender to allow the front wheel to move properly. A mechanic said a new radiator was needed for the trip back to New Jersey, but for simple driving around town, it should be fine, providing they remembered to put water and fluid into it.

"You have perfect lips, by the way. A man couldn't resist kissing them for long."

"You're a tease. I should have let you walk home in this cold."

Dameon smiled. "You'll know better next time."

Steam poured out of the front hood. Dameon pulled over. "Jamie, did you check the radiator before you left?"

"No, Father said it should be all right."

Dameon turned off the engine. "How long did you have it running, waiting for me?"

"An hour."

"That would be the problem."

"What?"

"You can't leave it running, sweetheart. Not until the radiator's replaced."

"Oh, will it still work? Around town, I mean."

"Should be fine, once we get some water into it." Dameon opened the driver's door, then proceeded to open the hood of the car. A huge billow of steam flew upward. Using the cuff of his wool coat, he opened the cap to the radiator, then threw some snow on it. It hissed and creaked, rebelling against the sudden cold.

"What do we do now?" Jamie asked, standing beside him.

Feeling a touch of mischief, he wadded up a ball of snow and flung it at her. For the next few minutes, a roaring snowball fight ensued. She ran and ducked and avoided as many of his snowballs as possible, all the while making her own ammunition on the run. One thing was certain: She'd done this a time or two.

Dameon took aim and fired off another shot.

She wiggled her hip to the right and avoided the missile. "Miss me, miss me, now ya gotta kiss me." She stuck out her tongue.

He charged at her and roared.

She squealed and ran away.

Step by step, he gained ground on her and tackled her into the snow. They fell into a snowbank, laughing.

The laughter stopped as he noticed her beautiful brown eyes on a sea of lovely porcelain skin. With the touch of his finger, he brushed away the hair from her eyes. "May I?"

She nodded her agreement.

He eased down his lips to meet hers. Heaven, honey, and fire coursed through his veins. The kiss was sweet but ignited into passion. A deeper kiss developed. Not wanting to break the connection, he pulled away, nevertheless. "Oh, Jamie, you're so beautiful."

❧

Jamie lay in the snow, not wanting to move. Dameon's kisses were sweet as honey. And for the first time in her life, she felt so at peace. She now understood her parents craving time alone with one another. She wanted the same with Dameon.

A desire to be closer to him burned within her. Rather than respond to it, she gathered a small handful of snow and rubbed it on his exposed neck.

"Oh, yeah." Dameon grabbed an even larger handful of snow and rubbed it on her neck.

Jamie laughed, then cried, "Stop, please stop."

He stopped and leaned over her. "You're beautiful, sweetheart."

She loved hearing him tell her how beautiful she was. "Why do you call me sweetheart?" she asked.

"Because you have a sweet heart. You openly care for others. It's how I've seen you from the moment we met."

She liked that. "Hmm, so what should I call you?"

"Dameon is fine." He got up and offered her a hand to help her up.

She took the proffered hand. "Thank you. But I definitely need to come up with a nickname for you."

"I'm certain it will come to you."

She let her mind ramble for a few moments. *Dameon, Dame—nope, that wouldn't do. Farmer, grower—no, he's a milk farmer. Let's see, cows, milk, cheese—cheese wouldn't work. Hmm, he came to speed skate. Of course, I never saw him skate.*

He was leaning over the engine. He was a handy fellow to have around. *Handy Andy.* Nah, that wouldn't do.

It should be a name of love, from one lover to another. His kisses were sweet as honey. Then again, honey was used all the time with couples. On the other hand, lover was far too personal and would definitely upset her father.

"What are you thinking?" he asked, wiping his hands off.

"Your nickname or, rather, love name. Your kiss was sweet as honey, but so many people use honey."

"Hmm, I thought your kiss was sweet as honey, too." He wiggled his eyebrows again. "Want to see if they are still sweet?"

"You're going to be hard to stop."

"Why would you want to stop?" He nestled up beside her.

"Because you gave your word," she whispered.

He stepped back. "You're right. I'll be more careful."

"Balance, honey. We just need balance."

He smiled.

"What?"

"You used it."

Jamie laughed. "I guess it just fits."

"Yeah, I guess it does. Come on. I think we can get to your house with the little bit of snow that's melted into the radiator. Besides, your father will be waiting with a shotgun if we take much longer."

"He didn't know where I was going."

"Don't be too sure of that. He knows."

Jamie slid back into the front seat and over to the passenger side. "You're probably right."

"Not a doubt in my mind." Dameon started up the car. It bucked but made it the mile down the road.

"Good night, sweetheart. I think it's best that you go straight to bed. We'll talk in the morning over breakfast," he suggested.

"Do you know how early you get up each morning?" she asked.

"A little before five. Why?"

"I'm not a morning person."

"Ah, that would be a problem living on a farm."

"Don't remind me." She sighed. "Good night, Dameon." She yawned. "I'll try and see you in the morning."

He waved her off and went about taking care of the engine, while Jamie went inside and warmed up.

"Mom. Dad. You're up?"

"Of course, dear. What took you so long?" her mother asked, holding her father's hand.

Dameon had warned her. She should have expected them to be waiting for her. "I left the car running while I waited for Dameon to come out of the club. On the way home, the engine overheated. He's putting in some water now. We had to wait for the engine to cool down before coming home."

"I'll go check on the car, Sophia." Her father got up and went outside.

Her mother patted the sofa for Jamie to sit beside her.

With her loving touch, she pushed back Jamie's bangs. "Do you love him?"

"How bad is the damage?"

Startled, Dameon banged his head on the hood of the car. "I think it will be all right. But I'd order that new radiator immediately." He wiped his hands on a cloth.

Henri Preston gave a stiff nod in response. Perhaps he didn't like being told what to do. *It surely couldn't be the cost, could it?*

"I'm glad you were there when the car overheated."

"I've worked on machinery most of my life. Running a farm takes a variety of equipment, and keeping them working seems to be a large part of the job. Especially since the Depression hit."

"It hasn't been easy on many." Henri turned and looked back at the house.

"Begging your pardon, sir, but why didn't you move into one of the houses closer to the country club? Why so far out of town?"

"Sophia and I enjoy our privacy, but economics played a factor, too."

"Ah. If there's a junkyard around here, we might be able to find a radiator that would work just fine at little cost."

"Really?" The excitement in Mr. Preston's voice was hard to ignore. Money was tighter than Dameon realized for this family. Or perhaps Mr. Preston had been keeping that information from his family. Jamie had never given any indication of a problem.

"Yes, sir. I told Jamie I would cut down my hours so we could spend a little time with one another. I'd be happy to look around and see what I can find."

"I'd appreciate that, Dameon."

"You're welcome, sir."

Dameon closed the hood.

"I'm afraid I know little about mechanical things."

"It would be my pleasure. It's the least I can do for your family giving me a warm bed to sleep in each night."

"Speaking about that, do I need to remind you about your word?"

"No, sir. I'm remembering. But with all due respect, I like your daughter."

A smile edged the side of Henri Preston's mouth. "I may have overreacted some last night."

"Truthfully, I'd probably have done the same thing," Dameon confessed. "If I were in your shoes."

"It's quite different when you're the one courting than when you're the parent of the one being courted."

Dameon let out a nervous chuckle. "I can only imagine. I spoke to God on the matter this very morning and suggested I should only have sons."

Mr. Preston roared and slapped him on the back. "Ah, but parents want their children to experience *everything* they experienced while raising them."

"You're positively cruel."

"Parents' revenge, son. Parents' revenge."

Dameon groaned. Perhaps children were something he should avoid having at all costs. Jamie's sweet face came into his mind. Then again, children were a blessing from the Lord.

❧

The next morning Dameon worked out a new schedule with Mr. Daschel, then tracked down a used radiator for the Prestons' car. Working with the few tools he could scrounge up around the barn, Dameon went to work removing the old radiator.

"Good morning, Dameon." Henri Preston's voice seemed almost cheery.

"Good morning, sir. I found a radiator and managed to get the man down to three dollars."

"Wonderful." Henri Preston reached for his wallet. "I'm sorry; I only have two dollars on me. I'll go back into the house and get the other dollar from Sophia."

"There's no rush. I trust you for it." Dameon winked.

Henri's shoulders slumped slightly. *Just how bad is their financial situation?*

With any luck, Dameon would have most of the money needed for the balloon payment, but he'd have to be very careful in his expenses to make it back home, and he'd still depend on the kindness of strangers.

Ten minutes later, Jamie returned with the dollar. "Daddy said to give you this. How's it coming?"

"Slowly. Wanna help?"

"Doing that?" She pointed to the open hood of the car. "You can't be serious." She narrowed her gaze onto him. "Are you?"

"Yup." He dropped the wrench into her hand. "Come

154

here and hold the wrench like this."

"It's heavy," she complained.

"Needs to be to do its job. Here, hold it like this." Dameon leaned over her and helped her place her hand on the wrench in the optimum spot for leverage. "Okay, you hold this as tight as you can while I use this wrench to try and free this nut from the bolt."

"All right."

Dameon worked his way under the car and tugged on the stubborn nut. Jamie lost her grip on the wrench and dropped it. Thankfully, Dameon saw it coming in enough time to shift his head to the side.

"Sorry. It moved."

Dameon chuckled. "Yeah, that's why I need you to hold it real tight."

"Okay, I'll try."

"Give it all your strength. You nearly beaned me with that wrench."

"I'm so sorry. Are you all right?"

"Fine, fine. I saw it coming and moved. Ready to try again?"

She nodded. He positioned her once again and caught a glimpse of her biting the tip of her tongue, trying to hold the wrench in place. *Lord, she's adorable.*

An hour later, they both cleaned the grease off themselves. "That was fun," she quipped.

"You're a fast learner."

"Thanks. But don't spread it around. Wouldn't want it known that I'm a grease animal."

"Monkey," he corrected.

"Monkey, right. You work well with your hands."

Dameon fought off his first response to be angry with her for the remark, knowing that she wasn't being intentionally insulting. "Thanks."

They leaned against the kitchen counter. "I don't want to go to work today, but I need to. I'm sorry we didn't get to have time to go to the games."

"There are a few more days of games." She looked down at her feet, then back up at him. "I enjoyed working with you."

Dameon tried to still the thumping of his heart. He loved this woman more deeply than he loved anyone else, but it wasn't logical. They came from different worlds and would never see one another again.

She took a tentative step forward and reached for his hand. The softness of her hand in his erupted a protective desire in him to wrap her in his safekeeping from now to eternity. He led her into his embrace. "Oh, sweetheart. I enjoyed working with you, too." He flicked her long bangs away from her eyes. "You know you have the most gorgeous eyes? A man could get lost in them."

She blinked and tried to look away.

"Please tell me why it's so hard for you to accept a compliment about your beauty."

She wrenched from his embrace and walked across the kitchen, not turning around to look at him. "You've seen my mother. How can I compare to her?" Jamie turned and faced him with tears in her eyes.

Instantly, he had her back in his arms. "You silly girl,

you. You're gorgeous. I've never known anyone to be as beautiful as you. Your mother is a fine-looking woman, but you are more beautiful. The contrast of your dark hair against your lighter skin tone, the deep chocolate color of your eyes that sparkle with flecks of gold. . . How can you possibly believe you are not her equal?"

"Do you really, really see me that way?" she pleaded.

"Oh, my sweet sweetheart. Yes, most undeniably, yes. A man—this man—could get lost in your beauty. But it goes beyond your looks. It's your heart, my love. Your sweet heart."

"But—"

He planted a kiss upon her lips to squelch the argument. She had to know she was beautiful. If nothing else could happen from their relationship, she had to know she was truly beautiful, inside and out.

The kiss deepened. His heart pounded. He needed to remain in control. Breaking off the kiss, he quelled the passion. He hoped.

❧

Jamie found it impossible to sit still the rest of the day. Dameon was working. She had no interest in attending the games. The Olympic Games had lost their thrill when compared to her growing love and attraction to Dameon. She didn't want to watch unless he was beside her. They seemed more powerful, more engaging with him there.

She'd admitted to her mother her growing affection for Dameon, and her mother cautioned her about allowing herself to feel too much for a man she had just met. To be wise, one must spend time with the Lord and seek His guidance.

But how could she pray when all she could think about was being in the man's arms, listening to his words, absorbing his kisses?

Her stomach churned at the memory of their last kiss. Thankfully, her father had not been in the house. He certainly would have sent Dameon packing for that kiss. It hadn't been that he'd done anything inappropriate; in fact, he'd pulled away before their passions overtook them, but. . .

Ah, that's why she needed to spend more time with the Lord. Her passions were out of control. She was running away with her desires and not thinking with her head. Taking the steps two at a time, she ran up to her room and pulled out her Bible.

She opened to the last place she had stopped reading the night before during her prayer time. "For what is our hope, or joy, or crown of rejoicing? Are not even ye in the presence of our Lord Jesus Christ at his coming?" she read from 1 Thessalonians 2:19. Would Jesus be glorified by the thoughts and desires she had for Dameon this afternoon?

Admittedly, He wouldn't. Her heart sank. She loved Dameon; that was beyond question now. But how could she love a man and still honor God without lapsing into the physical aspects of a relationship?

"Lord, I don't know how to balance my new feelings for Dameon and live an honorable life. My hope is to not dishonor You. My desires for Dameon have been less than honorable," she admitted. "He loves me, Lord. I'm sure of it. But we come from different worlds. He could not live in mine, as I'm fairly sure I couldn't live in his. What are we going to do?"

Jamie fell on her bed and cried. The only thought she had come up with was to end the relationship now before they crossed the line and broke one another's hearts.

She was a racer who had won one race, but the crown, the glory of the race, came at the cost of losing her heart. It wasn't fair. Life wasn't fair.

Jamie wiped the tears from her face and marched the long trek to the country club to break the news to Dameon. They had no choice. They had to end their relationship before it was too late.

Chapter 7

You decided this all on your own?" Dameon demanded. How could a few hours change his life so drastically? Earlier, he'd been contemplating marriage with Jamie; now she was breaking up a relationship that had hardly gotten off the ground.

"Dameon, I'm sorry. I don't want this, either, but I was reading and praying, and I believe it's what we have to do."

"Why?" He balled the dishcloth in his hands.

"Because our relationship can't be honoring God. We're two very different people."

That was it: their social class. Hadn't he been arguing with himself over the same issues? Hadn't he himself overlooked the problem and decided to move forward and get to know Jamie better? "I see."

"Dameon." She reached for his arm. He pulled it away. "I'm sorry. I don't want it this way but. . ." Tears that had been threatening to fall now poured down her face.

"Go home, Jamie. It'll be all right." The words he spoke were not in his heart. They were contrary to everything he felt and everything he wanted to do. What he wanted was to wrap her in his arms and hold her until all the fears went away. What he should do was let her leave and end their relationship before it truly began. She was right: They did come from different worlds, and neither one of them would be happy in the other's. He should have known better. She was forbidden fruit, and he shouldn't have been tempted by it.

"I'm sorry," she sniffled.

"I'm sorry, too." His voice cracked.

For a moment, he watched her leave. She was hurting, and it was probably all his fault. *I should have known better.*

Back inside the kitchen, he worked and worked and worked. He couldn't stop; he wouldn't stop until the very last dish in the place was done.

"Good night, Mr. Daschel. I'll be leaving in the morning."

"Are you all right, son?"

"Fine. Thanks for all the work; it really helped me."

"If you really want to help, you'll stay. As you know, I've been having trouble keeping dishwashers who don't get caught up in the games."

"I'd love to help. But it's time for me to head back home."

Mr. Daschel extended his hand, and Dameon shook it. "Thanks again for all the help."

Dameon put on his winter coat and left with Mr. Daschel, who locked up behind him. The snow was blowing, and the wind howled as he trekked back to the Prestons' farmhouse. "Perfect." He stomped back to the farm with his collar turned upward and his hands stuffed under his armpits for extra warmth.

A horn blared behind him.

❧

Jamie cried herself to sleep, sequestered in her room, refusing to speak with her parents. She pleaded with God to allow her to have peace over the decision she had made. But no peace came, only more confusion. She didn't want to dishonor God, but how could she love a man as much as she loved Dameon and *not* dishonor God?

"Jamie, open this door." The tone of her mother's voice meant she'd better obey or she'd be seeing the door open anyway.

She wiped her eyes and opened the door, keeping her head bent so her long bangs would cover her eyes. "Good morning, Mom. What's the matter?"

"Jamie Elizabeth Preston, don't you dare try and hide this from me. Now, fess up and tell me what's happened. Has he done anything—?"

"No, Mom, nothing like that. I'm sorry. No. Dameon was a perfect gentleman."

Her mother squared her shoulders and walked into the room with the regal elegance she always carried, then sat down on Jamie's bed. "Come here and tell me what's going on."

"Nothing."

"Jamie." She crossed her arms.

"Oh, all right, but you won't like it."

"I'm listening."

Jamie took in a deep breath. "After our talk the other night, and after Dameon and I shared a very. . .a. . .a passionate kiss. . ." Jamie felt her cheeks burn. "I realized that I wasn't being a good and godly witness. I wanted Dameon more than I wanted to be right with God."

"I see. So, what did you decide?"

"I broke up with him. It's the only way. I love him so much, Mom, yet I can't be a good Christian and have these desires."

Her mother smiled and cupped Jamie's face with her hands. "Honey, God gives us our desires. You can control them."

Jamie spent the next hour talking with her mother about how God's love gift works, what happens when sin takes over, how to balance her love for a man with her love for God, and how to keep her priorities straight.

"I didn't have to break up with Dameon?"

"I don't believe you had to. I think you overreacted. But you said something else that makes me wonder if it's more than your physical desires that are a problem. You mentioned the issue of social class. I know I brought it up as something to think about, but you do know that I would not say you had to marry a man within your social class, right?"

"But?"

"I was saying, be aware of the differences. There will be issues that will arise between you. You'll have to accept living within his means. And he can't be threatened by our wealth or, currently, our lack thereof." Her mother smiled.

"I jumped in and overreacted again, huh?"

Her mom nodded and asked, "Where is Dameon?"

"I don't know. Didn't he return last night?"

"His belongings are gone. He left a note thanking your father and me, but. . ."

Jamie interrupted. "Oh no. Where did he sleep?"

"I don't know, but there's another problem. The silver is missing."

❧

"Thanks for the ride." Dameon waved off Joey Thompson as the man drove away. They had traveled through the night and arrived in Albany, New York, in time for breakfast. Joey's heading south was a gift. The ride took days off Dameon's trip back home. Unfortunately, Joey was heading west from Albany and Dameon was heading east. If he could hitch a ride with someone else heading east on the highway, he could make it home in a couple of days, unlike his trip to Lake Placid, when he'd walked most of the way.

His pocket full of his hard-earned cash and his belly full, he asked some of the truck drivers if they were heading east.

"Excuse me, are you Dameon Grant?" a police officer asked.

"Yes, sir." *Why would a police officer be looking for me?*

"Would you come with me, sir?" The police officer escorted him out of the diner, leading him by the elbow. Outside the man asked, "May I look in your pack?"

"Sure." Dameon took off his pack. "What seems to be the matter, Officer?"

"There's a warrant out for your arrest."

"Excuse me?"

"You've been accused of stealing."

"That's absurd. Who would make such a claim?"

"It's not my place to say." The officer rifled through his pack, then placed him under arrest. Placing handcuffs on

Dameon, the officer escorted him to the rear seat of his police car.

Hours later, Dameon was sitting in a cell, crying out to God for some understanding of what had happened. Obviously, from the line of questions he'd been asked, someone had stolen something from the Preston home. The police had seized his money and were asking him where he'd sold the stolen silver. *Silver. What silver?*

He didn't recall seeing any—not that he had looked for any. He fought his anger, his frustration, and his desires. He loved Jamie, and now her family thought him capable of stealing, and after all he'd done to help that family. Dameon couldn't believe it. He bounced his foot up and down out of nervous frustration. *Lord, You know I'm innocent of these charges. Please help me.*

The metal door between the holding cells and the sheriff's office creaked open. "Someone's here to talk with you, Grant," a voice bellowed.

He looked up and saw Jamie walk through the doorway. He squeezed his eyes shut. The woman he loved was seeing him behind bars, a woman whose social class would never allow her to love him for who he was and not what his wallet produced.

"Dameon." Jamie's voice quivered. "They've asked me to ask you where you sold the silver."

Anger reared its ugly head. Dameon jumped up. "You believe that? After all we've been through, you believe I'd steal from your family? I can't believe your father would even think it. But here I sit behind bars." Dameon paced. "I can't believe you Prestons. Your holier-than-thou approach to life is unbelievable. If I didn't know better, I'd say your family is as poor as mine. Why I even bothered to help out you and your family is beyond me."

"Honey," Jamie whispered.

Dameon stopped pacing. Her voice was so calming. Her love name for him settled him instantly.

"I don't believe you stole from us. I've tried to tell my father that, but the police said you had a wad of cash in your pocket. Daddy's pretty convinced."

Dameon walked up to the bars and reached out for Jamie. "I earned that money. You know it, and if your father would stop long enough to look at the truth and think, he'd know it, too. Doesn't anyone use common sense in your family? How much could the silver have been worth—especially now? People are getting next to nothing for silver. I know. I sold off a tea set for Mother to help us try and make our balloon payment."

She took his hand and stepped closer. "I'm sorry, Dameon. I'm sorry about everything. I shouldn't have broken up with you. It was foolishness, and well, my father has trouble believing people sometimes. I do believe you. I know you would never steal."

"Thank you, thank you for that. My sweet sweetheart, what are we going to do?" Dameon reached through the bars and pushed her long bangs from her eyes. "I love you. I'm sorry; I shouldn't be saying it, but I do. I can't help it. I love you so much. I know this is rotten timing, and we'll probably never be able to be together, but you have to know.

I love you, and I would never do anything to intentionally hurt you or your family."

"I know." She slipped her eyelids closed, then opened them slowly. Their chocolate beauty made a man crave to be near her sweetness. "I love you, too," she confessed.

He tried to kiss her between the bars. Their lips barely touched.

"I'll try and get Father to come in and talk with you. If he sees you, he'll know without a doubt you couldn't have done this."

He leaned his head against the bars, and she wrapped her hands around his. "Not yet, please. Oh, Jamie, what are we going to do?"

Chapter 8

Jamie kissed Dameon's forehead. Somehow she had to convince her father to come and speak with him. "I'll be back as soon as possible."

"Wait, please, just one more moment." Dameon held on to her hand and caressed the top of it with his thumb. "I'm sorry. I wish I could be the man you need."

"Oh, you foolish man! Don't you know you are the man I need?" She squeezed his hand. "I'll be back as soon as possible."

Jamie stood up straight and squared her shoulders. With determined steps, she left the holding cell area of the sheriff's office and headed back to her parents.

Her father jumped to his feet as she entered the room. "What did he say?"

"He didn't do it, Daddy. And I believe him."

"Humph." He stomped back to his seat.

Her mother reached out and patted her husband's arm. "Why do you believe him, Jamie? The police claim he was carrying $175."

"But wasn't he working hard for that money? Didn't he work twelve hours and more a day?"

"True, but what about the silver?"

"He didn't take it, Mom. And I believe him. Why do you assume he did? Couldn't it have been stolen while he was at work? Didn't Mr. Daschel say Dameon worked until midnight last night?" Jamie walked over to her parents and took one of the other chairs in the waiting room and lowered her voice. "And just how much value does silver have these days? Dameon said he sold a tea set for his mother and was paid only a very small sum. Isn't it more reasonable that Dameon earned every penny he had in his pocket? And isn't it odd that a man who spent an entire morning tracking down a radiator and replacing it in your car would only ask for the three dollars he paid for the part?"

Jamie paused for a moment. "It doesn't make sense, Dad, does it?"

Henri Preston was a man Jamie always found to be fair—hard on people, perhaps at times, but fair—and always quick to agree when he was wrong, a trait she had inherited from him. He took in a deep sigh and let it out slowly. "I'll go meet with the boy."

Slowly, her father exited the room. Jamie stayed seated next to her mother. As much as she wanted to be with Dameon, it was something the two men needed to work out.

"Everything will be all right, dear." Her mother patted her arm.

"I hope so. I want Daddy to drop the charges. It's ludicrous to think that Dameon would steal from us."

"I think you're right. But isn't it possible that he was angry enough that he felt entitled to the silver for the work he'd done around the place?"

"I can't believe you'd think that, Mom. He never asked for compensation. Look at all he did around the house unasked for. The wood he chopped, the work on the hen-house, gathering the eggs, repairing some small things here and there. No one asked him; he just did it. I don't think he's the kind of person who would steal."

"You're probably right. I'm sorry for doubting him. It just happened so suddenly, and folks aren't always rational when they are angry."

Jamie wanted to argue with her parents that they shouldn't have doubted Dameon under any circumstances, but hadn't she wondered herself? It did seem likely that he had stolen the silver and disappeared. What really seemed odd was how quickly he had made it down to Albany. The trip had taken several hours for them to arrive.

Her thoughts were a muddle of confusion. How long would Dameon have to sit in jail?

"Mom?"

"Yes, dear?"

Jamie glanced down at her hands, folding and unfolding them. "Do you think I could be a good farmer's wife?"

&

Spending the night in jail for something he hadn't done—Dameon had never expected to live through that kind of humiliation. Henri Preston had dropped the charges but also impressed upon the police to keep Dameon overnight.

This allowed Henri Preston to escape with his daughter back to Lake Placid.

❦

Four days later, Dameon found himself back home, and for the first time in his life, he felt out of place on the farm.

A week after returning home while mucking out the cows' stalls, Dameon realized that he had left Jamie without a fight. He should have returned to Lake Placid and worked things out with Jamie and her parents. But shoulda, coulda, woulda wouldn't help now.

Dameon slid a shovel against the wooden floorboards, scooping up the muck. Parts of the farmer's life were not appealing, even after years of experience.

The games were over now. Had the Prestons returned to Princeton, New Jersey? Should he try to find Jamie? He bent down and scooped another shovelful of muck and tossed it in the wheelbarrow.

The sound of a car or truck pulling up in front of the house caught Dameon's attention. He had closed the barn door upon entering. The end of February could bring some of the coldest weather in New England.

He drew his attention back to his work. More than likely, it was someone to see his parents. Few people called on him since he had graduated from high school, and Dameon seldom found himself at the center of attention. He leaned down and positioned the shovel for another load.

The large barn door creaked open. Dameon stood up. "Dameon, you have a visitor," his father called out. He stood there with his winter coat wide open, grinning from ear to ear.

Who could it be? Dameon wondered. *Father certainly wouldn't be grinning if it was the banker here to collect on the balloon payment.* Dameon had raised enough to appease the creditors, or so he and his parents had been led to believe. His trip to the Olympics had paid off, but his heart was no longer with the farm. It was locked deep within Jamie. He stepped out of the stall, stomped the muck off his boots, took off his leather work gloves, and left them on the rail of the stall.

"Dameon."

His back stiffened when he heard Jamie's voice. He spun around to see if he was hearing things or if she truly was there. "Jamie." His heart soared. "What are you doing here?"

"I'll leave you young people be," his father said, walking off to the house.

Dameon saw the Prestons' car in his yard. "Did you drive here by yourself?" His legs shook as he took a tentative step toward her.

"No, my parents are with me. I needed to see you." She looked down at the ground.

Dameon's heart caught in his throat. A moment of ecstasy had vanished in less than a second. He'd hoped she'd come to be a part of his life. Of course, he had never asked her.

"Jamie," his voice quivered, "I've been trying to figure out if I should go to New Jersey and see if I could find you. I've missed you. I love you."

Jamie's precious brown eyes puddled with tears.

"Oh, my sweet sweetheart, come here." He wrapped her in his protective grasp. "Please, tell me you love me and want to spend the rest of your life with me."

She shook in his arms. "I've been terrified," she confessed. "My parents didn't know what to do with me. Daddy doesn't like to see his little girl hurt, and when he refused to let me see you again in Albany, I sulked. I sulked for days."

Dameon chuckled. "I was tempted to go back to Lake Placid, but my parents were counting on me. And the police *helped* me find a ride heading east."

"Dameon, there's something you must know. Father's been hit terribly by the Depression. We've little in liquid assets. We're heading for Greece in a couple of weeks."

He held her tighter. "No, please don't go. Stay. Please stay with me."

Jamie smiled and wiped the tears from her eyes. "I was hoping you'd say that. I can't imagine being a farmer's wife. I don't know the first thing about it. But I'm willing to learn if you can be patient with me. I'll need a lot of patience. I've been trained for social gatherings. I know how to entertain royalty, but I don't know the first thing about milking a cow."

"It's like opening ceremonies. It takes a little practice, but once you have the art down, it produces tremendous joy for many."

Jamie cocked her head to the right. "I seriously doubt that, but I'm willing to learn."

"And you'll have to teach me as well. I have no idea what it would be like to entertain royalty. I'd be the proverbial bull in a china shop."

She leaned back from his embrace and narrowed her gaze. "Tell you what, how about I take care of the china and you take care of the bulls?"

Dameon laughed. "But what about the cows?"

She opened her delicate mouth and closed it. He'd caught her on that one. Taking full advantage of the surprise, he leaned down and kissed her tender lips, then said, "My sweet sweetheart. I love you."

"I love you, too," she said with a giggle.

"What? What am I missing?"

"My parents met at the first Olympics."

"Really?"

"Yes."

"Hmm." Dameon snuggled her in his arms once again. "Do you think we've continued a family tradition?"

"Mother says so."

"And your father?"

"He's still getting used to the idea of his little girl growing up."

"Ah, that reminds me. I think it best if we only have sons."

Jamie jabbed him in the side.

"Ouch. What's that for?"

She aimed again.

"Never mind. I think I know."

The cowbell rang.

"What is that?" Jamie asked.

"That's my mother saying it's time for us to come in and face the adults."

"Ah, guess it's time I meet your parents." She winked.

"If I know my parents," Dameon added, "they will have had us married and with two kids before we get into the house."

"Oh? What about the honeymoon?"

Dameon stopped. "They wouldn't have thought about that."

"Mine would. What do you think about a trip to Greece?"

"I think I'm way out of my league. Until a few weeks ago, I never traveled any farther than into town for supplies."

Jamie held his hand. "Honey, together we have a hope in Jesus. He's our crown. Nothing this world offers means anything. I've learned that recently from our family's struggles during the Depression. Mother has far more wealth than Father ever had, but they are two of the most down-to-earth people I know, and it's because of their faith in the Lord."

"Yeah, the morning after your father caught us in the kitchen, he found me asleep on the floor in my room. I'd been up all night praying and reading the Bible, trying to figure out how I could repair the wedge I'd placed between your parents and myself. But I'd fallen asleep during my prayer time. Anyway, your dad seemed to soften when he saw what I'd been reading."

"Father mentioned he respected you and your beliefs in the Lord. He was angry in Albany, but I think he was angrier with himself for jumping to conclusions that weren't true."

"I went to the Olympics in the hope of helping my family." Dameon drank in the beauty of this magnificent woman. "But I found a far richer gift. I found God's gift to me in you. I love you, Jamie Preston. Will you please become my wife?"

"I love you, too, Dameon. And you're my gift, too. I never fit quite right in my parents' world, but I know it's a part of me and who I am. And yes, I'll marry you. Just remember, you take care of the bulls."

Dameon grinned and tapped her reddened button nose. "And you the china, my sweet sweetheart."

LYNN A. COLEMAN

Lynn A. Coleman is an award-winning, multipublished author and speaker. She is the co-founder of American Christian Romance Writers, served as president for two years and advisor for the group. Currently, she makes her home in Miami, Florida, with her husband of thirty years. They serve the Lord as pastors of Christ Community Church. Together, they are blessed with three children and eight grandchildren.

Olympic Goals

by Kathleen Y'Barbo

To Shirley Miller,
an awesome sister–in–law and sister in Christ.
Welcome to the family!

Author's note: The actual events surrounding the 1960 Olympic Trials in California and the Seventeenth Olympic Games in Rome have, to the best of my ability, been presented in the most accurate manner possible. Some artistic license has been taken in placing the fictional characters of Bonnie Taggart and Preston Grant and others into these events.

Chapter 1

April 1, 1959

Preston Grant strolled past the broad windows of Setzer's Main Street Drugstore and Soda Shoppe, then stopped to pick up a penny lying in his path. Without warning, the pharmacy's door flew open with enough force to send him sprawling to the pavement. As he straightened, a pink blur flew by, leaving the loveliest fragrance of lavender in its wake.

Her wake, he corrected, as the blur slowed a bit to reveal a feminine form with long legs and a runner's stride. A runner? Preston shook his head to clear the cobwebs. This was no runner. A pretty shopgirl, most definitely, but not a runner.

Yet she moved faster than any other member of the University of Massachusetts track team—all but himself, of course. As the fastest man on the UMass team this spring and an Olympic hopeful, however, he knew talent when he saw it.

And this woman had talent.

"Excuse me, sir!" a sweet voice called as pink high heels pounded a swift cadence on the sidewalk. "Please forgive me. I'll offer a proper apology just as soon as I catch Mrs.—" She disappeared around the corner along with the rest of her statement.

Dusting off his tweed trousers as he stood, Preston once again inhaled the sweet scent of lavender. Or perhaps he just imagined he did.

The girl, however, was no figment of his imagination, for he would soon have the bruises to prove it. The thought occurred that he might be the butt of an elaborate April Fool's Day hoax most likely perpetrated by his roommate, Tom, or possibly by one of the guys on the team.

No, he decided as he tucked the penny into his pocket. That just wasn't possible. The runner's legs were too shapely to belong to one of the guys, and that voice had been far too sweet to be anything but genuinely female. The girl, whoever she was, was real.

And this left Preston with a dilemma. Did he stay and wait for his apology or leave now and arrive at his meeting with the journalism department head on time?

To leave would mean keeping the most important appointment of his life, namely, the meeting that would decide whether his conditional acceptance into the master's program in journalism would become permanent or not. To stay meant he would miss the appointment that could seal his academic fate, but it also meant he would meet the woman who moved like the wind and smelled like lavender—all while wearing pink high heels.

A tough choice.

Preston cast a quick glance at his watch, then toward the corner where the pink phantom had disappeared. Wouldn't you know she had run in the opposite direction from the journalism building so there would be no chance of accidentally meeting her along the way?

Again he checked his watch. He should head left on Main, back toward the campus, but perhaps just a quick jog to the right at the corner would be in order. What harm would there be in taking a look to see if perhaps she'd turned to head back this way? After all, she *had* offered to make an apology, and it *would* be terribly rude of him not to allow her to do so.

It was the least he could do.

He smiled. "The very least."

Thus, a plan was formed. He could casually canvass the general area within a two-block radius of Setzer's and, if he hustled like the future Olympian he planned to be, still make it to his meeting with the dean just a minute or two late.

Five at the most, if he kept his conversation with the girl to a hasty hello and a promise to phone her tonight. Surely the dean would understand.

When he reached the corner, the woman in pink was nowhere to be found. Preston strained his neck to look beyond the bend to see if perhaps she'd gone that way. After all, there was an alley behind Setzer's Drugstore, and she just might have returned through the back way. Preston was about to head off in that direction when a hand clamped onto his shoulder.

"Aren't you supposed to be somewhere?"

"Tom?" Preston shook off his roommate's grasp and straightened his shoulders as he jogged toward the alley that led behind the row of shops. "Yeah, um, the meeting. I know. I was just looking for—that is, I saw this girl in pink high heels run past and I tried to catch her, but—"

"Really, Preston, I know you don't have a way with the ladies like me, but a track star who can't catch a girl in pink high heels?" Tom's laugh echoed down the empty alley. "Oh, I get it. April Fool!"

"You're the April fool, pal." Preston whirled around and stalked out of the alley toward Main. She could be walking through the same door she hit him with right this moment. Unfortunately, when he reached that door, the only person in sight was the Reverend Greene, who offered a crisp greeting before disappearing inside.

One last glance at his watch told him he'd be five minutes late now, no matter what. Preston sighed and turned to head down Main Street, his elbow throbbing. Maybe the dean and his committee would understand his tardiness if he showed them his bruises.

"Okay, okay. I give." Tom fell in step beside Preston. "So tell me about this girl."

Preston laughed and gave his roommate a side look. "Let's just say my first impression was a memorable one."

So memorable, in fact, that Preston had neither the attention span nor the interest for a lengthy meeting with the thesis committee. He managed to satisfy the dean's questions and finish the interview in record time without having to show them his injured elbow, but when he returned to Setzer's, the store was dark and the door locked tight. The only vision in pink was the advertisement for stomach ailment medication prominently displayed in the pharmacy window.

❧

The next two days were filled with morning classes and midday practices at the track, followed by afternoons working his part-time job as an assistant copy editor at the local paper. Although his intentions were good, he never managed to get to the pharmacy before the shop closed. A few times on his walks between the track and his dorm, he thought he might have caught sight—or, rather, the lavender scent—of the woman in pink, but without a clear image of her face, he couldn't be sure.

By the morning of the third day, he'd become so desperate, he even followed a lavender-scented coed with a blond ponytail to a dorm near the commons. When he noticed her staring at him out of a second-floor window on his trek to the cafeteria, he braved a wave. To his surprise, the coed waved back.

Rather than suffer through the beef stroganoff advertised as the lunch special at the cafeteria, Preston decided to skip the meal and race over to Setzer's for a soda and possibly an apology from a pretty girl. Unfortunately, he got neither, as the girl was nowhere in sight and the line at the soda fountain was longer than he expected. As Preston walked back to campus, his stomach growling and his mind churning, he began to wonder if he would ever come face-to-face

185

with the woman in pink.

"Hi," a decidedly feminine voice called as a blur in blue-and-white polka dots rushed past. Preston stopped short and turned to watch a blond ponytail disappear inside Setzer's. For a moment he debated chasing the ponytail—and its owner—into the drugstore based on the highly unlikely possibility this girl might be *the* girl.

If he followed the girl instead of logic, he would miss a practice, which would cause him to miss this weekend's meet, coach's rules. Even so, he debated a moment before turning his back on Setzer's and heading for the track. Along the way, a plan began to formulate. Perhaps there was a way to meet the woman who plagued his thoughts *and* still make all his obligations.

That evening at four-thirty, Preston pushed away from his desk at the *Chronicle* and strode toward the editor's office. His boss, a family man with seven daughters, listened to Preston's tale of woe with a smile. He handed him his weekly paycheck, then sent him off a half hour before quitting time to find the vision in pink—or whatever color she wore today—before the drugstore closed.

Preston arrived at the sidewalk in front of Setzer's at precisely fifteen minutes until five. His hand shook as he reached for the shiny brass handle on the door, the same handle that had left its mark on him a few days earlier.

"Okay, here goes nothing," he whispered as he yanked on the handle and stepped inside.

The strong scent of antiseptic assailed him—nothing like the lavender he wished for. And then he saw her.

Behind the counter, ringing up an order of baby aspirins for a young mother, stood the vision in pink—only today she wore yellow, the color of sunshine. At least he thought it was the same girl, although she did bear a strong resemblance to the pony-tailed coed from the dorm. Perhaps that was where he recognized her from.

The only way to know for sure was to either watch her run or get close enough to check her for the scent of lavender. Neither option seemed likely at the moment.

"Can I help you, sir?"

His gaze locked with hers, and his voice disappeared. So did his brain.

Managing to garner enough coordination to shake his head, Preston retreated to the foot products aisle to rethink his plan. Perhaps his original idea of storming the counter and making a joke out of demanding an apology from the woman who had bowled him down wasn't quite the tack he should take in this instance.

"Are you shopping or sightseeing, young man?"

Preston whirled around to see Mr. Setzer glaring at him from his perch at the far end of the counter. "Shopping, sir," he said as he turned to grab a red plastic basket from the stack at the end of the aisle.

The clock behind Mr. Setzer's head read five minutes before five when Preston wandered up to the counter to wait in line behind Pastor Greene. Without a clear plan, he'd run out of time. He looked down at the basket and counted half a dozen items he would never use and another dozen he had duplicates of at home. Contemplation of a quick trip down the aisles to return the items to their rightful places on the shelves was interrupted by Pastor Greene.

"Why don't you go ahead of me, son? I'm still making my mind up about these throat lozenges."

"Oh, yes, um, thanks," Preston said as he hefted the basket onto the counter, then dove to catch a roll of antacid tablets before they hit the floor. As he tossed them back into the basket, he braved a look at the girl behind the counter.

All doubt vanished. It definitely was *her*.

She reached for a pair of yellow rubber gloves sitting atop the basket, then froze. "Hey, I know you," she said as she pointed the gloves in his direction.

"Oh, really?"

"You're the guy from the other day." The prettiest shade of pink, very much like the color she wore at their first meeting, rose in her cheeks as she resumed unloading the basket onto the counter. "I believe I owe you an apology."

Preston's confidence rose, and he squared his shoulders and smiled at the vision in yellow. "How about you deliver that apology over dinner, Miss Sunshine?"

She averted her eyes but returned his smile. "I'd like that very much. By the way, my name is Bonnie."

Chapter 2

March 24, 1960

Bonnie Taggart stood at the edge of the University of Massachusetts track and watched the love of her life clear the last hurdle to sprint for the finish line. Clicking a stopwatch, she shouted out the time, his best yet. Preston Grant acknowledged her with a wave and a smile, then turned toward the bleachers to grab the towel he'd left hanging on the rail.

How she loved to watch Preston on the track. He was a natural—a future Olympic champion, for sure—while she, well, she was nothing but an accidental competitor at best. Somewhere this past year between deciding to subtly chase the handsome journalism graduate student and actually catching him, Bonnie had learned that she, too, had been gifted with the ability to run.

Just last week, when she'd become distracted by thoughts of her upcoming math test, she'd actually come a little too close to beating him on their morning sprint from the steps of her dorm to the university track. If the truth were known, she could have tried a bit harder and actually arrived at the finish line before him, but why in the world would she want to do that? Merely spending time with Preston had been her goal. If she beat him, he might find someone else to train with for the Olympics.

The Olympics. She shuddered at the thought. Pretending interest in the goal of making the Olympic track-and-field team had given her plenty of time with Preston, but what if she actually achieved the goal of earning a spot on the 440-relay team?

Surely the Lord had meant to give the gift of speed and endurance to someone more suited to the blessing. No more unlikely a woman ever graced a track than Bonnie Lou Taggart. Forget the Olympics. All she wanted to succeed in was being the best wife to Preston she could and, if God allowed, the best mother to his children. Of course, she would use the elementary education degree she hoped to receive at the end of the year to teach until the wedding, or possibly until the babies came.

First she had to receive a proposal, however, and Preston was too distracted to consider anything besides track and field right now. After Rome, perhaps, but not now.

Bonnie sighed. She'd been guilty of moments of distraction, as well, most of them directly related to her part in the upcoming Olympic Trials. If only she could tell Preston the truth regarding her fears.

But loving Preston meant loving the Olympics, for the Olympic Games had been a part of Grant family lore since before the turn of the century. From his grandma Sophia and grandfather Henri to his parents, Jamie and Dameon, there had been no doubt about the meaning of the ancient competition to the family. Soon Preston would take his place in that lineage, the first to actually compete in the games.

And bless his heart, he intended for her to participate, as well.

Moments later, the object of her thoughts trotted over, sweating despite the persistent chill in the springtime air. The towel lay draped over one broad shoulder, and his short, sandy brown hair ruffled in the breeze. As he neared, Bonnie's heart did its usual flip-flop.

How she would love spending the rest of her life waking up next to him. God could not have blessed her more if He'd given her the sun and the moon and all the stars.

"Good morning, sunshine," he whispered as he wrapped an arm around her waist and turned to lead her away from the track. "How did the makeup test go?"

Bonnie shrugged and snuggled into his embrace, ignoring the damp towel sharing space between them. "Oh, fine, I suppose, but I missed our morning run terribly."

Actually, she'd missed *him* terribly, not the run.

Preston chuckled. "You only skipped the original test because you *were* with me."

She looked up into brown eyes flecked with gold and returned his smile. Ever since Preston had taken an interest in coaching her, he'd insisted she participate in every track-and-field event within a day's drive of the school. "I know, but I hardly count spending the day at a university track meet as time spent together. When you weren't running hurdles, you were on the sidelines watching me."

While she adored the time spent driving alone to and from the meets, the actual contest always left her a bit disconcerted. She won far more times than she lost when she raced alone, and her 440 team was unbeaten this year. Those victories were certainly worth celebrating.

Still, all the wins in the world would not add up to one marriage proposal from Preston Grant. "Sunshine, you're going to give Wilma Rudolph some stiff competition as the fastest female runner in Rome," he loved to proclaim.

"Miss Rudolph can have the whole thing with my blessing," she longed to say in response, although she knew she never would.

Preston removed his hand from her waist and entwined her fingers with his. Again she returned his smile as they walked along in companionable silence.

What's taking him so long to propose?

His graduation was just a few months away, and if Bonnie hadn't cut her class load back drastically to facilitate her track events, she would be finished as well. Now it would take until next year to receive her degree, but to her mind, the time had been well spent—with Preston.

Preston had certainly talked all around the subject of marriage in the months since last fall when they'd realized the seriousness of their relationship. Just a week ago, he had expressed an interest in what she intended to do after graduation, then indicated concern when she told him of her plans to take a teaching job at the elementary school where she currently did her student teaching.

No wife of his would work once the children began arriving, he'd stated firmly. What he *hadn't* been firm about was just exactly *when* he intended to make her his wife.

"And so I told Pop I would be sure I got on camera to wave at him and Mama," she heard Preston say.

"I'm sorry, dear. Could you repeat that?"

He gave her his most patient smile and squeezed her hand. "Daydreaming again? I hope I was in it."

She felt heat rise in her cheeks. "Always," she stammered.

"Well, as I was saying, Tom's dad talked to the boys at CBS and promised me at least one close-up so I could say hello to the family back home."

"How exciting! I'm sure your parents will be thrilled to see you on television all the way from Rome."

"You'll be there, too, you know. How's about I get you a close-up, too? Wouldn't your folks love that?"

"Sure," she said with what she hoped would be some measure of enthusiasm.

The thought of enduring the Olympic Trials in order to make a spot on the team that would go to Rome made her knees weak. The Lord knew her reluctance to compete; He alone got her through each meet. Why had He allowed her charade of pretending to be a serious athlete to go so far?

Preston stopped short and pulled her toward him. "Okay, Bonnie, what's the problem?"

"Problem?" She broadened what she knew was a weak smile and averted her gaze. If she looked at him directly right now, she would cry, for sure. "I suppose I'm just a little nervous."

"If you weren't, I'd worry about you," he said as he gathered her into his arms. "It's going to be you and me competing together in Rome, just a couple of Olympians in love. If that's not romantic, I don't know what is."

She giggled despite herself as she reached for the disgusting towel and tossed it aside to kiss him square on the lips. "Preston Grant, you have absolutely no idea what romantic is, but I love you anyway."

Oh, how he loved her! Bonnie Lou Taggart was his blue-eyed beauty, with the long, lean frame of an athlete and the heart of a woman with whom he could happily spend the rest of his life. She loved the Lord first and him second, and both his mother and father adored her. Even his brother Henri grudgingly admitted he'd done well for himself in landing such a catch.

And best of all, she could run like the wind.

Watching Bonnie head around the track brought tears to his eyes. Moving with the speed of a gazelle, she made running seem effortless. Often, she emerged from a race barely out of breath. Sometimes he wondered if she might be holding back, perhaps not giving her all, especially in their morning races from her dorm to the track.

On any given day, she could beat him in a footrace, and he knew it. It was only the kindness of her heart that slowed her pace to just a step behind his every time.

One more reason why he loved her so.

He watched while she disappeared behind the double doors of her dorm, then, as was their custom, he waited until she appeared at her second-story window. When the glass pane rose and her radiant face appeared, he waved.

"See you tonight," she called.

"Tonight it is, sunshine," he answered before turning to head back to the gym for another hour of training before class.

Unlike Bonnie, running did not come naturally to him. But nothing would keep Preston from running in the Olympics. Nothing.

He shrugged off the weight of that statement with a roll of his shoulders and took a shortcut through the university library. For various reasons, neither his father nor his grandfather had participated in the Olympic Games, yet the event had taken on an almost mythical status in the Grant household. When Pop heard CBS would be broadcasting the Olympiad to the United States for the first time ever, he actually went out and bought a television set. Big plans were in the works for the whole family—possibly, the whole town—to watch him compete.

Again Preston felt the sting of inadequacy. What if he didn't make the team? What if he didn't go to Rome?

"No. God wouldn't let that happen. He promised I would go," he said loudly, startling a nearby coed from her studies. "Sorry," he whispered, but the girl answered with a glare.

God wouldn't let him fail, would He? All his prayers had led to one conclusion. He was meant to go to Rome, to compete in the Olympiad. Throughout the rest of the morning, during a practice in which he knocked over more hurdles than he cleared, and into his afternoon break back at the dorm, he contemplated the promise God had given him. The more he thought, the less sure he became over what God had pledged.

When his roommate, Tom McCoffey, strolled in, Preston told him of his dilemma.

"Are you sure you're supposed to compete? I mean, did God tell you that specifically?"

Preston leaned up on one elbow and eyed his roommate from the upper bunk. "He said I would go to Rome for the Olympics. That's all I know."

Tom settled into the squeaky desk chair and steepled his fingers. "So you know you're supposed to *go*, but you're not sure if you're supposed to *compete*."

"Yeah."

"Maybe you're supposed to take my dad up on his offer to work for the network." He wadded up a piece of notebook paper and tossed it toward the bunk bed. It landed square on Preston's chest, then rolled onto the mattress. "Hanging out with Dad and the CBS guys is good enough for me, and hey, it'll look pretty good on my résumé that I helped with the first ever U.S. Olympic broadcast. You could do the same, you know."

"I guess."

"You have to act fast, though," Tom said. "Slots on the crew are going fast."

"Thanks, but I'm going to have to pass." Preston fell back against the sheets and cradled his head in his hands. "I had a lousy day on the track, and now my ankle's killing me. My timing's off, and if I don't get some more practice in, I'll never get to where I want to be. I've made a promise to God to be the best. With the trials coming up quick, I have to wonder if He wants me running hurdles or not."

"Have you ever considered that maybe God's just trying to tell you to depend on Him and not on yourself? That maybe it will be the Lord who gets you to Rome instead of any effort on your part to 'be the best'?"

Preston reached for the wad of notebook paper and lobbed it toward Tom, who caught it and tossed it into the wastebasket beneath his desk.

"Point taken, Tom," he said. "But what about the call on our lives to do our best? Doesn't He expect us to do our utmost for His highest?"

"Not when our best is good enough for Him but not good enough for us." Tom rose. "You're your own worst critic, Preston, and that's my final say on the matter. Now, are you coming with me to the cafeteria? It's mystery meat night."

"As great as that sounds, I can't. I'm meeting Bonnie in an hour."

"Hot date?" Tom grinned.

"Strategy session, actually." Preston sat up and ducked his head to keep it from hitting the ceiling as he swung a leg over and climbed down from the top bunk. "Bonnie's been a little slow coming out of the blocks lately, and I'm convinced we can shave a few seconds off her time if I can get her to work on that."

Tom shook his head and folded his arms across his chest. "You're kidding, right?"

"No, I'm completely serious. Why?"

"All I can say is that if I had a sweet little number like Bonnie Taggart in love with me, I surely wouldn't be wasting evenings trying to 'shave a few seconds off her time.' " He clapped a hand on Preston's shoulder. "A girl like her needs affection, Preston. Flowers, candy, a nice evening out that *does not* involve the university track. Practice a little romance, my friend, or someday you'll lose her to someone who will."

Lose Bonnie? Never.

She'd been his from the moment he'd first told her hello almost a year ago. He'd known it and so had she. God had showed him in a thousand ways that He had put His blessing on the relationship, as well, so how could the silly things Tom mentioned really matter? Sure, he knew most other girls liked that sort of sentimental stuff, but Bonnie wasn't like most other girls. She was different, special.

And she was *his*, flowers and candy or not. Still, she *was* a woman, and women did have a natural affinity for the silliness of romance and sentiment. If she could run faster for him, maybe he could be romantic for her—just this once.

A plan began to dawn, and he smiled. He loved her, and after the Olympic Games, she would know just how much.

"So, Tom, you think this romantic stuff is *really* necessary?"

"Yeah, if you love her, I do." He gave Preston a quizzical look. "Why?"

"Because I've got an idea, but I'm going to need some help. The jewelry store where you work—how late is it open?"

Tom glanced down at his watch, then back at Preston. "Until six. Why?"

"You know how you owe me a favor for vouching for you with that cute little redhead in our psych class? Well, I need to collect on that favor, and I'm going to need your friend the jeweler to help me—and quick."

Chapter 3

Bonnie had just finished tying the laces of her sneakers when Preston's familiar voice called her name. "Be right there, sweetheart," she said as she raced to the window. "I just need to grab my—Preston?"

What she saw took her breath away. The love of her life stood beneath her window in the dark blue suit and striped tie she hadn't seen him wear since her grandmother's funeral.

"I hope you don't mind, but I took the liberty of changing our plans for the evening." He held up his watch. "Training's postponed until tomorrow night. Tonight we've got reservations at seven."

"Reservations?"

He nodded and gestured in her direction. "And as lovely as you look in that outfit, I doubt it would be appropriate for the Garden Room."

She inhaled a sharp breath. "We're going to the Garden Room?"

A meal at the finest—and most romantic—restaurant in town would set Preston back a week's wages. She'd always hoped to dine there with Preston, but she'd imagined it would be to celebrate their engagement.

Her heart jumped. Could this be the evening she'd been waiting for, the night that Preston would ask her to be his wife?

"Give me five minutes," she called.

Five minutes stretched to ten as Bonnie donned and discarded several dresses before she found just the right one—the pink organza frock she'd worn the first time she met Preston. Sliding her feet into matching pink high heels, she ran a brush through her hair and curled it into a French twist, then snapped a pair of pearl earrings onto her ears. Finally, she dabbed a bit of her favorite lavender cologne on each wrist and behind each ear.

A moment later, she flew down the stairs and emerged into the twilight to find Preston waiting patiently. "I'm sorry it took me so long, but—"

Preston stopped her apology with a kiss. "You look beautiful," he whispered against her ear as he linked arms with her and set off in the direction of the Garden Room. "Definitely worth the wait."

The evening's stars began to emerge as the pair strolled across the commons toward Main Street. They talked of silly, inconsequential things having to do with school and work, yet the conversation drew Bonnie in and held her. Spending time with Preston would never be anything but special, no matter how mundane the topics of conversation.

The Garden Room shone especially bright that night as Bonnie and Preston dined by candlelight with a beautiful centerpiece of white roses decorating the crisp white table linens. The Marv Davis Trio provided a lovely background of classical tunes as the menus were produced—hers, thankfully, without prices. When she couldn't place a thought, much less an order, Preston took over.

What seemed like mere moments later, the food arrived, presented grandly beneath silver servers. Preston raved over the taste of an overlarge steak, while Bonnie's excitement made her unable to enjoy the most delicious grilled flounder she'd ever been served. When Preston ordered two slices of the Garden Room's signature coconut pound cake, he ended up having to eat both servings.

Finally, the meal ended and the waiter brought the check. Bonnie waited in breathless anticipation as Preston reached for her hand. Her pulse raced, and her mouth went dry. How she would respond to the question he was about to pop, she had no idea.

When Preston cleared his throat, Bonnie reached for her water glass. A gulp of cold water later, she turned her attention back to Preston and waited for him to ask so she could say yes.

His fingers curled around her hand as his gaze locked with hers. The moment she'd dreamed of for ages was finally here.

A winter wedding would be nice. Something at Christmas or possibly New Year's Eve. Yes, New Year's would be just the thing. She would invite all their dear friends and family. Red poinsettias would decorate the church, and the bridesmaids would wear—

"Shall we, Bonnie?"

Bonnie mentally cleared away the wedding plans and focused her attention on Preston. "Shall we what?"

Preston offered his most endearing smile. "Go." He rose and offered her his hand, then looked perplexed and sank back onto his chair. "Unless you'd rather stay a bit longer."

"Oh, no, um. . ." She fumbled with her napkin and ended up dropping it atop the roses. So Preston's plan was to propose after dinner. Bonnie forced a smile and stood. *Of course. Why propose in a crowded restaurant when one could find a nice private place to declare one's eternal love? How wonderfully romantic.*

Bonnie followed Preston out of the Garden Room with a genuine smile. *Thank You, Lord, for such an extraordinary man. Help me to be the wife he needs.*

She breathed a deep sigh of contentment and leaned into Preston as they strolled toward Main Street. Straight ahead, the darkened windows of Setzer's glinted with the light of the streetlamp.

"Happy?" Preston asked as he squeezed her hand.

"Never happier."

"Me, too." He stopped abruptly and gathered her into his arms. "Do you realize we're standing in a special place, Miss Taggart?"

Bonnie's heart thudded against her chest. "Actually, I only have eyes for you, Mr. Grant, so I hadn't noticed."

Preston touched the tip of her nose, then pressed a finger to her lips. "This is where we met."

She stole a quick kiss, then smiled. "Yes, it is, isn't it?"

He settled her onto the steps leading to the front door of the old pharmacy and knelt in front of her. Again Bonnie's heart lurched.

"Bonnie?" he said as he reached inside his jacket.

"Yes?" Her head began to spin, and it took all her concentration just to keep her mind on what was happening. This would be the only proposal she would ever receive, and she fully intended to appreciate every moment of it.

As if moving in slow motion, Preston opened his hand to reveal a small black velvet box.

"Bonnie, you know I love you."

"Yes," she breathed in a whisper.

"And you know we've talked about how we both feel God is leading us to a relationship that will last forever."

All she could manage was a nod.

"Well," he said as he placed the box in her hand, "you were right when you said I'm not a romantic guy, but I try. A guy like me—I don't have a lot to offer a girl like you, at least not yet." He paused for what seemed like an eternity. "What I'm trying to ask is, would you wait for me until I can make something of myself?"

What? That wasn't quite what I expected him to ask.

"Of course, I'll wait, Preston," she said slowly. "I just don't understand what you mean about making something of yourself. To me you're the most amazing man I've ever met. What more could you do to improve on that?"

His look of relief sent her reeling. So did his kiss. Finally, he pulled away.

"Open it, sunshine," he said, gesturing toward the box.

Bonnie gave him another quick kiss, then slowly lifted the top to reveal a slender pink ribbon coiled atop the black velvet. As she lifted the ribbon, a shiny penny caught her attention.

"What's this?" She met Preston's gaze with a smile.

"Remember the first time we met?"

Heat flooded Bonnie's cheeks. "How could I forget? I was terribly rude. I ran right over you."

"And in those pink high heels, no less." Preston took the ribbon and placed it on her neck. "What you don't know is if I hadn't stopped to pick up this very penny, you and I might never have met. I want to spend the rest of my life with you, but first I have to. . ."

His words trailed off, and he looked away. At that moment, with the stars as a backdrop and Setzer's Drugstore and Soda Shoppe as the stage, Preston Grant had never looked more appealing, and Bonnie had never been more in love.

"Oh, Preston, I love you," she said as she fell into his embrace. "And I'll wait forever if I have to."

He held her at arm's length and shook his head. "Not forever. I promise."

Chapter 4

July 4, 1960

The morning of her Olympic Trials dawned bright with neither the chance of rain nor any other natural occurrence that might bring the competition to a halt before Bonnie's event took place. She stifled the urge to seek solace in the ladies' room and strode out onto the track with a confidence she did not possess. Instead, she held tight to the ribbon around her neck and prayed.

It might be Independence Day, but Bonnie felt anything but independent. In fact, she had never felt so dependent on the Lord in her life.

The July heat had not yet claimed the day, so she inhaled a deep breath of fresh California air and gave thanks that her event would be among the first. The rest of her team had gathered near the starting blocks, so she headed their way. Martha Rogers, her roommate during the trials, shouted a greeting.

"Coming," she answered. "Give me a minute to stretch, okay?"

"All right," her friend called, "but the race will start whether you're stretched or not, so hurry up."

From a throng of spectators in the stands, Dad's voice rang loud. "Give it your best, honey," he called. "We love you."

"We're proud of you," Mom added.

Bonnie searched the crowd until she found her parents sitting with Preston's mom and dad several rows up. The Grants offered smiles and shouts of encouragement, while Preston's brother, Henri, gave her a nod. Her own brother, Jim, had been unable to attend, but his wife, Patsy, sat beside Mom, holding a sign proclaiming victory for Bonnie and Preston.

Her fan club, that's what Mom had called them last night when she phoned Bonnie from the hotel. Well, this morning she needed all the fans she could get. With her whole future on the line and her mind not exactly on the task of winning, knowing there would be familiar faces to cheer her on did help a bit.

"We know you're going to do just fine," Dad shouted. "Win that race, Bonnie Lou."

Waving a reply to the little group, she trotted toward her teammates. If only she could be so confident. Thanks to Preston, she'd shaved crucial seconds off her time and conquered her penchant for getting a slow start off the blocks. After yesterday's practice session, he proclaimed her ready to take on the world—literally. According to him, there was nothing else she could do but show up and take the win for her team. Her training was complete; she was ready.

Martha smiled. "You all prayed up?"

"I'm not sure," Bonnie said.

"I'd be worried if you were." She grasped Bonnie by the hand. "Just keep your eye on the prize and watch the hand-off. Nothing else matters because the Lord'll take it from there."

Moments later, the call came for her event, the women's 440 relay, and all hope for doing anything on her own evaporated. " 'I press toward the mark for the prize of the high calling of God in Christ Jesus,' " she whispered as she assumed the position and waited for the start.

Those words never failed to bring comfort. The Lord put her in the race, and He alone would determine the finish. Her purpose was merely to press on toward the goal, to keep her eye on the prize, as Martha said.

"I love you, sunshine," drifted her way, and she glanced to her left in time to see Preston standing on the sidelines. "We're going to Rome together."

Yes, she would do this for Preston. She would achieve his Olympic goals, even if they weren't really hers as well.

And then, almost as if time shifted and slowed, the race began. Her legs felt like lead, and the crowd noise turned to a dull buzz in her ear. All she knew was the ground beneath her feet and the wind in her hair. Nothing else registered except the steady beat of her heart and the even cadence of her breath as her arms pumped and pushed her forward past first one competitor, then another.

Rounding the second turn, she began the mantra that always sustained her. "Press on, press on," she whispered in rhythm with her stride as she picked up her pace. The baton began to feel heavy in her curled fingers, and the blood pounded in her chest as the third turn fell behind her. Ahead Martha awaited, ready to take the baton, but mere yards seemed like miles today. In the lane next to her, a competitor caught up with her, then put on extra speed to break ahead.

"You can pass her, sunshine," she heard. "Put on the speed for the handoff."

With that cue, Bonnie dug into the track and forced her pace beyond what she knew possible to regain the lead. Somehow, the baton slipped into Martha's hand and her leg of the relay ended. She slowed her pace and walked off the track to allow her heart to match her breathing, turning her gaze toward her family in the stands.

Dad shouted something she couldn't understand, and Patsy stood waving the sign. Mom waved her hankie and leaned on Mrs. Grant's shoulder. Both women wore broad smiles. Only Henri sat quiet and still.

The sound of runners approaching drew her attention back to the action at hand. As the others took their turns handing off, Bonnie cheered them on until the race ended and her team had taken the victory. Celebrations ensued, and somehow, Preston appeared at her side to claim first an embrace, then a kiss. The flash of a camera shutter quickly separated them.

"Miss Taggart," a reporter called. "Congratulations. Would you care to answer a few questions for our readers back home in Boston?"

"Thank you," she replied as she leaned into Preston's shoulder, "but I'd rather not."

"C'mon, Bonnie," Preston whispered. "Talk to the man. He's come a long way to cover this."

"I suppose it wouldn't hurt," she said softly. "As long as you'll do the interview with me."

She looked up at Preston, but he failed to notice. He'd already begun smiling for the camera. "I wouldn't dream of letting you do this alone, sunshine."

"So, Miss Taggart," the reporter began, "to what do you owe your success?"

Bonnie smiled, then jumped when the camera went off again. "To the Lord and Preston Grant," she said. "One gives me strength, and the other gives me wings."

Those were the last words she had to utter during the entire interview. Like the trained journalist he was, Preston took over and fielded questions on every subject from her training schedule to her favorite breakfast food. The only question he refused to answer at length was in regard to a wedding date for the two of them.

In that case, he responded with a vague, "Wait and see."

Thankfully, the interview soon ended, and Preston escorted Bonnie to the edge of the track. His event would not be called for quite some time, but he refused to leave the track area. Always a part of the action and never in the stands— that was her Preston.

"How's your ankle?" she asked as they halted at the gate.

Preston brushed a strand of hair out of her eyes with the back of his hand, then allowed his fingers to trace the line of her jaw. "The ankle's fine." He placed his thumb on her lips, and she kissed it. "You worry too much."

Her fingers caught his. "And you don't worry enough."

"That's because you do it for me. Now tell me you love me, and let me go get ready to win this one for you, sunshine."

"I love you," she said, "whether you win or not."

He looked puzzled for a moment, then incredulous. He dropped his hands to his sides, then crossed his arms over his chest. "Are you holding out the possibility that I might not make it to Rome with you?"

"Of course not, sweetheart," she said quickly. "I can't imagine it any other way."

"That's better." One last embrace and a kiss, and he trotted to join the others warming up in the center of the track.

Bonnie couldn't help but notice Preston favored his left leg as he jumped over the low barrier separating the track from the practice area. She knew he'd been unhappy with his performance over the past few weeks and had stepped up his training regimen, refusing to take the trainer's advice and treat his tender ankle with care.

"Stubborn man." She allowed the gate to close behind her.

"Don't expect the Lord made them any other way. It's supposed to be part of their charm, but I believe it just makes 'em ornery."

She cast a glance over her shoulder to see Martha standing there, and Bonnie giggled. Her friend, the pretty Texan, certainly had a way with words.

Martha trotted to catch up with Bonnie as they headed for the stands. "Can you believe we're going to Rome? That's a long way out of town for this Dallas girl."

Bonnie's buckling knees stopped her short. "Oh my,

211

Martha. We are going, aren't we?" She grabbed for the railing and held on tight. Beyond Martha's puzzled gaze, she saw Preston make a successful practice jump over a low hurdle.

"Honey, you look like you swallowed a bug."

She forced her attention to return to Martha. "I'm fine, really."

Martha looked skeptical. "If you're fine, why can't you let go of that rail?"

"Well, I suppose I'm a little nervous." She paused to pry her fingers off the cold metal rail. "But that's normal, right? I mean, this *is* the biggest event of our lives outside the day we accepted the Lord."

"Now that's the truth." Martha guided Bonnie toward the stairs leading up into the stands. "How about we go sit down and watch the fun from the peanut gallery?"

"I'd like that." She nodded toward her family. "I'll introduce you to some very special people."

Their arrival in the stands caused a minor uproar with Mom, Dad, and Patsy all trying to hug her at once while Preston's mother chattered on about the race. Only the Grant males seemed relatively unaffected by their presence. Once the introductions were complete, Mom made room for her and Martha at the end of the row next to Grant's brother.

While Martha and Henri exchanged pleasantries, Bonnie's gaze scanned the field until she found Preston. He stood apart from the others, his head bowed as if in prayer.

All at once the importance of the day hit her full force, and she dared to think the unthinkable. *What if Preston doesn't make the team?*

212

When Martha touched her arm, she jumped. "You're about as skittish as a long-tailed cat in a room full of rocking chairs," her friend said. "What's wrong, pal?"

"I'm so nervous." She leaned against Martha's shoulder and took a gulp of fresh air. "For Preston," she added.

"Relax. It'll all be over soon."

Bonnie glanced at her mother's watch. "Not soon enough to suit me."

Martha nudged her. "Before you know it, you'll be in Rome with Preston, wondering what in the world you were so worried about."

She took a deep breath and tried to imagine competing in the Olympics with Preston at her side. As in all the times before, she failed.

Chapter 5

As a courtesy to its two Olympic hopefuls, the University of Massachusetts athletic director sent trainer Dell Woods along with Bonnie and Preston. What Bonnie did not know was that Dell had gone to the director and insisted he be included, not to be there for Bonnie in case of emergency, but to be there for Preston just so he could compete.

In the months leading up to the trials, Dell had been invaluable in keeping Preston on the track when the last place his tired body wanted to be was in training. When taping and ice didn't bring quick enough healing to his injuries, Preston depended on Dell's expertise.

He'd done nothing illegal. Many athletes used the same method to abate the pain. Still, Preston felt the Lord calling him to discontinue the treatments.

"Trust Me," he'd heard in his heart last night as he fell asleep contemplating the trials.

This morning he'd prayed—no, he'd pleaded—for the strength to make the team on his own. God had continued to answer in the same manner. *"My strength is sufficient for you."*

Of course, Preston knew that, but where was God when his knees ached, his ankle throbbed, and his muscles screamed for rest? Where was God when Preston stared up into the stands and saw the love of his life and the family without whom his Olympic dream never would have been possible?

Maybe he needed just a little something to get him started. It wasn't like he was an addict or some pill-popping beatnik. He had just inherited a questionable set of knees along with the fierce desire to be the first Grant in the family to be an actual Olympic contender. A bad combination, to say the least, but Dell had the answer.

Or at least he always claimed he did.

Dare he ask the question of the quiet and unassuming trainer? Thus far, Preston had only partaken of medications to numb the pain and allow him to continue to run past his body's endurance—all medically sound means to remain in competition. Never had he stooped to something that might give him an unfair advantage.

At least not yet, although Dell had certainly offered on more than one occasion. Right now he knew for certain Dell possessed the very tools to secure a spot for Preston on the U.S. hurdles team. The spot would give him a platform to share his beliefs with the world and to fulfill his—and his father's—dream of becoming an Olympian.

What was so wrong about getting just a little help? It's not like he would depend on anything but his own talents once his place on the team was secure.

Please, God. You understand, don't You? After all, You're the one who gave me the desire to compete.

God's silence spoke volumes. With a nod toward the trainer, Preston jogged in the man's direction.

Dell met him halfway and slapped a hand on his back. "Looking good, Grant." He leaned in and lowered his voice. "How are you really, buddy?"

Preston shook off Dell's hand and stared him down. "I'm fine." He paused. "A little nervous, but fine."

"Need anything to help you get through this?"

Yes. He nodded at a passing teammate, then turned his attention back to Dell. "No thanks."

The trainer cocked his head to the side and seemed to be assessing Preston. While his face wore a smile, his demeanor showed no humor. "You sure? I watched you this morning, and your left ankle looked a little wobbly. I could fix that."

Preston's shoulders sagged with the truth. The course of the rest of his life hinged on the results of the next race. Everything he'd hoped for, dreamed of, and worked for would culminate shortly in a race that to the rest of the world would be merely entertainment.

To Preston, however, it was his life.

"No," Preston finally said. "I'm not sure of anything right now."

"That's what I thought. Come with me. Uncle Dell will take care of what ails you."

Lord, stop me, because I can't stop myself. I just have to make the team. He fell into step beside Dell and headed for the locker room. Seconds later, a member of the press corps stepped into his path.

"Preston Grant, right?"

Preston nodded and gave Dell a side glance. "Yes, and this is Dell Woods, trainer at the University of Massachusetts."

Dell gave the middle-aged reporter a broad smile, then turned his charm on the camera crew. "Nice to meet you fellows," he said. "If you'll excuse us, Preston and I were just about to get in a little last-minute training before the big race."

The reporter turned his attention to Preston. "I was hoping you might give my viewers a moment of your time, Preston."

"Can't," Dell said. "Maybe afterward, when he wins."

"My strength is sufficient." Preston squared his shoulders. "Hey, Dell, I think I'll skip the last-minute training." His gaze locked with the trainer's. "Thanks anyway."

Rather than answer, Dell stared a moment longer, then shrugged and turned to walk away. As the trainer paused to look over his shoulder and laugh, Preston resolutely turned his back and faced the newsman and his crew.

Putting Dell Woods out of his mind, Preston shook hands with the fellow from CBS and smiled. The reporter, a small-time guy from the local affiliate, had just pulled a silver pen out of his pocket and asked him what he would be doing if not for the Olympics.

"Why, I suppose I'd be doing what you're doing, sir," he said. "The Olympics runs in my blood, pardon the pun, so if I couldn't run the hurdles, I guess I'd have to interview the ones who can."

"Well, that's a fine ambition, son," he said.

The reporter asked a few more questions regarding his training schedule, what he ate for breakfast, and whether he thought the upcoming election would bring a win for the Republicans or the Democrats. Each query went dutifully answered until the man asked Preston about his love life.

"I would venture to guess that there are any number of pretty coeds out there who would love to know if there is a future Mrs. Grant in the picture. Anyone special out there you want to say hello to back in Massachusetts, Preston?"

Preston allowed his gaze to drift past the reporter to the stands where Bonnie had just turned to laugh at something her mother said. A thought occurred. Why wait until Rome? He could haul Bonnie out of the stands right now and profess his undying love right here in front of this television reporter and his camera crew. What a story that would be. It might even make the national news.

And then her gaze met his, and she lifted her left hand to wave. He upped his smile a notch and watched her touch her fingers to her lips and blow him a kiss. Pantomiming the act of catching it, he wrapped his fingers around the imaginary kiss and held it to his chest.

What a woman. Mere national coverage would not do for the profession of his love. No, he would wait until he held the attention of the entire world. He would wait for Rome.

"Mr. Grant?"

His attention shifted back to the reporter. "I'm sorry," he said with a shake of his head. "What was the question?"

Before the newsman could answer, the loudspeaker crackled and the voice of the track announcer called his event.

Preston shook the man's hand and sprinted away, shouting a word of thanks over his shoulder as he left the reporter and camera crew standing alongside the track. Moments later, he stood at the starting blocks with his event only seconds away.

He sought his father in the crowd and turned to face the stands. With his right hand raised high, he pointed toward his dad as if to say, "This one's for you, Pop," then punctuated the gesture with a smile for his mom. Finally, he met Bonnie's gaze and blew her a kiss. Just as he had done earlier, she caught it and held it to her chest.

Hurdles, real and imaginary, lay stacked on the track in front of him in neat progression. Each one would have to be met, challenged, and defeated for him to become an Olympian. The air snapped and crackled with an electric excitement, and even the sun seemed to shine a bit brighter. It all came down to one man, one race, and one very big God.

When he turned to fit his feet into the starting blocks, all thoughts faded save one. God must bless him with the best time of his career. After all, his decision not to take Dell up on his offer of extra help meant that God would gain full victory should Preston win a slot on the team.

And as the starter's pistol sounded, Preston had no doubt He would do just that.

✦

Bonnie clicked the stopwatch with shaking fingers, then forced her attention to the runners on the track. Preston neither led the group nor trailed but rather maintained a position in the top third of the runners. As was his custom, he rounded the first turn, then began to put on speed.

"How's he doing?" Preston's dad shouted.

She tore her gaze from the knot of runners on the track and focused on the stopwatch. Her heart thudded. Somehow Preston had shaved a full two seconds off his best midrace time. "He's doing great, sir. Best time ever."

Mr. Grant nodded and turned his attention back to the race. Bonnie attempted to do the same but found herself unable to watch the runners as they sailed over each hurdle.

"You all right, Bonnie?" Martha asked.

She offered her friend a weak smile and a nod. "Still nervous."

Keeping her attention on Preston had never been easy during a race. She was more nervous during the competitions than he ever professed to be. Generally she clamped down on the stopwatch, then stared at the sweeping hand rather than at the hurdling man. When the race ended, she always cheered—with Preston none the wiser.

Today she found this hard to do. Finally, with one lap left in the race, she excused herself from the group and darted down the risers and out of the confinement of the stands. If she couldn't watch, she would pray. Besides, when it was all over, she could find Preston much easier from her trackside vantage point.

The crowd noise faded to a dull roar beneath the stands as Bonnie leaned against a heavy post and closed her eyes. Clutching the stopwatch, she began to pray.

Please let him go to Rome, Lord. It means so much to him, and I just can't go without him.

Sneaking a peek at the stopwatch, she realized the race

should be nearing its end. Surely she could brave a glance at the event long enough to see the finish. With the stopwatch firmly in hand and a prayer still on her heart, Bonnie stepped out into the California sunshine in time to see Preston racing to approach the final hurdle of the race with a solid lead.

As runner met hurdle, Bonnie prayed and waited for Preston to sail over the iron bars to certain victory. Instead, she watched him fall to the ground in a heap.

Chapter 6

Something was wrong. He shouldn't be lying here.

Running, yes, that's what he should be doing. Someone groaned. Was it him? Preston couldn't be sure.

Must stand.

Must run.

Must win.

He had a dream—a goal.

Olympic dreams.

Olympic goals.

Preston opened his eyes, then slammed them shut again. The whole world and all its contents had turned upside down and spilled across the track, pushing him with great force to the ground.

Where were the other runners? What had happened to the race? One moment he'd captured the lead from the farm boy from Boise, and the next he lay. . .where? On which side of the finish line had he landed?

Preston strained to determine the answer but failed

miserably. A bitter taste filled his mouth, and the sting of gravel met his fists as he tried to take hold of the shifting earth. His legs ignored his brain's cry for help and mocked him by refusing to move. One hand shook; the other lay still, three of its fingers curled in an abnormal direction.

Dell's voice hummed somewhere above him, as did the eerie hush that did not generally characterize a stadium full of fans. The California breeze kicked up and blew over him, but he barely felt it.

Bonnie faded into sight, then departed, only to return. "Sunshine?" he managed through the grit and metal in his mouth.

"Preston, I love you."

He held tight to those words even as he slipped into darkness.

❧

Bonnie crowded into the backseat of the taxi and wedged herself between Mama and Mrs. Grant while Mr. Grant took the front seat. The rest of the family followed in a second cab as the little procession—first the ambulance with Dell Woods riding alongside Preston, then the two cars—raced toward the emergency room. Martha promised to maintain a vigil beside the phone in the Grants' hotel room. The job of alerting family and friends back in Massachusetts fell to her, and she took on the challenge armed with a long list of phone numbers.

The thought of the dear Texan fielding phone calls in her distinctly Southern way from staid New Englanders almost made Bonnie smile. Almost, but not quite. She might never smile again until she could be sure of Preston's complete recovery.

"I just don't know what happened," Mrs. Grant said. She looked at Bonnie as if searching for an answer. "He was doing so well. He almost won."

He almost won. Bonnie suppressed a sob and allowed a shimmering of tears free rein as she touched the pink ribbon around her neck. *He almost won—but he didn't.*

Mr. Grant sat stone-faced, his gaze riveted upon the flashing lights of the emergency vehicle directly in front of him. "It's my fault," he said softly. "I pushed him too hard."

"You never did any such thing, Dameon." Mrs. Grant reached across the seats to place her hand on her husband's shoulder. "If anyone is at fault, it's me. I'm the silly goose who raised him on stories of his father's and grandfather's Olympic dreams." A tear slid down her cheek and landed on the sleeve of her prim white sweater. "I always encouraged his goals, but I never thought they would end like this."

"We don't know if they've ended yet," Mama said. "Let's just see what God has in mind. Preston's still a young man, and there's always 1964."

Mrs. Grant gave Mama a grateful smile and settled back in the seat. "I suppose you're right." She stared out the window at the California landscape passing by at high speed. "We must believe He has a purpose in all of this."

"This certainly isn't how I expected to spend the Fourth of July," Bonnie whispered. "I thought we'd be celebrating together, Preston and I. I thought. . ."

Mama gripped Bonnie's hand tighter as the ambulance

raced through yet another red light and made a sharp left turn. "He's going to be just fine, honey." The cab lurched to a stop beneath the canopy of the hospital's emergency entrance. "God's going to take care of him. You just wait and see."

"I know." Bonnie slid across the seat and out the door in time to watch the orderlies bundle Preston into a side door marked "Authorized Personnel Only."

The next few hours passed in a haze of bitter coffee, quiet prayer, and, finally, restless silence. After the first few meager attempts at conversation, the little group maintained a stillness that lasted until a nurse called the family into a small room where the attending physician waited alongside Dell Woods.

Bonnie, still clad in her running attire, filed into the tiny room but refused her mother's offer of a chair. Instead, she leaned against the ugly green wall and listened while the doctor pronounced the end of Preston Grant's Olympic career.

To be sure, Preston would be fine. He'd broken three fingers on his left hand and would likely feel some minor but lasting effects from the ankle he'd shattered. The odds were high, however, that he would make a full recovery.

What he would never do, the doctor assured them, was run the hurdles.

The ankle would never hold up under the constant pounding of landing on the track after a hurdle, and to top it off, the doctor flatly stated Preston should never have been allowed to participate in the trials with old knee injuries and a sprained ankle still untreated.

Old knee injuries and a sprained ankle? Bonnie stared at Dell in disbelief. Was Preston running injured? He'd said he felt fine.

And what of Dell Woods? Why hadn't he noticed Preston's condition? After all, he *was* the trainer, the man paid to keep UMass athletes in good shape so they could compete.

A thought dawned, and she tried in vain to push it away. Still, it tickled and teased its way to the forefront until she could no longer deny it.

When the doctor finished his speech, the Grants began their barrage of questions. Bonnie, however, moved toward the door and gestured for Dell to follow.

"Hey, I'm sorry about your boyfriend," Dell said when she stopped abruptly in an alcove off the main lobby. "He could have won that race. He could have really been something in Rome."

Bonnie whirled around and resisted the urge to take the trainer by the throat and shake the life out of him. "Get out of here," she said through her clenched jaw.

Dell affected a broad smile and shrugged. "Hey, I know you're upset. I am, too. It's hard to watch a career die a natural death right in front of you."

"His career *didn't* die a natural death. *You killed it.*" Bonnie enunciated each word of her pronouncement with care, never moving her attention from his face. "You were hired by the school to keep him running and—"

"And that's just what I did." He took a step toward her, all signs of his good humor gone. "So what is it you're getting at, little lady?"

Bonnie took a deep breath and let it out slowly. Every inch of her body hummed with the anger that begged to find release in a good jab across the trainer's smug face. Instead, she willed herself to remember that God, not she, would exact revenge.

"Thank you for your services, Mr. Woods," she said stiffly. "I don't expect they are needed anymore. Perhaps you should head back to school before the athletic director misses you."

"But he knows I'm here," Dell said. "He sent me." The last words were flung at her as if he dared her to respond.

A pair of nurses strolled past, and Bonnie waited until they were out of earshot to reply. "Yes, but did he send you here to do what you've done to Preston?" This time she took a step toward him. "I'm sure the doctors would have no problem documenting the cause of his current condition."

"I have no idea what you're talking about." But as he made the statement, the look on his face told Bonnie he did.

"He had talent, and he could have run the race on his own. He might not have come in first place, but I believe he was good enough to make the team." She paused while an orderly strolled past, pushing an elderly woman in a wheelchair. "Whatever you did, whatever you gave him, it let him run when he wasn't supposed to. It made him not feel the pain." Dell looked away, so she continued. "He wanted this so bad, bad enough to do just about anything to achieve his goal."

The trainer captured her wrist and held it in a steely grip. "You said it, Miss High-and-Mighty. Your boyfriend knew you had the natural talent to go all the way to Rome on your own. Unfortunately, he also knew he didn't."

Bonnie jerked her arm free and rubbed her wrist. "What's your point?"

"My point is, if you're looking for someone to blame, blame Preston Grant. He's the one who wanted to go to Rome bad enough to end up where he is."

"He's right, Bonnie."

Bonnie whirled around to see Preston's brother, Henri, walking toward them, wearing a worried look. Instantly her heart lurched. "What's wrong? Has something happened to Preston?"

Henri took her by the elbow and guided her away from Dell. "He's waking up, and they're about to move him from recovery to a room. Mom and Pop are up on the fourth floor with him right now."

"Then take me to him."

Preston's brother shook his head. "I can't do that. You're not family."

"That's absurd." Bonnie shook off his grip and picked up her pace, heading for the bank of elevators at the end of the hall. When the doors opened, she stormed in and pressed the button marked "4." Before the doors could close, Henri climbed in with her and pulled her out.

"What are you doing?" she sputtered as he led her toward a side exit.

"Saving you heartache." He lifted a hand to call a taxi. "Go back to your room and wait. There's no need for you to stay here."

The cab stopped short at the curb, and Henri reached to open the door. "Driver, would you see that this young lady gets back to the stadium and rejoins her team?" When the cabbie gave Bonnie the once-over, then nodded, Henri thrust a few bills at him through the open front window.

Henri straightened to face Bonnie once more. "In you go. I'll tell your parents where you went when I bring them back to the hotel."

Bonnie refused to go a step farther. "Honestly, Henri, I don't know what is going on here, but I absolutely refuse to leave this hospital or the man that I love."

"What if he doesn't want to see you?"

An elderly gentleman strolled up and pointed his walking cane toward the taxi. "Young folks, are you going to use that cab?"

"I don't know about him, but I'm certainly not." With that, Bonnie turned and raced toward the hospital's side entrance.

Never had she been so thankful for the speed God had blessed her with as when the elevator doors closed with Henri nowhere in sight. Leaning against the cold wall of the elevator, Bonnie pressed the button for the fourth floor and began to pray.

Through the silent entreaties, a single phrase rang out. *What if he doesn't want to see you?*

Hadn't Henri asked her that question moments ago? Perhaps she misunderstood. Surely Preston would not refuse to see her.

The doors spilled open into a large hallway with signs pointing to the right and left. Bonnie followed the one marked "Surgical Recovery" until she reached a pair of large silver doors. Ignoring the now-familiar "Authorized Personnel

Only" sign, she pressed through to find a large desk attended by a rather stern-looking trio of white-uniformed nurses.

A thin, birdlike nurse of middle age peered at her over her glasses and inquired, "May I help you?"

Fear snaked up her spine and lodged in her brain. The place smelled like antiseptic and sickness. How could Preston be a part of it? "Yes," she finally managed. "I would like to see Preston Grant, please."

The nurse cast a sweeping glance at Bonnie's unusual attire, then shook her head. "I'm sorry. Mr. Grant's just come out of recovery and is with family right now."

She squared her shoulders and stared the nurse down. "Well, *I'm* family and I would like to see him, please."

Reaching for a clipboard, the nurse pursed her lips. "And what is your relation to the patient?"

Bonnie took a deep breath and let it out slowly. "I am his fiancée."

Well, she was. Almost. And she had the penny to prove it.

Doors burst open behind her, and Henri appeared at her side. The nurse shifted her attention from Bonnie to Preston's brother. Henri paused to give Bonnie a hard look. Finally, he shook his head. "It's all right. She's family, Nurse."

The nurse took one last look at the pair, then nodded. "I thought she might be another of those pesky reporters. Not five minutes ago, security caught a fellow trying to sneak into Mr. Grant's room with a camera. My guess is he thought our patient would make good front-page news. Well, I certainly am not going to let that sort of invasion of privacy happen on my watch."

"Yes, ma'am." Henri gave Bonnie a side glance and grinned. "We appreciate that you're doing such a good job."

Bonnie rolled her eyes in response. "Yes, thank you," she managed.

Trailing Henri and the nurse down the labyrinth of narrow green hallways until they reached room 407, Bonnie tried to still her racing mind. "Press on," she whispered. Somehow the words that usually gave her comfort during competitions now ministered to her in a different way. Whatever waited on the other side of the door, Bonnie knew she would meet the circumstances with God's help.

Henri placed his hand on the door, then paused to look down at Bonnie. "Remember, I warned you, kid," he said as he pushed the door open and disappeared inside.

Chapter 7

Bonnie approached the blanket-wrapped figure slowly, capturing every detail of the scene but believing none of it. Preston lay motionless, a tangle of wires connecting him to an IV pole and a stack of machinery beyond. Mrs. Grant leaned against the bed's metal safety rail while Mr. Grant perched on the edge of a chair. Neither seemed to notice Bonnie.

Her gaze fell on Preston's bruised face, and without warning, the room tilted. Henri steadied her and propelled her forward with a few quiet words of encouragement. Somehow she managed to remain upright long enough to receive a hug from Mrs. Grant before grasping for the rail.

Henri leaned close to Bonnie and lowered his voice. "They had to operate to set his ankle. The doc said he would be a little loopy until the anesthesia wears off, so don't take him seriously if he starts talking out of his head."

"All right."

"Hey, Pres," he said a bit louder. "Look who's here."

Preston's eyelids fluttered, then opened only to fall shut

again. "Sunshine?" came out on a long breath. "That you?"

"That's right. It's me, Bonnie." She released her grip on the rail to smooth the sheet across his chest, then lay her hand over his. "You gave us a real scare, sweetheart."

"But you're going to be fine," Mrs. Grant added, sliding Bonnie a side glance. "Isn't he, Bonnie?"

"Yes, that's right," Bonnie quickly added. "You'll be back to normal in no time."

Back to normal? Bonnie cringed. Nothing would ever be normal again, at least not until Preston was up and running, chasing another Olympic dream.

With four years' worth of time standing between them and the next Olympic Summer Games, Bonnie hoped that while Preston would be chasing dreams, she would be too busy being Mrs. Preston Grant and chasing a couple of Grant babies to even think of running any races.

Funny how chasing her dream didn't involve much actual running at all. If only Preston could say the same.

Preston's father rose and placed a hand on Mrs. Grant's shoulder. "Why don't we find some hot coffee and a bite to eat, dear?" He nodded to his elder son. "Come with us, Henri."

"Of course." Henri opened the door for his parents, then turned his attention to Bonnie. "Can I bring you something?"

"No, thank you."

Henri nodded. "Just promise me you won't take anything he says seriously, kid. He's been saying things that don't sound like my brother."

"I promise."

A moment later the door *whooshed* shut behind the trio,

and Bonnie found herself alone with Preston, who seemed to have fallen into a deep slumber. Rather than wake him, she inched the chair closer to the bed and leaned her head on the rail to pray.

Father, make him well again. Give him strength of body to heal and strength of mind to understand why You chose this path for him.

"Bonnie."

She jerked her head up at the ragged strength in Preston's voice and focused on his face. He seemed to be studying her, eyes clear though still half closed, and the fingers of his right hand drumming a pattern against the white sheets.

"What is it, sweetheart?"

"I don't want you here."

Poor dear. He's still under the influence of the anesthesia. In a few hours, he'll be fine.

Bonnie attempted a smile. "I don't mind, really. Now why don't you get some rest? I'll be right here when you wake up." She gestured to the table beside the bed where a month-old copy of *Reader's Digest* lay atop a copy of *Life* magazine from last fall. "I've got plenty to do, and nowhere else I'd rather be."

Preston looked past her to stare at the door and the nurse's station beyond. "I didn't finish the race, did I?"

What do I say? Bonnie looked past him to the window and the street beyond. The last rays of the sun danced off the hoods of cars in the parking lot and carved a brilliant path over the windowsill and across the pale green linoleum floor. Like an upside-down rainbow, it climbed the wall and ended not with a pot of gold but at the edge of Preston's medical chart, hung from a peg beside the door.

"Bonnie?"

She forced her gaze to return to the man she so dearly loved. "You were incredible, sweetheart. Your time in the first half was your best ever. I had to look twice to see if the stopwatch was working properly."

He almost seemed to grin when he turned to face her. "Really?" he whispered.

"Really."

Any trace of happiness faded without warning as his gaze turned penetrating. "But did I make the team?"

Bonnie knew she could lie and make him happy for the moment, but even if he didn't remember her deception tomorrow when the effects of the anesthesia were gone, she would. Eventually, Preston would know the truth. How much better for that truth to come from the one who loved him most.

"No. You fell just short of the finish line," she said softly. "I'm so sorry, sweetheart. You didn't finish the race."

He seemed to ponder her statement. "And you. Did you qualify?"

She'd never felt so ashamed of an accomplishment in her life. Often she'd wondered why God chose to gift her with athletic ability, but rarely had she questioned His results. Assuming the Lord had used her talents to bring her to Preston, how could she now believe He would use the same to divide them? Surely Preston would understand.

Bonnie lifted her gaze to the ceiling. "Yes, I made the 440-relay team."

For a moment, silence filled the room, broken only by the wail of an approaching ambulance and the chatter of night birds in the trees outside the window. Bonnie waited, praying for something—anything—to say. Finally, she dared a glance at Preston, who lay still, eyes clenched shut.

"Preston? Say something, sweetheart. Anything."

But he said nothing. He just lay there too pale and still to be her beloved Preston.

When Preston opened his eyes and reached for her, Bonnie let out the breath she hadn't realized she'd been holding. Gathering her hand tighter in his, Preston pulled her toward him. Bonnie leaned as far over the bed rail as she could, standing on her toes to place her lips against his.

While he allowed the kiss, he did not participate. In fact, he did nothing but hold tight to her hand. Even though the muscles in her calves began to tremble, Bonnie continued to strain toward the prize that was Preston Grant.

"We'll get through this," she said as she gingerly placed a kiss on his bruised cheek and another on his forehead, where a bandage covered a good portion of his face.

Preston released her fingers to grasp her arm. "But Rome."

"Shhh." Bonnie touched his lips. "Forget Rome. If you're not going, then neither am I."

His battered features contorted, and he stared at her as if she were a stranger. "Get out," he said as he pushed her away with a force that belied his weakened condition.

Bonnie caught the bar and righted herself, cold fear hitting her in waves. Henri said the anesthesia had made Preston confused, but the look on his face told her he seemed to know what he said. Still, she held on to the hope she could reach him.

"Sweetheart, it's me, Bonnie." She inched closer. "Surely you don't mean that. I love you." In desperation she pulled the penny from beneath her shirt. "Remember this? We made a promise to each other. Well, I meant it."

When she took his hand, he jerked away to slam it against the call button. At the sound of the nurse's voice, Preston turned his face toward the wall. "The woman. Get her out."

"The woman?"

It took the nurse and a security guard to forcibly remove her from the room. When they shoved her into the elevator with a warning not to return to the fourth floor, Bonnie finally gave up and gathered enough of her dignity to be able to walk toward the hospital exit with her head held high. Surely tomorrow would be a better day.

Tomorrow she would return and try to talk some sense into Preston. If she timed things just right, she might not have to meet up with any of the staff members who had participated in her banishment.

But as she hailed a cab and climbed inside, Bonnie knew her biggest challenge lay not in getting past the watchful eyes of the nurses, but rather in getting past the pain of the man she loved.

❧

July 7, 1960

"I don't care what you say; I know you love that girl." Henri slammed his fist against the bed rail so hard the whole bed shook.

Preston bit back a yelp at the shaft of pain shooting from his bandaged ankle and focused on his older brother. "I never said I didn't love her. Love's got nothing to do with it."

Henri lifted a brow and stared down at Preston. "So why don't you just swallow your pride and see her?"

"It's not about pride," he said, but as he spoke the words, he had to wonder if they were true. Hadn't he told Bonnie he would marry her once he made something of himself?

"It's been three days. It's a wonder she's still trying. I know I wouldn't under the circumstances."

Three days.

Vaguely he remembered their disastrous first visit after his surgery. Through conversations pieced together from his mother and brother, he gathered he had been less than friendly to Bonnie. According to the security guard now stationed at the end of the hall to fend off reporters and the woman he loved, he'd been downright mean.

Well, so be it. Any man would feel a bit cranky given that all of his dreams had come to an end in one humiliating fall just a few yards short of the finish line. And how much more did it hurt to know that while he fell short of his goal, Bonnie had gone on to achieve hers?

That stung worse than any physical injury.

No, the doctors told him his ankle would heal, as would his broken fingers and scratches. What might never be the same was his ego—and his broken heart.

The door opened, and a bright-eyed nurse's aide strolled in with a pair of crutches tucked under one arm. "Ready to try out your new legs, Mr. Grant?" she asked as she leaned the wooden contraptions against the bed and began to struggle with the metal rail.

Preston sighed and reached over to help the aide release the rail. He looked over the top of her head to Henri, who stood with arms crossed over his chest and an irritating smile on his face. "Do I have a choice?"

The aide seemed perplexed. "Well, I suppose I might have read the chart wrong. Would you like me to check with the nurse?"

Henri stepped over to grab the crutches and thrust them toward Preston. "No, that won't be necessary, miss. I'm sure my brother's ready to get up out of that bed and start living again."

But was he? At that moment, Preston really didn't know.

Sitting proved to be less of an ordeal than standing, but both activities were nothing compared to trying to walk. His head swam, his ankle throbbed, and his pride—yes, he had to admit pride was indeed involved—well, it hurt the worst. Not only had he failed to achieve his lifelong goal of making the U.S. Olympic team, but now he could barely cross the room under his own power.

"All right, that's enough for now, little brother." Henri guided him back to the bed and eased him into place under the blankets. "You get some rest. This afternoon, you and I are going to do this again, and this time I'm not going to let you get away with a little stroll around the room."

Henri walked to the window and stared down at the hospital gardens below. "Yes, indeed, I believe you and I will be going for a walk in the gardens after lunch."

If he'd had the energy, Preston might have argued the point. Instead, he fell willingly into the blackness of sleep.

⚜

He awoke to the clatter of lunch being unceremoniously served on his bed tray. A lump of something white covered in brown gravy lay nestled next to an oily pile of green peas and a mound of what could be meat loaf. Atop the mess lay a slightly burned piece of toast and a pat of butter that had begun to run onto the meat concoction. To complete the picture, a dish of tapioca garnished with half a cherry sat beside an empty glass and a small carton of milk.

Stifling a groan, he pushed the tray away and rolled back to face the wall. Even if he'd had an appetite, one look at this food would have killed it.

"Oh, no, you don't," Henri said. "Get your lazy self up and eat something so we can beat it out of this hospital room and into the sunshine."

Sunshine.

Bonnie.

Preston shook his head and pulled the covers tighter over his head. *No, I can't think about her. Not now. Maybe not ever.*

"Hey, I'm not kidding." Henri hit the end of the metal bed with something hard.

Peeking over the blanket, Preston saw his brother holding crutches. The last thing he needed right now was for the big lug to try and cheer him up with some walk in the park. He'd been lucky to walk to the bathroom this morning. No one and nothing could get him outside.

"Go away," he muttered. Again his brother hit the bed

with the crutches, this time with enough force to make the mattress shake. He met Henri's gaze through narrowed eyes. "I said, go away."

Wielding the crutches like a bat, Henri aimed them at the bed one more time. "I can do this as many times as it takes to get you out of that bed."

Preston pretended indifference and pulled the covers back over his head. "Suit yourself."

The door swung open, and footsteps crossed the room. Tempted to identify the latest intruder, Preston elected instead to remain still and hope for solitude.

"Well, hello, Miss Taggart," Henri said. "How did you get in here? No matter. I'm sure my little brother will be thrilled to see you. May I say you look lovely today, a real vision."

Bonnie? Here?

Scrambling to his elbows, Preston paused to overcome the combined wave of pain and nausea that followed. Finally, he allowed Henri to help him complete the process of sitting up only to realize he and his brother were the only ones in the room.

"Where's Bonnie?"

Henri chuckled and rolled the lunch tray back into position in front of Preston. "I'm sure I could find her if you'd like to see her. Why don't you see how much of this you can keep down while I go look for her?"

If he'd had the strength, Preston would have decked his brother right then. How dare he have him play the fool at a time like this?

"You know, I was in love once."

Preston blinked, then stared. "And when was this?"

Henri shrugged. "Oh, not so long ago." His face turned serious. "I was stupid."

"You, stupid? Wow, that's hard to believe," Preston muttered as he reached for the fork.

Clang!

Preston dropped his fork square into the mashed potatoes and turned his attention to Henri, who once again held the crutches in the air. "Will you stop hitting the bed?"

His older brother looked ready to swing again. "I'll stop when I decide you're going to listen to me."

Affecting a bored look, Preston dropped his hands to his lap and stared. "All right, I'm listening."

Gesturing to the lunch tray, Henri shook his head. "Listen *and* eat."

Using his spoon to retrieve the errant fork, Preston cleaned the utensil as best he could with his napkin. All the while, Henri watched in silence, his fingers still wrapped around the crutches. Finally, when Preston could delay no longer, he stabbed his fork into the meat loaf and took a small bite.

To his surprise, it tasted much better than it looked, so he took another bite. Out of the corner of his eye, he saw Henri lean the crutches against the nightstand and sink into a chair beside the bed. Preston offered his brother a bite, but he waved it away with a swipe of his hand.

"Suit yourself," he said as he returned to his meal.

A moment later, Henri steepled his hands and let out a deep breath. "You know I don't talk about God much, little brother."

Preston stopped chewing long enough to nod. The truth be known, Henri Grant was a man of few words. Basically, he made it his business to talk as little as possible.

But then that was Henri.

"Well," his brother continued, "it's not because I don't believe in Him. It's just that. . ." His voice trailed off, and he looked away.

"I know," Preston offered. "You don't have to say it to believe it. I mean, you go to church just like the rest of us and—"

"Must you always interrupt?" Henri slammed his fists together. "Just because you're set to be a newsman doesn't mean you always have to be the one doing the talking. Just eat and learn, little brother. If you do, you just might avoid making the same mistake as me."

Preston stuffed an overly large forkful of peas into his mouth. "Sorry," he managed after he swallowed. "Go ahead."

Their gazes locked, and an intense look came over Henri as he gripped the metal arms of the chair. "Okay, but I never told this story, so don't you dare make fun of me, Preston. I'd have to hurt you worse than you are now if I even get an idea you're laughing at me."

"I promise." He set down the fork and turned his complete attention to his brother. "Really."

"All right. Well, you see, there was this girl." Henri paused, and for a moment Preston wondered if he would continue. "She was beautiful." He thumped his chest. "Not just on the outside, but inside, where it counts."

Preston nodded.

"I fell for her the first time I saw her." A look of sadness passed over Henri's face as he met Preston's gaze. "A man's pride is an awful thing. One minute you're on top of the world, and the next you've hit bottom only to find out it's your own fault. The way I see it, you're on the road to doing the same thing I did."

"And what's that?"

Henri shrugged. "You're about to lose the best thing that ever happened to you."

The truth of the statement hit Preston full force. Just as he had in his more lucid moments over the past few days, he pushed the thought away and focused on his brother instead. "And when did all of this happen, Henri?"

"Last week."

"Last week?"

Henri nodded. "I'm afraid so."

Preston reached for his robe and winced as he paid for the effort. "What would you say about striking a bargain, big brother?"

Chapter 8

Bonnie leaned against the trellis and let the sun shine against her closed eyes while a light breeze teased the edge of her pleated skirt. Beneath her blouse, she could feel the weight of the penny against her chest. Beneath the penny lay her broken heart.

She'd come to this spot alone each day since her banishment from the hospital, mostly to pray, but also to get away from the excitement and happiness that permeated the dormitories belonging to the female participants in the Olympic Trials. Most of the team going to Rome had gathered last night to plan and celebrate. Bonnie chose to spend the evening writing a letter to Preston. If she could not reach him through the spoken word, perhaps she could reach him through the written word.

And she *had* to reach him today. There would be no tomorrow in which to attempt the feat. Tonight the train would take her back East, far away from the Olympic Trials, from California, and from Preston Grant. In the last few hours before she had to leave, she had come to this place in hopes that God would finally hear her plea—or possibly answer her prayer—before she sought out a nurse or orderly to deliver her letter.

Most days, she truly believed in God's timing and was willing to wait on Him without worry or question. Today, however, He would have to hurry to get all this accomplished before five, when she had to board the train for home.

She took a deep breath and let it out slowly. *I'm here again, Father. I'm waiting and listening.* If only she waited and listened long enough, maybe the Lord would let her in on the secret of why all her dreams had to end in this beautiful place.

"Excuse me. You're Bonnie Taggart from the Olympic track-and-field team, aren't you?"

"Oh!" Bonnie jumped to her feet, then shielded her eyes from the blinding sun. Reeling backward, she grasped the trellis to steady herself.

"Forgive me," the man said. "I didn't mean to startle you." He thrust his hand toward her and shook hers vigorously. "Would you mind if I sat with you for a moment?"

A kind-faced gentleman of middle age, graying hair, and average height came into focus. He wore a green cardigan sweater over a starched white dress shirt and dark slacks. Under one arm he carried a small black notebook, and the tip of a silver pen gleamed from his shirt pocket.

He must want an autograph. Bonnie gave him another long look. He *did* seem harmless enough, and there *were* plenty of people around.

"Well," she said slowly, "I suppose that would be fine."

"Thank you, Miss Taggart. I assure you I won't keep you but a moment."

Bonnie settled back on the bench, and the stranger took a seat next to her, placing the notebook in his lap. "So, are you a fan of the Olympics?" she asked.

The gentleman chuckled. "You could say that." He paused and his smile faded as he drummed thick fingers over the top of the notebook's cover. "Actually, I'm a reporter for the local CBS affiliate." He reached for his pen. "I interviewed Preston Grant a few days ago, just before the race that ended his career. I couldn't help but wonder why a fellow Olympian comes to the hospital gardens every day but never goes inside to visit her UMass teammate."

She rose. "If you'll forgive me, sir, I think I'll be going."

"Wait, don't go."

This time it was Preston and not the reporter who spoke.

Bonnie whirled around to see the man she loved hobbling toward her on crutches, brother Henri at his side. He seemed somewhat pale, and even from a distance Bonnie could see he must be in considerable pain.

Henri stepped ahead of Preston to take the reporter by the elbow. "How about writing a story about the nosy reporter who got thrown off hospital property by a patient's older and wiser brother?"

"But, sir, I assure you I had the lady's permission to—"

Bonnie watched the pair disappear down the path, then slowly turned her attention to Preston. "Hey, sunshine," he said with a forced grin.

"Hey," she responded.

"Long time, no see." A butterfly flitted between them, and Preston continued to look in its direction long after it had disappeared into a hedge of flowering hibiscus. Without returning his gaze to Bonnie, he sighed. "But then I guess that's my fault."

So many ways to respond. "I guess," she finally said.

He met her stare and leaned on unsteady legs. "I owe you an apology. I was a real. . ."

Preston's voice faded as he lurched forward. Bonnie reached him just in time to keep him from landing on the path.

"Here, come and sit down," she said as she guided him with difficulty to the bench. By the time he managed to settle into a sitting position with his leg extended and the crutches beside him for support, beads of perspiration dotted his face and what little color he possessed was gone.

"You smell nice. Lavender, right?"

"Yes." Bonnie touched the sleeve of his robe, then quickly pulled her hand away. "It hurts, doesn't it?"

Preston looked past her and nodded. "I thought I was doing myself a favor numbing the pain. Now I see. . ."

Again she reached for him, this time allowing her fingers to graze the back of his hand before resting on his arm. "No need to say more, sweetheart. I know all about how you trained while you were hurt, how you wanted so bad to make the team that you pushed your body beyond its limits." She paused, not sure whether to go on. Finally, she added, "About Dell Woods."

Something akin to pain crossed his handsome features.

"I didn't think taking something to numb the pain was really cheating. I mean, I just didn't have the luxury of taking time to heal, so I. . ." He shuddered. "You're so good at what you do—a real natural, sunshine. I never wanted you to know that I wasn't. Even so, I never took anything illegal. I promise."

"Oh, sweetheart." Bonnie's fingers curled into a fist, gathering up the fabric of his robe. "I understand."

Sighing, Preston's gaze locked with hers. "I wish I did."

Never had she seen Preston like this. Not even their last conversation in the hospital frightened her like this. Then she could blame the anesthesia. Now she had no one but herself to blame. Her Olympic success amplified his Olympic failure.

There was only one remedy for what ailed Preston Grant. Thankfully, the cure was within her grasp and easily done.

"Preston," she said softly, "I love you more than anything in this world except the Lord Himself. You know that, don't you?" When he nodded, she continued. "Then it's settled. If you're not going to Rome, then neither am I."

❧

Preston forced himself to meet her gaze but couldn't quite muster a smile to match hers. "That's ridiculous. You're going to Rome, and that's all there is to it."

Bonnie's smile sagged at the corners. "But I don't understand. I love you. I can't possibly go to the Olympics without you." She reached for his right hand and entwined her fingers with his. "There, it's settled. So why don't we talk about something else? Say, what about that new fifty-star flag we've got now? Isn't it something?"

Stars and flags were the least of his concerns. Getting Bonnie to Rome was all that mattered. Forces out of his control had changed Preston's Olympic goal. Bonnie's, however, was still within her grasp. She might not realize it now, but if she gave it up for him, she would grow to resent it—and him.

And that was no way to begin a marriage.

Marriage. Preston once again studied the bright pink blooms of the shrubs and thought of spending the rest of his life with Bonnie Taggart. *Bonnie Taggart Grant,* he mentally corrected. Yes, the idea still held great appeal.

In fact, it was the only thing in his life that still did outside of the Lord. He couldn't mess that up, too, not like he'd messed up his shot at going to Rome.

The pink flowers swayed in the breeze. Pink. The first time he met Bonnie she'd been wearing that color. She'd bowled him down that day, and to some extent, she still did every time he saw her.

Preston's mind jerked back to the present. Bonnie was staring, searching his face. She wanted his approval for her idiotic plan to drop out of the Olympics. He had to do something. He didn't intend to shout, and yet when he found the words to answer Bonnie's statement, they erupted with such force that all his strength left with them.

"Stop it, Bonnie. You *are* going to Rome, and I'm not going to listen to another word of protest on the matter. You and I worked too hard to fall short of your goal. Don't you understand that's what it's always been about?"

Bonnie's lower lip quivered as the color drained from her

face. Slowly she released her grip and brought her fingers up to cover her mouth. A lone tear fell, and with it Preston felt his heart break. With a silent prayer for strength, he pressed on with the words he hoped would send Bonnie to Rome, knowing they could very well cause him to lose her in the process.

"Why are you crying? Winners don't cry."

She lowered her hand to her side as another tear rolled down her cheek. "But I thought. . ."

Preston struggled to his feet, ignoring the pain in his ankle as well as in his heart. Someday when Bonnie stood on the platform to receive the gold medal she deserved, she would thank him for releasing her to follow her dream. Someday, but from the looks of her, not today.

"You thought what, Bonnie? That I spent all that time training with you for a reason other than to see you go to the Olympics?"

"I don't care about winning races. I care about you. About us." She paused. "We made a promise to each other. I thought you loved me," she said in a whisper that barely traveled the distance between them.

"I do. That is, I did. What I mean is. . ."

His voice faltered, and he looked away as he held on tight to his crutches. Nothing in his life had ever been as hard as this. Selfishness and pride made him want to gather her into his arms and hold her until the rest of the world with all its problems disappeared. Logic and love caused him to press on.

"Sunshine, have you ever thought that maybe God gave you this talent so you *could* go win races?"

Again she captured his gaze—and his heart. "But I just can't go without you."

Preston closed his eyes. *Lord, You know how much I love her. Please don't let her see how difficult this is for me.*

A wave of nausea hit him hard. If he stayed another moment, he might not make it back to his room without help. The thought of Bonnie witnessing his humiliating weakness brought him directly to the point. "Go to Rome, Bonnie," he said, clenching his jaw. "Who knows? We just might see each other there. Now leave before I call security."

"But, Preston, I—"

"Remember that day outside Setzer's? If you could move that fast in pink high heels, nothing can stop you on the track in Rome, so stop pretending you can't do it."

"But I'm not pretending," she said in a shaky voice. Her shoulders sagged and her lower lip quivered. As she brought her fingers up to capture a tear, Preston longed to hold her once more, to kiss away the pain he'd brought her.

"Will you just go, Bonnie? I don't know how much plainer I can make things for you." Preston fought another wave of nausea by leaning against the arbor's wooden frame. "You're a runner, so go. *Run.*"

With that, he turned and hobbled as far as the hospital entrance before collapsing into an empty wheelchair. As a nurse scurried toward him, Preston cast a glance over his shoulder to watch the only woman he'd ever loved disappear down the garden path and quite possibly out of his life forever. *Oh, Lord, why did You let this happen to me? You alone know how badly I want to be with her in Rome. Please, do something—anything!*

"Say, aren't you Preston Grant?"

The reporter Henri had supposedly sent packing had returned and now elbowed his way past the nurse to kneel beside the wheelchair. Before Preston could protest, the man shoved a business card into his hand and rose.

"Call me, young fellow. I just spoke to my boss, and we might have a business proposition for you."

Chapter 9

August 24, 1960

Preston looked up from his script to watch the lighting crew work. In a few hours, dawn would break and he would begin a whole new day—and a new life as a reporter for CBS. The trek from injured athlete to rookie reporter had been a swift one. It seemed as though he'd barely been released from the hospital before the local CBS affiliate's general manager had him on the phone with an offer to represent the station. Preston suspected Tom's father had something to do with the offer, but neither Tom nor his dad would admit to it.

Standing to stretch the kinks out of his shoulders, he gingerly took a few steps across the empty track. As he picked up his pace, he let his mind roam free, chasing dreams and memories of Bonnie Taggart and an Olympic goal he'd exchanged for a much more exhilarating goal—being the husband of an Olympian.

Before he realized what had happened, Preston was

running for the first time since the trials in July. And it felt good—really good.

He rounded the turn and sprinted toward the finish line, imagining what it would be like to actually compete. Funny how he couldn't manage nearly as much enthusiasm for the dream as he once had. Instead, he began to think about Bonnie.

He'd battled within himself as to whether to tell Bonnie he would be in Rome, after all. Once he made the decision to take the CBS job, he'd gone back to his apartment and picked up the phone to call her only to realize he had no idea where to find her. Her mother might have been of help, as would the coach at UMass, but he knew if he found Bonnie, he'd never be able to wait until they met in Rome to see her again.

When he saw her, it had to be special—as special as she was to him. He'd been such a selfish fool, thinking of himself instead of Bonnie. Henri's story of losing a girl to pride had stuck with him, and he prayed that God would help him make his situation right, as He had with Henri.

As the days passed, a plan began to formulate, and Preston could only pray that the plan came from God. It just had to.

He'd made too many arrangements to have them fail now. He'd had plenty of time to think about his selfish pride and what life was like without Bonnie Taggart. No, he had a ring in his pocket and the Lord on his side. Nothing short of the Lord's intervention could get in his way.

Preston sailed over the tangle of lighting cords and past

the shiny hulk of the CBS camera, guarding his tender ankle as he landed. To his delight, the pain that had persisted over the past weeks was gone. Another answered prayer! At this rate, he just might consider another run for the Olympic team. As Mom had told him on more than one occasion, he was still a relatively young man, and 1964 would come around before he knew it. Running the hurdles was out. His busted ankle would never hold up under the stress of the repeated landings on the track.

No, lately he'd begun to think he might enjoy running on a relay team. After all, he'd trained with a relay runner. Why not consider becoming one, too?

He laughed out loud and picked up speed. The idea was nothing more than a crazy dream. God had him pegged as a journalist who happened to know how to run. His Olympic goal for 1964 was to go to the games as a paid employee of CBS and not a volunteer intern. Tom's dad had as much as indicated there was a job waiting for him at the network in New York when he returned from Rome.

The idea of a steady income *and* continued involvement in the sports world held a certain appeal. It would also go a long way toward buying that little place in the suburbs that he and Bonnie would fill with love and little Grants.

Again he had to laugh. What a life he had ahead of him. "Thank You, Lord, for all Your blessings. One more lap, and I'll come to my senses and go back to work."

Just one more lap.

In the meantime, he went over the details of his plan. Tomorrow morning, the teams would march into the stadium in the opening ceremonies, and he planned to be there, microphone in hand. His first interview would be a pretty track-and-field runner named Bonnie Taggart, and the first thing he would ask her was to be his—

He never saw the freshly laid television cable until his foot caught beneath it. Preston went flying face-first toward the ground. As he landed, he heard a snap.

After that, everything went black.

◈

Bonnie's vision blurred as she swiped at the tears rolling down her face. Six weeks after saying good-bye to Preston, and she still couldn't get him out of her mind—or her heart. She toyed with the pink ribbon still around her neck. How many times had she removed the silly thing only to put it right back on again?

To think he might have found an interest in her simply because of some athletic talent they shared was beyond belief. When she left California, she had been absolutely certain Preston would call within the week. When that week went by, then another, she'd begun to wonder. Now she sat in her flat at the Olympic Village on a beautiful August morning still wondering.

Tomorrow she would take part in the opening ceremonies of the Seventeenth Olympiad, and mere days after that she would compete. Already she'd met the young American boxer Cassius Clay, Crown Prince Constantine of Greece, and an Ethiopian bodyguard who planned to run his races barefoot, among others. Bonnie sighed. Even among the most interesting of competitors, she barely managed to think of anything or anyone but Preston Grant.

"Still fretting about that Grant fellow?"

Bonnie jumped. "Martha. I didn't hear you come in."

Martha smiled and sank onto her bed as she allowed her pocketbook to fall to the floor. "I guess not. You're so busy pining away you don't even realize you're missing what could be the most exciting experience of your life."

"I suppose." She curled her feet beneath her and rested her head in her hands. "I can't help it. I just want to go home."

Martha shifted from her bed to Bonnie's and draped her arm around Bonnie. "I know you want to go home, but right now, I believe God wants you here." She paused to offer a broad smile. "Or at least I do. Now how about you quit your moping, and let's get out there and see what we're missing? It isn't every day two small-town girls get to go see the sights in Rome."

"See the sights?" Bonnie shook her head. "But we're not supposed to leave the village without letting our chaperone know."

Martha rose and crossed her arms over her chest. "I happen to have it on good authority that our chaperone's busy having breakfast with Crown Prince Constantine's mother and will be busy for at least three hours. I'll be glad to explain our little visit to town just as soon as she's available. Now, do you want to see the Pantheon or not?" She offered a conspiratorial grin. "I promise to have you back before lunch."

"Oh, all right," Bonnie said as she gathered her purse and stuffed her Brownie camera inside. "I suppose a little sightseeing wouldn't hurt."

"That's the spirit." Martha linked arms with Bonnie and led her out into the hallway. "Speaking of hurting, did you hear about the fellow from CBS who got injured early this morning?"

Bonnie shook her head. "No, what happened?"

"Well, I heard the guy was running around in the dark like a fool and tripped over a cable laid across the track. Broke his leg, I believe, or maybe it was his ankle. Some reporter, I think." She shrugged. "Have you ever heard of such a thing? And I thought being an athlete was dangerous."

"Is he going to be all right? The reporter, I mean."

"Oh, he'll probably just get sent home to recuperate." She stopped short and turned to face Bonnie. "Say, how about you and I offer up a little prayer for that poor fellow before we hit the town?"

"Good idea," Bonnie said. "Did you happen to catch his name?"

"No, I didn't, but the Lord knows who he is."

The story of the injured American haunted Bonnie as she followed Martha on a frantic, three-hour tour of Rome. Perhaps it was because it reminded her of Preston and his spill on the track in California. By the time they hailed a cab outside the Olympic Village and headed toward the center of the city, wondering about the reporter turned into thinking of Preston. The sight of the Pantheon took her breath away, but all she could think of was how much more spectacular the memory would be if Preston were with her.

At the Trevi Fountain, Bonnie watched Martha perform the silly ritual of turning her back to the waters and tossing a coin into the fountain. "To insure you come back to Rome," she said.

Come back? Why in the world would she want to return? She hadn't wanted to be here in the first place.

Her fingers tore the ribbon from her neck and, in one swift move, tossed the penny it held into the center of fountain, pink ribbon and all. She might not ever see Italy again, but the dumb penny that represented the love she'd wasted on Preston Grant could rot here, for all she cared.

✍

September 2, 1960

The crowd inside the Stadio Olympico roared, then quieted as the next event was announced. Banners from the participating countries snapped in the crisp breeze as runners stretched and practiced and, in Bonnie Taggart's case, prayed.

Bonnie said, "Amen," then fit her feet into the starting blocks and cleared her mind of all other thoughts save to press on toward the prize. To her right, a young woman from Great Britain knelt, tying the laces on her running shoes, while to her left, a cadre of reporters stood with cameras at the ready. It still amazed Bonnie that today's events would be shot on Hollywood film, then flown back to the U.S. to be broadcast from CBS Studios. Today the Olympians would compete, and tomorrow the citizens of the United States could watch the games in the comfort of their own living rooms. What an amazing modern world she lived in.

Again the reporters caught her attention. One of them,

a man of average height leaning on a pair of crutches, looked vaguely familiar. The shadow of a massive television camera balanced precariously on a sturdy metal tripod obscured a good portion of his face, but what she saw looked rather like. . .

No, it couldn't be. Her mind must be playing tricks on her.

"Runners to your positions, please."

Jerking her attention away from the press, Bonnie focused on the official and waited for the starter's pistol to sound. When it did, she tucked the baton into the crook of her arm, dug into the track, and shot forward.

Moments later, she successfully handed the baton off to Martha, and Bonnie's moment of Olympic glory ended. "That wasn't so bad," she whispered as she watched Martha overtake the British runner to garner a few precious seconds for the team.

Unfortunately, although the team presented its best time ever, the victory went to others. While camera crews from around the world swarmed the winners, a lone cameraman rolled his television camera toward Bonnie while a reporter hustled alongside him.

Actually, the reporter didn't exactly hustle, for he struggled with a cast on one leg and a pair of crutches that kept him from moving slightly faster than a crawl. Still, he surprised Bonnie by calling her name.

Bonnie stared. Preston Grant was struggling to make his way toward her on a pair of crutches while juggling a large microphone with the CBS logo emblazoned atop it. The same logo that appeared on his blazer.

She froze. "Preston?" Her gaze fell on the familiar face of the cameraman. He, too, wore the CBS blazer, along with a broad smile. "Tom?"

"Sure is, Bonnie," Tom said.

Preston offered her his most endearing smile and thrust the microphone toward her. "Preston Grant, CBS Sports. Miss Taggart, could we have a moment of your time?"

"A moment of my time? Of all the. . . Humph." Bonnie turned and stalked away. After six weeks of complete silence, he showed up out of nowhere in Rome as a reporter for CBS? The nerve of that man.

Then it hit her. Crutches. Preston was on crutches—again.

Casting a glance over her shoulder, she saw Preston and Tom in the middle of an animated discussion. Tom noticed her first and gestured in her direction. Preston's gaze followed to lock on Bonnie.

She wanted to slug him and hug him all at the same time. Bonnie stalked toward him, praying God would either give His permission or stop her.

From somewhere behind the pair, a spotlight blazed. Tom aimed the camera at her, and Preston held the microphone out in her direction.

"Hey, sunshine. Long time, no see," he said when she stopped just inches from him. Bonnie said nothing.

Preston upped the wattage on his smile. "How about saying hello to the folks back home?"

She tried to ignore it—and him—as well as the thumping of her heart, as she strode past.

"Bonnie, sweetheart, talk to me, please," he called, catching the attention of those around them.

Well, that was the absolute last straw. Bonnie turned to face him with fire in her eyes.

"Talk?" She shook her head and squared her shoulders as she put her hands on her hips. "If anyone has some talking to do, it's you, Preston Grant. You tell me you love me and promise me I won't have to wait for you forever; then you just disappear out of my life?"

At least Preston had the decency to look uncomfortable. "Yes, well, about that. You see, I, um, had a goal and it required, um. . . Well, suffice it to say I hit a few snags along the way."

"A goal?" Bonnie shook her head. "This conversation is over." Again she headed past him toward the exit.

"Wait! Please, Bonnie, don't leave yet."

She kept walking.

"I was an idiot. I love you, Bonnie Taggart, and I don't care if the whole world knows it!"

This time she stopped but couldn't quite make herself turn around and face him.

"That's right, Bonnie. I love you. I always have. I wanted to wait to propose until I felt worthy of you, and I figured being an Olympic champion might accomplish that."

Bonnie began to pivot slowly in his direction, eyes closed to prevent the tears from falling. It didn't work.

"Now I know that all the achievements in this world won't make me worth a woman like you." He paused. "But I'm still willing to try."

Her eyes opened to focus on Preston, who knelt before her. "Bonnie Taggart, in front of God and all the CBS viewers, I'm asking you if you will be my wife."

And the Olympian said yes.

THE GARDEN ROOM'S WORLD-FAMOUS COCONUT POUND CAKE

2 cups sugar
1 cup shortening
1 teaspoon vanilla
1 teaspoon butter flavoring
6 eggs
2 cups sifted flour
1 can (3.4 ounces) coconut
Pinch of salt

Preheat oven to 325 degrees. Cream shortening and sugar; then add vanilla and butter flavoring. Fold in eggs one at a time; then gradually sift in flour and salt. Fold in coconut, and pour into 10-inch greased and floured tube pan. Bake 1 hour, 20 minutes, or until toothpick inserted in center comes out clean. A few minutes before cake is done, begin making sauce.

Coconut sauce:
1 cup sugar
2 teaspoons coconut flavoring
½ cup water

Stir together in saucepan and bring ingredients to a boil for 1 minute.

To assemble cake:
Remove cake from oven, and brush or pour sauce over hot cake in pan. Return to oven for 4–5 minutes. Remove cake from pan immediately and let cool.

KATHLEEN Y'BARBO

Kathleen is an award-winning novelist and sixth-generation Texan. After completing a degree in marketing at Texas A&M University, she focused on raising four children and turned to writing. She is a member of American Christian Romance Writers, Romance Writers of America, and the Houston Writers' Guild. She also lectures on the craft of writing at the elementary and secondary levels.

Olympic Cheers

by Gail Sattler

Dedicated to Lyne,
who I know is as much a joy to her students
as she has been to me during the writing of this story.
Merci. Je n'aurais pu le faire sans vous.

Chapter 1

B rian McDermot inhaled deeply from his place in the line at the entrance to McMahon Stadium. He tilted his head back and stared up at the huge expanse. His most recent job had been as a member of the crew of workers who had added an extra twenty thousand temporary seats to the structure for this single event. Prior to that job, he'd been employed in the building of the Olympic Saddledome. After many years, it, too, was ready to serve its grand purpose.

This was it. The first day of the 1988 Calgary Winter Olympics.

Brian exhaled and watched his breath form a white puff in the cold winter air. The trouble was, the temperatures wouldn't get any better for the duration of the opening ceremonies, for which he held a ticket. McMahon Stadium, where the opening ceremonies would take place, was an open-air facility. City officials had hoped the current chinook would last through at least the first day of the Olympics. Unfortunately, it hadn't happened. Winter had returned. It was cold.

Again, he looked up at the building. As he did so, he patted the pocket where he had all his Olympic tickets safely zipped. Born and raised in Calgary, he regularly attended the Calgary Stampede, which had gained world-wide recognition. However, having the Winter Olympics in his own backyard was a once-in-a-lifetime event. Being an average working man, he'd spent more than he really could afford, but he wasn't going to miss out. Starting today, he was officially on vacation, and he planned to spend most of it on the Olympics or Olympic-related activities.

He continued to shuffle forward in the line. Children and adults chattered around him in English as well as in many foreign languages. People from all parts of the world had come to his hometown. Everyone was eager to be a part of the spectacle of the opening; then, after that. . . Brian smiled at no one in particular and thought, *Let the games begin!*

The excitement in the crowd was almost a tangible thing. Like him, some people were alone, but many were together in pairs or larger groups. Brian had chosen to attend alone for many reasons.

Aside from the prices of the events, most of his friends weren't interested in anything other than the hockey games. If Brian wanted to watch hockey, he could simply sit in his living room and watch a game on television. This was more than a series of international hockey games—this was history in the making. Hockey. Biathlon. Bobsledding. Figure skating and speed skating. Cross-country skiing, alpine and freestyle skiing. He could hardly wait to see the ski jumping. The few times Brian had tried skiing, he had barely been able to get off the bunny run. For the next sixteen days, the best of the best in the world were competing, and he was going to be there.

He couldn't afford tickets to all the events. Even if he had that much money to spend, he wouldn't have been allowed to purchase so many. Tickets were sold well in advance, and to be fair to the world, the Olympic Ticket Committee had figured out a way to sell the tickets to include as many people from as many countries as possible. Brian had managed to secure a ticket for the opening ceremonies but not the closing ceremonies. This was his one event for the day. Tomorrow, on day two, he had wanted tickets for the hockey game between Canada and Poland, but when he received his package of tickets, that event hadn't been in the lot. Instead, on day two, he would be attending the men's downhill alpine skiing, which had been his second choice.

That night and every night, he would go downtown to check out what was going on at the Olympic Plaza. The highlight of each evening would be the laser and fireworks shows. These would be visible from most parts of the city but were best viewed from the Olympic Plaza. Also, this was when and where the gold, silver, and bronze medallions would be awarded. The best thing about this part of the Olympics was that it was free.

Once past the entrance, he made his way to his reserved seat. A lightweight poncho had been placed on every chair for all attendees to wear over their winter clothing, which would effectively color the audience. Across the stadium, huge circles of bright colors had started to appear as everyone in the crowd donned their ponchos and sat. Soon the audience opposite him would become the Olympic Rings in bright red, green, black, yellow, and blue, surrounded by white, which was the background color that would be worn by 90 percent of the attendees. The aerial view would be spectacular. In case he missed it, he'd already set his VCR to record the nightly newscast. He made a mental note to watch for the helicopters.

Brian turned to face his seat and picked up his poncho. He hadn't known what color he would be until now, but he had seen in the newspaper what had been planned. His poncho was red.

Brian smiled. Since the Olympic Rings were on the other side, that meant he was going to be part of a Canadian maple leaf.

As a Canadian citizen, he liked that idea. One day, he would be able to play the tape of the evening news and point out to his future children and grandchildren exactly where he had been on February 13, 1988, at 1:30.

Brian straightened and held up his poncho, but it didn't fall from its fold. After a slight shake, it still didn't come loose.

Brian grimaced. He wanted to slip the poncho on, sit down, and watch the picture develop in the crowd. He stepped back as far as space would allow in the cramped area, raised his arms to chin height, and gave the poncho a quick snap.

In a rush of movement, it billowed wide open, just like a fresh sheet when changing the bed on laundry day.

Suddenly, the right side of the poncho crumpled as it hit something.

"Zut alors!"

A program magazine flew into the air.

Brian quickly turned his head.

Beside him, a woman flailed her arms, then began to topple.

In his mind's eye, Brian saw the woman falling into the hard, raised back of the plastic chair in the row ahead of them.

He'd worked with those chairs. Both from setting them up and assembling them, he knew how hard they were and how much it would hurt to land on top of the jutting backs.

Without hesitation, Brian flung the poncho to the ground and lunged toward the woman. He grabbed her with both arms, trapping her in a bear hug to prevent her from going down.

Together, they swayed for a moment until they regained their balance.

Brian looked down, down into the greenest eyes he'd ever seen.

"I'm so sorry," he muttered. "Are you okay?" He didn't expect an answer because he wasn't sure she understood him, but he hoped she could tell from his expression how he felt about almost knocking a stranger down in the crowd.

The woman's eyes widened even more, just like a deer caught in the headlights. *"Monsieur, veuillez me lâcher, ça va bien."*

Brian suddenly became aware that he hadn't released her. He didn't know what she'd said, but he did recognize the *ça va bien* from way back in high school, when taking French was compulsory, as meaning, "I am good."

He loosened his grip, and when he was sure her feet were planted firmly on the ground, he released her fully and backed up a step. A lady in the row behind them reached forward to return the woman's program.

"*Merci.* Thank you," she mumbled, then turned to Brian. "I am fine. I am not hurt. I am only surprised."

Brian couldn't remember ever having felt so embarrassed or so guilty. He'd never hit a woman in his life. Of course, his habit of snapping his sister in the rear end with the dish towel when they were kids didn't count.

His mind went blank, unable to think of a suitable response. Rather than say nothing, he picked up his poncho and smoothed out a few imaginary creases, as if they would matter. "I see your poncho is red. Mine is red, too. We're the only two red ones in the row, and then it's back to white on both sides of us. That means we're the stem of one of the maple leaves."

"Yes. I have seen the plan. It will be a good thing to see from a plane, will it not?"

He nodded and turned to face her. "Judging from your accent, you're a visitor here." He extended one hand. "My name is Brian. Welcome to Calgary, Alberta, Canada, my hometown." Slowly, she accepted his hand and smiled hesitantly. Instantly, Brian relaxed. "So, *bonjour*," he said in his best French accent, which was pretty much all he knew besides "my name is Brian" and "how are you?" which he figured would be repetitive, making his attempt at her language insulting. "Pardon my bad French. You speak English way better than I speak French."

She smiled hesitantly. " 'Ello," she said, her accent very thick but perfectly understandable. "My name is Sophie, and I come here from France. Your *'bonjour'* was very fine. You did well."

"I don't know how much difference there is between Quebec French and France French, but I figured that *bonjour* is simply *bonjour.*"

"You are right. I do not mean to be rude, but let us take our places. I must take many pictures."

Brian slipped his poncho over his head while his new acquaintance did the same.

He watched her out of the corner of his eye. No one had helped her, and no one had seemed overly concerned with his feeble rescue attempt. It told him that she was alone, too.

Without saying a word, as soon as she was seated, Sophie reached down and opened a small suitcase that was on the ground by her feet. Inside, safely nestled in preshaped foam, was one of the fanciest cameras Brian had ever seen. She picked up the camera body, attached a huge telephoto lens, took some light readings, then stood and snapped a number of pictures. Brian had no idea how many; he only heard the whirring of the auto-winder, telling him that it was a lot.

Brian pulled his inexpensive instamatic camera out of his pocket, snapped a few pictures from his seat, and quickly returned his camera to his pocket.

She sat, switched to a wide-angle lens, stood, took more

pictures, then sat, this time with the camera in her lap

He could no longer remain silent. "Nice camera," he mumbled.

She turned to him. "Yes. Yet it does become heavy after a while. At the outdoor events, I will take only one lens so I do not have so much to carry."

"How many events are you going to?"

She patted her pocket. "Many. This is very exciting to watch, but I must take many pictures in order to remember. Jean-Pierre is the photographer, but we are not always going to the same events. That way we can get the most pictures."

"Photographer?" He looked down at her camera. If that wasn't the camera of a professional photographer, he didn't know if he wanted to guess at the other one.

She nodded. "Yes. I have come here to observe and learn. My job is in advertising. I am in a committee back home, and it is our job to do promotions for the 1992 Winter Olympics in Albertville. I am here to see what is done, to take pictures, and to write articles so we may soon begin to invite the world to Albertville. Four years will go by very quickly."

"That's very interesting. I worked for years to make the Olympics here but not in tourism or anything like that." He swept his arm in the air to encompass the expanse of McMahon Stadium. "Over the last few years, most of the work I've been doing has been in either new construction or expanding existing structures to get the city ready to host the games. The Saddledome, the Olympic Park, and the Olympic Oval were designed and built specially for the Olympics."

"Then you must know something of the preparation needed before the games?"

He nodded. "My boss was on a number of committees, both professional and volunteer, so I heard a lot about the stuff they did. He and his wife and a number of people went to Sarajevo in 1984. I'd guess they did the same thing then that you're doing now."

"Most probably."

He looked all around them. "I know that a lot of the promo for this also promotes the city of Calgary as well as the games. There's a lot of things happening at night. To-night, and every night, there will be fireworks, bands and other entertainment, street vendors, pin trading, even square dancing. They're also going to light a fire on top of the Calgary Tower to make it look like a huge Olympic Torch."

"I would like to see these things."

"Most of it will be centered at the Olympic Plaza start-ing tonight. I'd love to show it all to you."

She paused, tilted her head slightly, narrowed one eye, and openly studied him.

Brian forced himself to breathe as he realized what he'd just said. He only wanted to see the history that was hap-pening in his community. He hadn't considered being a tour guide for someone he didn't know. Yet prior to the games, much of the local advertising and hype material released prompted all residents of Calgary to welcome the world to their hometown. For the last few months, the sermons at church had shifted in theme to include a lot about evange-lism and sharing one's faith in a nonthreatening way, as well as about simply being a good witness in a crowd.

Last Sunday, with a show of hands, everyone in the congregation had openly promised to share the love of God with anyone they came in contact with, both residents and tourists. At the time, Brian had raised his hand and followed along with his pastor's prayer, just like everyone else, not thinking it would really happen. He'd planned to sit comfortably in his assigned seats or stand around in the cordoned areas for the events that were standing room only all by himself.

He hadn't foreseen nearly knocking over a stranger. Especially a stranger from another country. A stranger whom both his church and his community told him he was supposed to be nice to.

He watched Sophie as she took her time considering his offer. He figured she was about thirty, which was three years younger than he. When he'd caught her, her head had barely come up to his chin. He couldn't tell now by looking at her, but knowing how her parka had compressed when he had caught her, she was as tiny as she was short.

Brian tried not to blush, even though nothing had been said. He'd already held this woman in his arms before they'd even been introduced. In hindsight, the reason he hadn't seen her when he flipped his poncho open was that not only was she a foot shorter than he was, but she had also been bent over with her heavy camera case.

While she wasn't pretty, she was by no means ugly, although it was hard to tell when she was bundled up in a hooded parka and covered with a bright red poncho.

Since she was openly studying him, he studied her. He couldn't tell what her hair color was, but unless she dyed it, it would be the same color as her eyebrows, which were a light brown. Her nose wasn't delicate, but it suited the rest of her face. Her chin was small and slightly pointy but nothing unusual. Her oval face was well structured but by no means outstanding.

But her eyes. They were the most captivating eyes he'd ever seen. Before he'd had time to look at her face, he'd looked deeply into pools of vivid green, the greenest eyes he'd ever seen. Already, he knew he would be thinking of her eyes long after they parted that night.

"If you would let me give your name and your phone number to my partner, then yes, I accept your invitation to see your city."

Brian gulped. He had been hoping that she would think he wasn't really serious, that he'd only asked to be polite.

He pictured himself in church, his hand raised, making the same pledge as the rest of the congregation.

A verse he'd read a few days ago in the book of James roared through his head. *"But let your yea be yea; and your nay, nay; lest ye fall into condemnation."*

He'd made a promise to God.

Now he had to keep it.

He cleared his throat. "Great. Everything is starting. We'll talk more about it later."

Chapter 2

Sophie Dupuis tried to turn her attention to the action on the ground in the center of the stadium, but her thoughts kept wandering back to the man beside her.

My heavenly Father, have I gone insane? What have I just done?

She didn't hear an answer, but she didn't really expect one. She'd learned many times that God seldom answered prayers in the obvious ways or in the ways she expected.

She never would have thought she would one day be involved with the Olympics, as had so many of her family members over time. Yet here she was, sitting in the frigid temperatures of a Canadian February, camera in hand at the opening ceremonies, gathering information.

Now she had just agreed to see the sights and sounds of an Olympic city with a stranger.

She couldn't deny that it was important to know what happened in an Olympic city after the events of the day had ended. She didn't live in Albertville, but the advertising company she worked for had been hired to do a series of brochures and other promotional material. They thought it prudent to see what Calgary was doing and had spared no expense. They had purchased many event tickets for her and Jean-Pierre. For the opening ceremonies, since they knew what had been planned with every person attending to wear a colored poncho, they had seats on opposite sides of the arena. For many of the other events, they would be side by side, where she would be taking notes and Jean-Pierre would be taking pictures. Yet because of the expense, the committee had chosen for them to go to some events separately, for variety, over the sixteen days.

She had her program and she had done plenty of research, but no amount of research could come close to being shown the city and local Olympic-related events and festivities by a resident.

Sophie glanced at Brian, then quickly turned back to watch the parade of athletes taking their places at the front of the stadium.

Brian had not interacted or spoken to the man in the seat beside him, which told her that this Canadian had come alone. She didn't know if it was because his wife didn't want to attend, if they could only afford one ticket, or if he simply was unattached. Because he wore gloves, she couldn't see if there was a ring on his finger.

She certainly didn't want to be escorted by a married man, but she was unsure of the wisdom of being accompanied by a single man who wasn't held accountable to anyone, either. Yet ever since the agency had booked the flight for her, she'd prayed for help in finding a unique presentation for the promotions. Even though their meeting had not been ideal, she had met a local person willing to show her more than she could ever see simply by following the official program and guidebook meant for tourists. The committee at home had told her not to allow herself to mix with the official Olympic Committee in Calgary, because they would only show her what they wanted her to see. Now an ordinary resident would be showing her the true-to-life happenings of what the city did while the games were in progress. She would see everything from the ground up. God really had answered her prayers.

So she had to trust Him and pray that she could trust her new escort as well.

Sophie would have felt better if Jean-Pierre would accompany them, but from the moment they'd arrived, Jean-Pierre had complained bitterly about how tired he was. Their plane had been delayed twice, and they'd arrived in Calgary's airport only that morning. Being prone to motion sickness, Sophie had a ready supply of medication on hand, which had the added benefit of helping her sleep. Jean-Pierre, however, complained that he could never nap in flight or sitting anywhere, which included in busy airport terminals. Knowing Jean-Pierre was awake and alert beside her, Sophie had slept everywhere she could during the long journey and many stopovers.

But now, as soon as the opening ceremonies were over, Jean-Pierre would be going back to the hotel, where they had adjoining rooms, to sleep. He had told her to simply follow along with everyone else. Maybe they would meet up later, or maybe they wouldn't see each other until nighttime, when she returned to the hotel.

She wanted to tell Jean-Pierre she'd had a change of plans but didn't know how to contact him. He would be on the first shuttle bus back to the hotel while she was trying to wend her way through sixty thousand people. Her only option was to wait, then phone him at the hotel, except she didn't know where she could find a pay phone. Even if she did, she didn't know how long it would take before he would be back at the hotel. She certainly didn't want to wait and call him from the restaurant, because she didn't want to wake him up.

Her thoughts drifted to a new type of telephone her boss had just purchased. The price was high, but the technology was amazing. The base unit of the phone was plugged into the wall, but the handset had a pull-out antenna and was not attached to the other part. Instead, it was almost like a walkie-talkie, yet it was a phone. Sophie could not afford such a thing, but she had been to her boss's home, and he had proudly shown her his latest acquisition, then allowed her to use it. She wished she could have such a telephone to call Jean-Pierre across the stadium, but such a thing could never happen.

A touch on her arm brought her out of her musings.

Beside her, Brian pointed down. "I don't know if you know this, but do you see the girl up there who is about to receive the torch? The two athletes giving it to her are both from Calgary, and they're Olympic medal winners. The girl's name is Robyn Perry, and she's only twelve years old."

"That is quite a responsibility for such a young girl."

Both Sophie and Brian sat transfixed as the schoolgirl received the small torch from the athletes, then lit the big torch at the front of the stadium.

"Did you see the Calgary Tower yet?"

"No, I did not."

"You can't see it from here, but right now, as they're lighting the Olympic Torch, they're lighting a flame atop the Calgary Tower. That's a big building downtown, shaped kind of like the torch. They're going to have a flame burning on top of the Calgary Tower, downtown, for the whole time the flame is burning on top of the real Olympic Torch."

"That is very fascinating."

Brian pointed back down to the center of the stadium. "Look what they're doing now."

Very few words were exchanged as the events followed on schedule. They watched singers and dancers, including a troupe of a thousand children dressed in blue, miming images of Olympic sports as well as dancing. The entire ceremony was breathtaking and perfectly planned, almost making Sophie forget the frigid temperature.

When it was all over, they remained in their seats while the crowd began to disperse.

Sophie turned to Brian, who was paging through his program book.

"I know it is only afternoon, and there are many hours until the lasers and show of fireworks," she said as she packed her camera back into its case. "But I do not know how to find you again. I was going to follow the crowd to see things until nighttime, when I meant to go back to my hotel. But now I will not be doing that. Where can I meet you when it is starting to become dark, a place that I will be able to find you?"

"What about Jean-Pierre?"

"Jean-Pierre must sleep. He does not expect me back."

"Not that. I meant, will Jean-Pierre mind if another man shows you around?"

"That I do not know. It would have been a good thing for Jean-Pierre to come to listen to all you are going to say, but it was his choice to go to sleep. I would like to phone the hotel and leave a message to say what I am doing and who I am with."

Brian glanced from side to side. "That's probably a good idea. If you're hungry, I can take you downtown and buy you dinner. So we can get acquainted. It's also a public setting, so you don't have to be nervous."

She checked her watch, which she had set to the local time before they landed. She hadn't eaten since the plane that morning, and even if it wasn't any particular mealtime, she was hungry. "Yes. I would like that very much."

"Tonight we'll go back downtown for the fireworks and laser show. Tomorrow I have a ticket for the men's downhill skiing. How about you?"

"Jean-Pierre and I have tickets for the hockey game between Poland and Canada."

Brian froze. "You should enjoy that. I really wanted to go to that game, but the luck of the draw wasn't on my side for tomorrow's lineup. Not that I don't want to go, but it was my second choice. The alpine skiing is in the morning, and I

285

haven't missed church on Sunday since I was in my teens."

Sophie froze. "Church?"

"Yes. I go faithfully every Sunday. Also, I play guitar for the worship team, so that gives me added incentive to be there. I mean, aside from the obvious reason of going to worship God." He cleared his throat, and his voice dropped. "Do you believe in God, Sophie?"

"Yes. I also go to church every Sunday at home. It will be strange not to go, even away from home."

He nodded. "I know how you feel. I guess in a way I'll be away from home, too. I'll be out at Nakiska." He cleared his throat and stood. "We should probably get going. It's a long way to where I parked my car."

Sophie's mind raced. She knew that just because a person said he believed in God and went to church didn't necessarily make him a good or trustworthy person, but the fact that he went every Sunday, standing at the front as an example to others, instantly eased her mind about going through a strange city with this man she didn't know.

She wanted to experience as much as she could about Canada in only sixteen short days. This was something she hadn't thought about before, but just like she'd told herself earlier, God didn't always answer prayers or give gifts the way His children expected.

She opened her mouth, but the wrong words came out. "The committee thought it would be best for Jean-Pierre and I to not go to all the same events. We have many tickets together, but many are not. Tomorrow we were to sit together, but maybe we can trade tickets. I would love to go to a church service in a foreign language. Maybe Jean-Pierre would like to go to the skiing, to go to something different than I am going to; then you could come with me to the hockey game."

"Wow. I'd love that. That's the game between. . ." Brian's voice trailed off. "But what about Jean-Pierre?"

"I do not know how to contact him, and he will be very angry if I wake him up. When we arrive at the restaurant, I will call the hotel and leave a message for him. Let us go now. Not only do I need to make this telephone call, but also your cold weather has made me hungry."

Because public parking wasn't allowed at event locations, Brian had driven partway and parked his car in a lot. He'd then taken the public transportation system to McMahon Stadium. Now, without his car, they had to take the bus to get to the Olympic Plaza. Brian acted as a perfect tour guide in the short distance from the Olympic Plaza to the downtown core.

While Brian talked, Sophie wished dearly she could be taking notes. Jean-Pierre, as a professional reporter, always carried a tape recorder in his case with his camera, but all she had was a pen and paper in her purse. She knew better than to try to write anything down. Between the uneven ride with all the starting and stopping in traffic and her unfortunate tendency to get carsick, she knew that if she didn't look out the window, she would embarrass herself terribly. So instead, she just listened and enjoyed the short ride.

Soon they got off the bus and walked a short distance to a small bistro. "Hmmm," Brian muttered. "It looks like it's going to be crowded, but I expected that. There were a lot of people at the opening ceremonies, and most of them can be expected to go downtown afterward. We might have to wait."

"I do not mind. That will give us more time to talk."

He smiled. "My first thought was to take you somewhere that wouldn't be so crowded—someplace I know the food is great and a little out of the way. But that's not really what you're here for. You're here to get the feel of the Olympic crowd." He waved one arm in the air toward the door. "So here we are."

Sophie first phoned the hotel with instructions on how to leave the message for Jean-Pierre while Brian put their names on the waiting list. Despite Brian's worries, they were soon seated at a table.

After they were settled, Brian leaned forward and folded his hands on the table. "I can't tell you what exactly was said, but I can tell you that a lot of newspaper space has been taken up about all sorts of Olympic things. Of course, first were the celebrations and initial planning when the city got the bid. Then came the nitty-gritty of all the organizing; then the construction began. For a long time, we've seen profiles on the athletes, as well as on the different sports. I would guess that you already know a lot about the history of the games. Probably way more than me, since this is your job."

"Yes. But the Olympics are also close to my heart. Over the years, many of my family have been involved in the games. Some have been spectators, there to cheer their friends as they participated in the games. Some have been involved in administration, like me. Also, I have a relative who actually was an Olympic athlete. *Ma tante* Bonnie, she is a relative from the United States. She ran in the games in 1960, but she did not win a medal. I am very proud to say that I was named after *mon mémé* Sophia; that is my great-grandmother. Sophia Papadopoulou was her name before she wed with *mon pépé* Henri, my great-grandfather Henri Preston. *Pépé* and *Mémé* were in the group of people who founded the first modern Olympic Games in 1896."

"Wow. You definitely know more of the history of the games than I do. I can't say that I even know the names of my great-grandparents, much less what they did in their lives. It's actually pretty sad. I'm going to have to ask my parents and see if they know."

"Family is very important to me. One day I will be married and have, how you say, a house with a fence of white."

"I think you mean a house with a white picket fence." Brian smiled. "You were very close, and I knew what you meant. You speak English very well, and your accent is very charming."

Sophie felt herself blush. "It is not always so good. Some people treat me like I am not smart because of my accent."

Brian made a soft snort. "I know people like that. Have you ever noticed how people who do that don't speak a second language themselves? I wish I could speak a second language, especially as fluently as you."

"It is because of my English that I have been given this job. Jean-Pierre is also good with English. Jean-Pierre also speaks German."

"I can hardly wait to meet Jean-Pierre. I guess I'll meet him when I take you back to the hotel."

"I do not know. If he is sleeping, I will not wake him.

Jean-Pierre can be *grincheux*, how do you say? I think your word is *crankled*, when he does not have enough sleep."

Brian's lower lip quivered; then he caught it between his teeth for a couple of seconds. When his expression became completely serious, his lips relaxed, and he cleared his throat. "I think you mean 'cranky.' It means *easily irritated*." He paused again to catch his bottom lip between his teeth, thinking of the appropriate match between the word *cranky* and the *grinch* part of her French expression.

He cleared his throat. "Speaking of cranky, how are you doing with the jet lag? I have no idea how many hours there is in the time difference."

"I have counted before I left home. It is eight hours difference. But I am fine because I did much sleeping on the plane."

"Then are you ready to start taking in all I'm going to tell you? To tell the truth, seeing the Winter Olympics happening is both kind of happy and kind of sad for me. I've spent so many years getting ready. With all the work and excitement, now that it's here and my work is done, it's almost anticlimactic, but at the same time, it's quite a rush."

"For me, my work is only beginning. There has been much planning, and building has already started, but now it is time to think more of the advertising and reaching the world to buy the tickets. But for today, I do not think this is good. On the way here, I wish I could have been writing, but I could not. Jean-Pierre has a tape recorder, but I do not have one. Also, even if Jean-Pierre does not want to trade tickets with you tomorrow, I would be very honored if you can see me again to tell me more about what happens in your fine city before the Olympics began."

"Well. . .I guess so. I don't have any plans for the next sixteen days except to enjoy the Olympic Games. Just to clear this up, I don't have a wife or girlfriend who will mind me spending my time with another woman. What about you?"

❧

Her mouth opened, but no words came out. She wasn't sure she could describe the status of her relationship with Jean-Pierre. But she also knew that even if he became angry, it wouldn't matter. He had to understand because she had a job to do and a willing volunteer. "There is no worry. Jean-Pierre and I, we are not married. There are many stores here. Can we do shopping, and I can buy a tape recorder so I can take everything you say home with me?"

He blinked at her quick change of subject, then replied, "I suppose so."

"And I will need to buy many cassettes. At the office, I have a Dictaphone to type everything onto paper. I think this is a very good idea."

Sophie's mind raced at the possibilities. If she could tape everything Brian said, she wouldn't have to take the chance of missing anything in the process of writing. Also, this way, when it was time to talk about other things and just spend time with him as a friendly Christian brother, she wouldn't have to worry about being distracted at something she might have missed writing down. Everything would be on tape. She was on a sixteen-day business trip, but that didn't mean she wasn't allowed to have free time or have any fun.

She folded her hands on the table and looked up at Brian. Now that they were inside and they had removed their winter parkas, she could see the man with whom she would be spending much of her time over the next several days. He was as opposite to Jean-Pierre as could be. While Jean-Pierre had hair so dark it was almost black, Brian's was light blond. The first thing she'd noticed about him in those long seconds that he'd held her while she regained her balance was his light blue eyes. Now that she could see his hair color, his pale hair matched his pale eyes. Even his skin tone was fair, not that the combination made him any less appealing. Brian McDermot was a very handsome man, even with messy hair.

Unconsciously, Sophie raised one hand and made a futile effort to calm her own hair, which was a mess from being covered with the hood of her parka.

She obviously didn't know Brian well, but she could see that he was a man of conscience and of kindness. When he stopped her from falling after he accidentally knocked her down, she could see every thought as if it were written in words above his head. He'd felt guilty and very concerned for her safety. Most other men would have ignored her for the rest of the time in order to not have to deal with the obvious embarrassment. Yet Brian had not only introduced himself, but when he found out her reason for being there, he'd offered to give her a personal guided tour.

If the same thing happened to Jean-Pierre, regardless of the price of the ticket, he probably would have gotten up and left. Jean-Pierre didn't like to deal with things that made him uncomfortable.

"Tomorrow night they'll be awarding medals in the Olympic Plaza. Do you think Jean-Pierre will want to join us?"

"I do not know. I have a feeling that we might start together, but Jean-Pierre, he will soon become separated from us. He is a reporter, and he will be glad to observe; but I think he might want to talk to people and ask questions, not just walk around and be in the crowd. He does love to ask questions. That is why this is a good job for him."

"It sounds like you've known him a long time."

"Yes. We spend much time together. We were very happy to come to Canada together for this job."

Sophie waited for Brian to ask if Jean-Pierre would have difficulty with the possibility of Sophie and Brian attending church while Jean-Pierre went off to see the alpine skiing Sunday morning, but the truth was that he would not. While Jean-Pierre sometimes attended church services on Sunday morning with her, most of the time she went alone. Jean-Pierre was a believer, but he did not share her enthusiasm in the Lord's work or the wonder of His Word. It was the only thing in their relationship that remained difficult for Sophie.

She had dated Jean-Pierre off and on for years, but as much as she liked him, that one thing separated them. Jean-Pierre did not in any way discourage her from her faith—the opposite was true. He openly encouraged her to serve the Lord in whatever ways she wanted, both socially and in works of ministry. But the fact that he did not participate caused her concern.

The waiter appeared, carrying a carafe of coffee. "Howdy! Would you like some hot coffee, folks?"

Sophie rubbed her cold hands together in anticipation. *"Mais oui!"*

He smiled, acknowledged Brian's nod, then turned back to Sophie. "I see you're from out of town. Welcome to Calgary. I hope you enjoy your stay."

When he finished pouring both cups, the waiter left a handful of creamers and a couple of menus and departed to serve another table.

Immediately, Sophie cradled the hot cup in her hands and lifted it to her lips. Before her first sip, she closed her eyes and inhaled, enjoying the warmth of the fragrant steam on her cold cheeks.

She opened her eyes to see Brian doing the same, except his eyes were open, and he was watching her and grinning. "This really hits the spot, doesn't it?"

Sophie quickly scanned the tablecloth. She didn't see any spots or stains—the white tablecloth was quite pristine. She hadn't seen any stains on Brian's clothing, either. She didn't know where the stain was that he was referring to, but no matter where it was, she couldn't see how striking at a stain with coffee would be a good thing. Adding dark coffee would make any stain worse. It didn't make sense. Yet he was smiling like this was a good thing. Sophie didn't understand how, but she smiled back anyway.

Brian sipped the coffee, then set the cup into the saucer. "I've been here before, and I had to wait for my coffee. This must be an idea by the restaurant owner. The business owners have been hyped for a long time about the Olympics. These next several days will be paramount. It's up to people like that waiter to make the visitors welcome and encourage them to come back again on future holidays."

"Yes. This also gives me an idea to suggest that in the restaurants people will go to after an outdoor event that waiters carry around hot coffee to serve immediately. The waiter was also nice and friendly. The Olympics bring good things for much longer than the short amount of time for the games."

"Yes. My job for the Olympics was done sooner. Remember, I've been involved in the building trade, and I worked on some part of the construction of all the buildings in the city that will be used for the Olympic events. So for me, my work is over, and I'm seeing the fruits of my labor, the first being the addition of the twenty thousand temporary seats at McMahon Stadium where we just came from."

"And my job is really for the 1992 Olympics, so it has barely begun."

"We should eat quickly, go shopping for a tape recorder, and I'll show you around."

While they ate, Brian told her about the Calgary Stampede, which was an international rodeo event held every summer. She listened more than she talked, and they were finished in less time than she'd ever spent in a restaurant.

Brian quickly paid the bill, and they were soon once more outside.

"There's a store down that way that sells electronics. We'll make a quick pit stop in there; then we'll be on our way."

Chapter 3

Instead of the electronics store, Brian found himself standing next to a rack of ladies' purses at the big department store. He shuffled back and forth on his feet, hoping no one he knew would see him there.

To distract himself, he watched Sophie trying to explain to the clerk what she wanted.

"I do not see what I am looking for, but I need *un fourre-tout*. One that fits much things."

The woman picked up a large purse. "This is the biggest we carry."

She shook her head. "Not a purse. I am sorry; I need. . ." Her voice trailed off while she searched for the right word. "I need something much bigger. Do you have something that would fit, say, two of my purses inside?" Sophie held out her purse, which wasn't small by any standards. Absently, Brian's hand drifted to his back pocket, over the top of his wallet.

He wondered what women carried in their purses that they needed to be so large but kept his thoughts to himself. There were many times he wished he had more room so he could at least carry a checkbook and a few odd items. At church, he caught many of his married friends asking their wives to keep things in their purses, but Brian didn't have that option. One day, God would match him up with the woman who would be right for him; but until that happened, he would continue to lose change, misplace his keys, and wish he'd put an extra blank check in his wallet.

"Maybe if you went upstairs to the book department. There might be a book tote that would be right."

"*Merci*. I will try that."

Brian led her up the escalator, then into the book department, but they didn't see anything appropriate. The few book totes they found were not a wise choice. She needed something that closed firmly on top, since they would be in a crowd much of the time. As much as the police force had increased their servicing for the duration of the influx of out-of-town guests, a woman carrying an open tote was an obvious invitation to pickpockets.

Sophie sighed as she ran her fingers along a very attractive but very open tote. "I always think of these things to say too late. The words in English I needed to say to the lady in the department for purses is holdall, but I think you call it a bag for the beach. No, I forgot to turn the words around for your language. It is a beach bag that I need."

Brian tried to hold back his laugh, but he couldn't. "Beach bag?" he sputtered through his laughter. "You're not going to find a beach bag anywhere this time of year. Not far from here, we've got snow on the ground and solid ice runs for the bobsledding. And don't forget the skating rinks for the skating events as well as the hockey games." Suddenly, Brian's smile vanished. "What's your favorite NHL team?"

"I do not understand NHL. What manner of sport is this?"

"It's short for National Hockey League, but the teams that participate are from both Canada and the United States. Follow me." He led Sophie out of the store and down the street to one of the large sporting goods stores, where he escorted her through the store and to the hockey department, smiling and nodding to dismiss the clerks who asked if they needed help. He selected, then held up a duffel bag displaying the bright red letter C with orange licks of a fire on the side—the logo of the Calgary Flames hockey team.

"This is what you need. Not only will it hold everything you need, but you'll also have a good souvenir of Calgary to take home."

She blinked at the bright colors of both the bag and the logo. "I think if I accidentally leave my seat without it, I will see that bag from far away."

"That's a good bonus. Let's go. We still have more shopping to do."

She paid for her new purchase; then they began their walk to the electronics store.

"It is starting to get dark."

"Yes. That means soon it will be time for the laser and fireworks shows. I hear they're going to be spectacular."

"Will we be able to see them?"

"Yes. I'm going to take you to the Olympic Plaza, which is down that way." Brian pointed to his right as they continued to make their way to the shopping area. "Not only is the plaza going to be the best place to see the lights, every night they're going to award the medals of the day there. That way, you don't have to have tickets purchased. They figure ten thousand people can stand in the plaza, but that also means it's another open-air event, which again makes us victims of the weather. We'd better hurry to get to the store before it closes."

They made it to the store with plenty of time to spare. Brian felt they paid a little more here than they would have at the department store, but this was a specialty store where the staff knew more about what they sold. They recommended a different microphone, which was of primary importance.

As Brian stood back and watched Sophie pay, he inwardly shuddered. The person she planned to record was him. He didn't like the sound of his voice when he heard it on a tape recorder. He hadn't willingly recorded his voice for many years, not since he was a child and his parents gave him a tape recorder for Christmas. Back in those days, it had been a small, reel-to-reel unit. He remembered spending many hours rewinding the tapes when he dropped them and they became unraveled. He figured that whoever invented cassette tapes was a genius.

As the clerk checked Sophie's signature on her traveler's check, Brian mentally shook his head at his little side trip down memory lane. Yesterday at work, his last day before his holidays, his boss had given the whole crew a big talk about how they had worked together to shape history. Now he was going to help Sophie with her task in making history. It started now—now that she had her tape recorder.

The clerk inserted the batteries and plugged in the microphone, and Sophie tucked everything into her new Calgary Flames duffel.

They both reached down for her camera case at the same time.

When his gloved hand wrapped over top of hers, Sophie's face turned an adorable shade of pink that had nothing to do with the cold weather.

"Please, you have so much more to carry now. Besides, I'd feel like a jerk with you carrying your purse, the duffel, and this big camera case." He shuddered to think of the weight she would be lugging around.

"That would be nice of you to carry it now. Tomorrow, I will take only the camera and not so much extra lenses, and it will fit into this new *fourre-tout*, also. It will not be so heavy or big tomorrow. Now let us go."

When they reached the traffic light, Sophie reached into the bag, pressed the button to turn on the tape recorder, and pulled out the microphone. She asked her questions into the microphone, then held it near the side of his face so he could talk as they walked.

He had to give her credit. As she asked the questions, she tried to be discreet with the microphone, but he couldn't shake the feeling of being nervous.

When he actually stammered while trying to speak coherently, Sophie started to giggle.

He cleared his throat and stiffened, hoping to regain some of his dignity. "What?"

"You say you play guitar at the front of your church. Surely you sing into the microphone, too. Do you not?"

"Of course I do. But this is different."

"I do not understand this difference."

"At church I'm with friends and my Christian brothers and sisters. In the back of my mind, I'm aware that they're recording the service, but I'm just one small part of the big picture. I'm just a voice singing harmony in the background. I can't explain. It's just different." He rammed his hands into his pockets as they continued to walk. "I didn't think this was going to be so hard. I need to think about what I'm saying, but with the microphone in front of me, I feel I should be talking all the time, not letting the thing record silence while I'm thinking."

She smiled, and again Brian lost his train of thought. "Do not worry. I will be listening to you with my Dictaphone. I will be going fast over the silences, then play slowly when you are talking. Do you know the Dictaphone?"

"I've never worked in an office. I can't say that I do. All I know is that executives make a tape of their letters, and the secretaries type them."

"I wear headphones, and there is a foot switch where I start and stop the tape or go backward if I miss the words and must listen again. It is easiest to type if the person speaks slowly and leaves parts where there is no voice. You are doing very fine."

Her graciousness impressed him. He didn't think he was doing "very fine" at all.

"So please do take your time to think. I have many cassettes."

He bit back a smile at her uneven English. In the short time since they had been together, he'd come to like Sophie a lot. He'd already become accustomed to her odd phrasing. He liked the musical flow of her accent and the way she carefully considered her words to make herself understandable. The more time he spent with her, the more he could see the struggles of someone for whom English wasn't her first language.

Language barrier aside, he enjoyed her easy manner and cheerful disposition. Yet when it was time to talk business, she remained focused and detail oriented in her choice of questions. He knew that when she got back home, she would have a spectacular presentation to give her committee, even without the photos Jean-Pierre was allegedly going to take.

Thinking about the elusive Jean-Pierre, Brian missed a step. He'd heard some things about Jean-Pierre but not enough to form an opinion. So far, the most important thing he'd learned was that there was more of a relationship between Jean-Pierre and Sophie than simply business.

They walked through the Olympic Plaza to pass the time until the shows started. Being in a crowd, Sophie turned off the tape recorder. They walked slowly, taking in a few street bands and other entertainers. She took a few pictures of one of the bands whose members were dressed in typical Calgary Stampede style, with Stetson hats and cowboy boots. Brian didn't particularly enjoy country-and-western music, but he waited with Sophie until the band took a short break so she could obtain their permission and contact information, just in case the photos were used in any of her promotional material.

As Sophie tucked her forms into her purse, Brian bought a couple of corn dogs from one of the vendors, a good treat because it was something they could eat without removing their gloves.

When the fireworks and laser shows began, they stood back and watched, too mesmerized with the spectacular display of modern technology to talk. At the big bursts, most of the people in the crowd responded with "oohs" and "aahs," but Sophie responded with *"Hein!"* and *"Que c'est joli!"*

Brian let himself smile openly, letting everyone around him think he was smiling at the fireworks, which were over too soon.

Even though they had spent only one day together, Brian already had mixed feelings about when this 1988 Winter Olympics would end. He didn't want to face the thought that he would never see Sophie again.

Until then, he would enjoy every minute he could spend with her.

Because the crowd dispersed at the same time and they were in close range of other people and other conversations, Sophie didn't bring out the microphone or ask him more Olympic-related questions. Instead, she told him about her home in France and some of the funny things that happened on the long flight, including the stopovers from Paris to Calgary.

Her tales only served to remind him that it had been a long day. They took the C-train to the parking lot where Brian had left his car, and from there he drove her back to the hotel. She became quieter in the car while he drove. She managed to stay awake until they reached her hotel—but barely.

Brian escorted her up the elevator and to the door of her room, where she told him to wait while she went inside. She walked to a door that joined her suite with the other room to find a note, which had been passed under the door.

As she read it, a full smile appeared on her face, momentarily wiping away the exhaustion of a long day.

"It is from Jean-Pierre. He says he would be delighted to trade tickets with you for tomorrow." She held the ticket up with one hand and clutched the note in the other, crumpling it in her excitement. "This means we can go to church together! I am so very happy about this!"

Brian smiled while he pulled his former day two ticket out of his pocket and made the swap. "This is great. Now you get some sleep, and I'll be back in the morning."

❧

At church, Brian accepted a bulletin, then stood to the side as Sophie also accepted one. When the couple handing them out suddenly figured out that the two were together, the woman's eyebrows quirked, but fortunately she said nothing.

Brian introduced Sophie to a few of his friends as they made their way into the sanctuary. A few of them elbowed each other, but to his relief, they gave Sophie a polite greeting and nothing more.

Everything else was normal as Brian escorted Sophie into the sanctuary, except Brian saw it from a different perspective. Usually he was practicing the difficult sections with the rest of the worship team; then immediately before the service, he went with the other team members into another room to pray together. Looking from below and in front of the stage rather than from the stage itself, he noted with interest that the sanctuary was rather noisy. People either stood or sat in groups, talking and laughing. Most parents who had brought smaller children were trying, some more successfully than others, to herd their offspring into chairs and get them to sit quietly until the service began.

He knew his church was more informal than most, so he had to assume that Sophie's church in France probably wasn't as active before the service. Because she appeared uneasy, instead of joining anyone he knew, he led Sophie straight to some empty seats, far away from where the youth group usually hung out.

After they were settled, Sophie leaned toward him. "I have noticed that many people are watching us strangely," she said softly. "Why would this be?"

He tipped his head and whispered back, "This is the first time in years that I haven't been up at the front with the worship team. I'd already made arrangements for someone else to play today because I had plans to go up to Nakiska for the men's downhill skiing. Of course, my plans changed. I'm here anyway, but I don't need to be at the front. People are surprised because they're not used to me walking around before the service." He didn't want to mention the other—and probably more primary—reason was not only had he not come alone, he'd come with a woman.

"That makes much sense."

"Are you okay with the bulletin in English? If you want to take notes, there are lines on the back."

305

"I can read English fine, but I am slower to write than I am to speak in English. When I am trying to write fast when I am listening to English, I will write some words in English and some in French. It can be a difficult thing. When I write down notes of what you say, that I will write all in French."

"You mean while you're listening to someone in English, you can write in French? Are you going to do the same with everything you ask me, too? How do you do that?"

She grinned from ear to ear. "*Très lentement*. Very slowly. This is why this is good for me to have the tape. I can play the tape many times, translate your words into my head, then write in French in good sentences instead of just making notes like I will be doing today."

Brian mentally shook his head while he imagined the process. "Your Bible is in French, too. I never thought of that. This is going to be really hard for you. I hope you don't have a hard time following, jumping between languages. I'm really sorry for suggesting this."

"*Mais non!*" she exclaimed. Several people turned their heads, causing them both to hunch their shoulders and drop their voices to whispers. "I will be fine. If your minister does not speak too fast, I will not have a problem. The only time it might be difficult is when we are finding which verses to read. Most people do not know this, but there are times where in the Francophone Bible, our verse will be one before or after yours, in your Anglophone version. So if we are looking at, say, verse seventeen in a chapter, it might be seventeen in yours, but it also could be verse sixteen or eighteen."

Brian blinked. "You're kidding. I thought it would be universal."

Sophie shook her head. "I do not know why this is. The numbers might sometimes be different, but it is still God's Word. I will understand the words of your minister as he speaks; then I will simply read the verse in my own Bible." Sophie patted her Bible, which she held in her lap. "It is a Louis Segond *révisé*. Similar to a King James Bible in that it is quite formal."

Brian glanced up. "The service is about to begin. Maybe you should find the key verse now, in case it's a different number."

"This is a good idea."

He flipped through his own Bible. "Here it is. 'And he will appear a second time, not to bear sin, but to bring salvation to those who are waiting for him.' Hebrews 9:28" [NIV].

Sophie flipped through hers. "I have found it. The number is the same. *'Apparaîtra sans péché une seconde fois à ceux qui l'attendent pour leur salut.' Hébreux 9:28.*"

Not for the first time since he'd met Sophie, Brian wished he had paid more attention during his French classes back in high school.

"Welcome, everyone!" the pastor's voice boomed from the speakers mounted on the walls. "Please stand, and let's worship God together."

The room darkened, the congregation shuffled to their feet, the music started, and everyone began to sing.

Of course, Brian knew every note of every song, making him painfully aware that Sophie didn't. He was pleased to see that she did know a couple of songs. However, she still struggled fitting the rhythm of the English words to the tune.

Brian found his attention divided for the entire service. As nice as it was to have a break and be with the rest of the congregation for the worship time, he found himself paying too much attention to comparing the difference between how the music sounded on stage, through the monitors, versus how everything sounded through the main speakers.

Once he got over that, he found himself distracted by listening to Sophie. For one song in particular, she not only knew the tune, but she actually could sing the words with the melody correctly. He'd listened to her speak so much, and he'd thought she had a musical voice just talking. But in listening to her sing, he was so entranced, he forgot to sing himself.

He reminded himself that he was there to worship God, not to listen to his guest.

When the pastor began speaking, he followed along with the notes, but he kept peeking over at Sophie to see if he could judge her level of comprehension by her expression. When he had spoken to her and saw her concentrating more, he tended to slow down. Of course, the pastor wouldn't know to do that.

After he was assured that she was able to follow along, he kept glancing down at her Bible to see the same verses written in another language. Some of the words he recognized from school, but he couldn't piece together the meaning of a single sentence. He caught himself comparing the words from her Bible to the same verse in his own, just like he did in the morning with the English and

French words on the cereal box.

Brian squeezed his eyes closed and snapped his Bible shut. He reminded himself again that he was there to listen to God speaking to him through the pastor's words, not give himself a language lesson.

By the time the service ended and they stood for the closing hymn, he was mentally exhausted. After the pastor's closing "Amen," Brian motioned for Sophie to sit down instead of file out of the pew.

"I hate to do this. I wanted to introduce you to some of my friends after the service was over, but I think we should go grab a quick lunch, then hurry to the Saddledome. The game starts at two-thirty, and we have to allow time to get there."

Sophie checked her watch. "Yes. Of course you are right."

Brian took her not to the place he wanted but instead to what was the fastest. Rather than talking about the service, he told her about how the city of Calgary had arranged for transportation to and from the events. There was to be no parking at any of the events. Instead, everything was accessible by public transport, either by bus or by the light rail system, which ran downtown, called the C-train.

"Well, here we go. On to our first real Olympic event."

Chapter 4

S eated on the C-train, they were with too many people to be taping Brian talking, so Sophie simply sat back to enjoy the ride.

They hadn't gone far when Brian turned to her. "What did you think of the church service? Was it similar to back home?"

She smiled. "Yes, it was the same in some ways yet different in many others. It was very pleasant, and it was good to be able to worship the same God so far from home. Thank you for taking me."

One corner of his mouth quirked up. "Actually, I was kind of nervous. I wasn't sure how you felt."

His honesty impressed her. "It was very good. I am anxious to tell my friends at home about how it goes at church services in Canada."

"You do realize that not every church is like mine. Mine is rather informal. There are lots of churches around where the men wear suits and ties and the ladies dress up."

"There were some people who dressed in nicer clothes,

but many wore jeans like us." Even though she had brought a couple of good outfits, she had chosen her clothes today for what she would be wearing at the hockey game—jeans, her warm boots, and her warm parka. She also carried her bright new Calgary Flames carryall, which contained her camera, her purse, and the cassette recorder—complete with extra batteries and an extra tape. Because the church was warm, she'd stuffed her hat, a scarf, and mittens into it, as well.

Brian checked his watch, then looked out the window. "We've made good time. We're almost there. Do you watch much hockey at home?"

"Not much, no."

"I hope Jean-Pierre is enjoying the skiing. With this sudden wind coming up, it's going to be cold up there." Brian cleared his throat and his voice dropped. "Does Jean-Pierre like watching hockey?"

"Yes, he does. But for this, we are working, and he was very excited to be thinking of all the great pictures he would get of the skiing."

"I guess I'll meet him tonight when I take you back to the hotel. Unless he's sleeping by the time we get back."

Sophie laughed. "He will not be sleeping. That was only for one day because of the long journey here. He always complains that he cannot sleep on the plane."

"It sounds like you know him well."

"Yes, we have been together many years."

Two men in the seats behind them chose that moment to start arguing about who was going to win the hockey

311

game, Poland or Canada. Not knowing much of the history of the individual teams, Sophie and Brian both listened. She hadn't known that the Polish team had been together only five weeks before the Olympics started. In that case, Sophie anticipated a rather boring hockey game. But being with Brian would make it all worthwhile.

Watching the game turned out to be a surprise. She had expected the Canadian team to be much better than the Polish team, but the skills of the players were well-matched. It was her job to watch the crowd as much as the events, but she found most of the time she was watching Brian. He cheered and groaned along with the rest of the spectators throughout the game. At the final buzzer, Canada won by a narrow margin of 1–0. Brian stood, pulled his hat off his head, and waved it in the air while calling out a big cheer with probably every other Canadian in the arena.

While the crowd celebrated the victory, Sophie stepped into the aisle and took a few pictures of the excitement that was happening all around her. She couldn't help but take a picture of Brian from the side.

Quietly, she tucked her camera back into the Calgary Flames bag, then stood at Brian's side. "What will we do now?"

He rested one hand over his stomach. "All this excitement has made me hungry. Besides, it's suppertime. Let's go to the Olympic Plaza, buy something for supper, and hang around there until the laser show and medals."

"That sounds like a good idea. I am hungry, too."

"It's not far, and we've been sitting for a long time.

Would you like to walk? That way we can get away from the crowd for a while. It'll take ten to fifteen minutes, depending on how fast we go."

The thought of being with Brian when they didn't have to be lost in a crowd caused something strange to happen to Sophie's stomach, making her think that she was hungrier than she realized. "Yes. I would like that."

They weren't the only ones with the same idea, but it did allow them to get away from the main crush of people.

"How are you enjoying your time here so far?"

She didn't know how to answer. It was a business trip. She had known that as part of her job. She was there to observe and take notes, not to have fun. Yet she was having fun. She told herself that it felt different than she had expected because on the first day of real events, she'd first attended church with a new friend.

A new friend she was becoming very fond of—very fast.

She looked up at Brian as they walked. Since he was expecting a reply from her, his head was turned toward her, as well. He remained silent, and she wondered if he was curious about why it was taking her so long to reply.

She didn't have an answer. Aside from the setting and the aura of excitement in the crowd, she was enjoying her time in Calgary so much because she was with Brian. She knew it was bad to mix business with pleasure, but being with a person who actually lived in the city of the Winter Olympics was an opportunity she couldn't turn down for any reason. She had to pay less attention to Brian as a person and more as an information source. Her company had made a major investment in sending her to the Olympic Games. She couldn't allow personal distractions to interfere with her obligations.

"I am learning a lot about your city as well as the games. Thank you for being my guide."

His smile faltered for a second, then returned. "With the games in full swing, there's going to be a lot more action today than yesterday. There's going to be a lot happening at the bars, but I don't think we need to see that. Also, many people will be taking side trips to Banff, the Columbia Ice Fields, and Lake Louise. They're not far from here, and there are a lot of tour packages for people."

"I need to spend all my time with the Olympics and attractions in the city. This is my job to do."

"Of course. I was just saying that there are other things for visitors to do and other places for them to go."

When they arrived at the Olympic Plaza, Brian looked up into the sky. "I know it's not that late, but it's February, and it's not going to be daylight for much longer. Is there anything you want to take a picture of right now?"

"I will be submitting some pictures, but Jean-Pierre is the photographer. Jean-Pierre's work will be much better."

He patted his pocket. "Then I'll come right out and say what I meant. Your camera is much nicer than mine. I'd love it if you'd take some pictures for me; then I'll pay for double prints on a few rolls. Starting with the roll you took last night."

She smiled. "My company would be more than happy to give you any pictures you want for your help."

She really hadn't planned on taking that many pictures. The camera was to be used for events that Jean-Pierre would not be attending so they could get the most pictures of the most events. Last night she'd been caught up in the excitement of the crowd and had taken many pictures, but from now on, she hadn't planned on taking many. However, she had seen Brian's camera. He'd been very quick, but he hadn't tucked it back into his pocket quickly enough. There were times when she wished she had an instamatic camera that didn't need to be focused, but she didn't want to tell him that for fear he would think her condescending.

"Stand over there, by the flags, and I will take your picture."

When she was done, she tucked the camera back into her carryall. Tonight, Sophie bought a couple of pieces of single-slice pizza, and they continued through the plaza. She recognized some of the same street entertainers from Saturday evening, but many were different.

Before darkness fell completely, she reached into her pocket and pulled out a small bag. "I have brought pins from home for trading. I have many hundred, so most I will give away to the different traders. But the first ones, I will give to you."

Brian pulled off one glove to examine the two pins. "I'll put the one for the 1992 Olympics in my collection, but this one of France, I think I'm going to wear. Can you pin it on me?"

Sophie pulled off her gloves and stuffed them into her pockets. "I think it would be best on the edge of your hood, by your chin, so it does not make a hole in the parka." She reached up, but he was too tall for her to attach the pin properly.

"Wait." Keeping his back straight, Brian did a partial squat. His knees bent outward, and he steadied himself by pressing his hands into his thighs. "Don't take too long. I don't know how long I can stay like this."

She stepped closer and began feeling with her fingers for a good place to push the pin in, then froze. In his current position, his face was, for the first time, lower than hers.

She looked down into his eyes. She likened their positions to the first time they met, with him looking down at her, in close proximity. Now, it was the same thing in reverse.

He had beautiful eyes. Happy eyes. Little crinkles showed he smiled often.

His warm breath fanned her fingers.

Her heart began to pound.

She couldn't help but like him. He'd been nothing less than a perfect gentleman. He was helpful. Kind. He was active in his church. A good Christian man. He respected her job and her language. She laughed at his jokes, and he laughed at hers. She'd felt an instant connection from their first conversation. Sophie didn't believe in love at first sight, but she couldn't deny that something was happening. Something beyond her control. If it were possible, she liked him even more today than she had yesterday.

But he lived across a very large ocean, far away from her home in France.

Sophie didn't believe in long-distance romances. They weren't practical. Both parties were hurt when the inevitable breakup happened. And the breakup would happen. It always happened when the distance was too far to travel. Neither of them could afford many international phone calls. Sending letters took too long. From the first moment they met, their time together was measured. In fifteen days, she would be going home.

She had no intention of having a holiday fling. She was in Calgary on business, and it was going to stay that way.

As she moved her fingers to fasten the clip of the pin, she brushed the warm skin of his cheek.

His eyes widened at the contact.

Her hand trembled, and she fumbled with the clip of the pin. Just as she managed to grasp it, still unconnected to the post, Brian's hand covered hers, pressing her closed fist to his cheek, which had now become slightly scratchy.

He turned his head and brushed his lips against her wrist.

Her heart stopped, then started up in double-time.

Brian turned back to her. His voice came out in a rough whisper. "I've never felt this way in public before, but I wish I could kiss you properly."

Sophie gulped. The darkening pink of the winter sky somehow muted the murmur of the people around them. "I feel this same way, too."

Slowly, he straightened his legs while still holding her hand but lowering their hands as he regained his height. Before she could think of what he was doing, he leaned forward and lightly brushed a kiss on her lips. She didn't even have time to close her eyes, and it was over.

"I'll do that better when I drop you off at your hotel tonight."

The start of loud music saved her from having to reply.

317

The laser show lit the sky as the last of the daylight disappeared. She tilted her head back to watch. Brian gave her hand a gentle squeeze, then released it. "You'd better get your gloves back on, or your hands will never warm up."

She quickly slid her hands back into her gloves. The second they were secure, one of Brian's arms slipped around her waist. She looked up at him, the lasers dancing in the sky above and behind him. He smiled, then jerked his head in the direction of the lasers above to encourage her to watch the show.

The second she raised her head, his grip around her waist became firmer.

She thought she should move away, but being close to him made her feel warmer, even though it didn't make sense. The only thing that would keep her warm tonight was her parka.

The show continued for a pleased crowd; then the music faded. Speakers boomed from the raised stage. Someone made a short speech, then proceeded to give out medals to the athletes who had earned them that day. After the last medal was awarded, Brian gave her a gentle squeeze, which made her turn her head to look up at his face.

"This probably sounds stupid, but I'm going to say it anyway. I'm already dreading the moment the Olympics are over and you'll have to go home. I wish the Olympics could last forever."

A blast of fireworks above her head echoed what she felt in her heart. "Let us just take this one day at a time and not think past each day as it happens. Let us enjoy the Olympics together and not let anything spoil it."

"That's a good idea. Let me start by continuing the tour."

"Tour? But we are standing in one place."

He pointed to one of the tall buildings where the fireworks were being set off. "That building over there is the AGT Building. That's the phone company here in Alberta. And that building over there, where that last blue bunch of lasers was coming from, is the Pan Canadian Building. I forget the name of the other building, but there's a really nice restaurant in it. I should take you there."

"I do not think that is a good idea. Actually, I think we should go back as soon as the fireworks are over. I have a ticket tomorrow for the luge at the Olympic Park. I will have to get up early. What do you have a ticket for tomorrow?"

"I have a ticket for the cross-country skiing, but if I start phoning early enough, I might be able to find someone who will trade with me."

Sophie's foolish heart fluttered. "I would like that."

"Good. The show's over. Let's start making our way back."

She nodded. "Yes. And if we are lucky, you will finally be able to meet Jean-Pierre back at the hotel."

Brian's smile disappeared. "Oh," he muttered. "Yeah. If we're lucky."

Chapter 5

B rian stood to the side as Sophie inserted her key into the lock of her hotel room.

"I can hear the television," she said as she turned the doorknob. "Jean-Pierre is in his room. This is a good thing."

Brian reserved judgment.

Halfway through the C-train ride back to where he'd parked his car, he'd picked up Sophie's hand and held on to it. He'd always thought holding hands was for teenagers, but he needed a simple way to show her how he felt.

She hadn't pulled away. They had talked easily about everything and nothing in particular, their hands joined as if it was simply a natural thing to do.

She would never know how hard it had been for him to make the initial movement. Yes, he'd kissed her quickly in the plaza; and, yes, he had slipped his arm around her and held her close when they were watching the fireworks, but that was an almost surreal moment. Being at the fireworks and laser show and being in the middle of the excitement for the medal awards was almost like a fantasy world. Not that being in such an atmosphere would have been an excuse, but it gave him hope that his thoughts about Jean-Pierre might have been wrong.

On the C-train, life was as normal as it could be. They were heading back to the hotel and back to real life. And back to Jean-Pierre.

But she didn't pull her hand away. Jean-Pierre's name had come up in the conversation a few times, but even thinking of him, her hand remained nestled in his.

She'd said she'd known Jean-Pierre for many years. It was obvious they had a close relationship. But if she was still holding Brian's hand when talking about Jean-Pierre, then the relationship wasn't as close as Brian had previously thought or feared.

Sophie pushed the door open. Brian stepped into the room behind her. The first thing that caught his eye was a camera, countless lenses, and a quantity of other miscellaneous photography equipment spread haphazardly all over the bed.

Brian knew Sophie had taken her camera with her but left all her extra lenses at the hotel. He didn't realize that she had a spare, and it seemed odd that she would have left everything out. The rest of the room would have been spotless except for a cup with some old coffee in the bottom of it and a half-dozen cream containers and empty sugar packets on the carpet next to the bed.

Sophie rested both fists on her hips. *"Ah non! Quel fouillis!* I had told Jean-Pierre he could borrow my lenses, but he

321

has scattered everything and left his own camera and much in here. I will not be cleaning up the mess of Jean-Pierre!"

Brian bit back a grin. In her anger, her French accent had become thicker.

So he wouldn't snicker at her accent, Brian studied the mess. There were more camera parts and accessories than he knew what to do with. He didn't know what some of the pieces were for. "I guess Jean-Pierre knows a lot about cameras."

"Yes. He has been a professional photographer for twenty years. He has much more than this at home. Many times, we borrow each other's equipment, but I do not like his mess in my room."

Despite her obvious annoyance, Brian instantly relaxed. In his mind's eye, he pictured someone who could have been at the same job for twenty years—an older gentleman who had seen Sophie's potential and nurtured and guided her in a professional manner into the world of corporate advertising.

Sophie walked to the messy bed, looked down at the mess on the carpet, then continued past. "I will ignore this litter and knock on the door that is between our rooms. Jean-Pierre is anxious to meet with you."

Brian smiled, now looking forward to meeting Sophie's mentor.

Sophie rapped on the adjoining door. "Jean-Pierre? Can you open the door? There is someone here I would like you to meet."

A shuffle sounded from the other side, followed by the click of a lock. The door swung open.

In walked a man not with silver hair but with thick dark hair, stylishly cut. The man appeared to be approximately the same age as Brian, but that was where all similarities ended.

Jean-Pierre's deep brown eyes sparkled, and his smile would have done any dentist proud. He wore jeans and a long-sleeved, button-down shirt that somehow accented a fine physique rather than hid it. He stood tall, proud, and masculine, like a rogue pirate except with short hair and no eye patch.

Jean-Pierre was so handsome, he was stunning. In fact, Jean-Pierre was the most handsome man Brian had ever seen, over and above all the movie heartthrobs whom women drooled over.

Jean-Pierre extended one hand. "*Bonjour!* You must be Brian. I have been anxious for this moment to meet with you."

Brian pictured women dropping in a faint at the sound of Jean-Pierre's deep, melodic voice.

Hesitantly, Brian reached out and returned Jean-Pierre's handshake. "Pleased to meet you, too," he said, glad he was indoors so that a bolt of lightning wouldn't strike him down as he spoke.

"Sophie has told me much about you. You are kind to show her your city while we are visitors."

Brian didn't feel very kind. He felt. . .jealous.

Sophie turned to Jean-Pierre. "I would like for us to have coffee together so we may talk, but you have left a mess in my room."

Jean-Pierre turned to Sophie. *"Ne t'en fais pas. Je vais tout ranger."*

Sophie glanced at Brian, then back to Jean-Pierre. "Please do not be rude to our guest. Speak so he may understand you."

Jean-Pierre turned to Brian. "My apologies. I needed to pick the right lenses for the fast movement of the luge. But then I heard something interesting on the television to make me be choosing my lenses later."

Brian's heart dropped with a thud. He remembered Sophie saying she would be attending some of the events alone but not all. The original plan had been for her to attend many of the events with Jean-Pierre, so many of the tickets she had were half of a pair. That was how Brian had managed to see the hockey game with her today. He'd traded tickets with Jean-Pierre.

Since Jean-Pierre was in the process of selecting his camera equipment, it didn't appear likely that he would be open to trading for day three.

Jean-Pierre walked to the bed but instead of picking up his camera equipment, he picked up a pillow, moved it, and sat on the corner of the bed.

Brian gritted his teeth. Jean-Pierre's level of comfort at being in Sophie's room, both with and without her, showed a familiarity and ease only achieved with the confidence of a long relationship.

He felt like he didn't belong there. Even though he was in his hometown, in this small room he felt like an outsider.

Jean-Pierre leaned down and picked up the coffee cup. "I was wondering where I had left this. I did not manage to finish it before I heard the news starting."

Brian listened to Jean-Pierre's speech patterns. Jean-Pierre was not as fluent in English as Sophie, but he remembered Sophie saying that Jean-Pierre also spoke German. Brian couldn't speak a second language, never mind a third, so he had no right to criticize.

Sophie began to slip off her parka. "I think it is time to hang up my coat. There is a machine to make coffee here in my room. I will make some; then we can both warm up. I will return."

While Brian slipped off his parka, Sophie walked across the room, then began making the coffee. He kept one eye on her, not wanting to be left alone with Jean-Pierre. He didn't know what to say, so he said nothing.

Jean-Pierre showed no such hesitation. "For what do you have a ticket tomorrow? Sophie had said you might be joining us at the luge if you can find someone to trade."

"I have a ticket for the cross-country skiing."

"I hope you can somehow be with us. Do you know the history of luge?"

"No. I only know that its origins are similar to our casual sport of tobogganing. I've done a lot of tobogganing over the years. I was born and raised here in Calgary."

"I was born in Rambouillet, which is a small city near Paris. From there I have been to many countries."

"Sophie says you're a reporter and you've been a photographer for many years." Brian couldn't compare the exciting life of a world-traveled reporter to his own humble job of construction.

"I got my first job taking pictures when I was in high

school. It is something I have been doing for my entire life."

Brian had started building things when he was twelve years old and helped his father build a doghouse. But he wouldn't exactly count that as his first job. "I guess you got lots of good pictures at the skiing today."

Jean-Pierre shook his head. "Unfortunately the winds, they were strong, and the event was canceled. I will be seeing it at another day. I had a good day instead to see the Olympic Plaza. I have also taken good pictures of your train, which your city has invented for the Olympics. Public transportation is an important thing."

Brian hadn't thought too much about public transportation. He drove his car to work and back because he didn't have a nine-to-five job, and he didn't stay too long in any one location before he had to go to the next contract.

"The coffee will soon be ready," Sophie called from across the room.

Jean-Pierre turned toward the adjoining door. "I will get a new cup from my room."

Brian watched Jean-Pierre disappear. The man looked good, even from the back.

Sophie appeared beside Brian. "Do you think you will be able to get tickets for the luge tomorrow? There is not much time."

"Are you sure about this? What about Jean-Pierre?"

"He will be going, too. Why is it you ask?"

Brian swiped his fingers through his hair. "Do you think he will mind me going?"

"He should not mind."

Brian opened his mouth, but no words came out. He'd seen the way Jean-Pierre watched everything Sophie did. Regardless of the way Sophie felt about Jean-Pierre, which Brian still hadn't fully determined, it was obvious that Jean-Pierre had feelings for Sophie. In fact, Brian suspected that the only reason Jean-Pierre was being so accommodating was because Brian could provide information they otherwise couldn't obtain, at least not so easily.

But Brian wasn't there to please Jean-Pierre or even to answer to Jean-Pierre. He was there because Sophie had invited him. He didn't believe in something so silly as love at first sight, but he liked her—he liked her a lot. He wanted to spend as much time as he could with Sophie because their time together was limited by the days of the Olympics.

There was no time to waste on indecision. If after the Olympics were over, they still felt the same way, even though it wasn't ideal, they could exchange letters and see what happened. Brian could even phone her when he could afford the extra money on the phone bill.

"I just got an idea. I have a few friends to call to see if anyone wants to trade tickets for tomorrow. I know one person from church was complaining about getting a luge ticket instead of what he really wanted. I don't know if that was for the luge event tomorrow, but there's only one way to find out. Can I use the phone?"

❧

Sophie shuffled her feet while they waited for the next athlete to begin his trial. She'd seen bits of luge on the news, but this was the first time she'd see the sport in person. She hadn't realized how fast the action was until the first athlete whizzed by at a death-defying speed, lying on his back on a sled, feetfirst, with no protection except for a helmet, which wouldn't have been the first point of impact in the case of an accident.

When the first man whizzed by, Jean-Pierre had been prepared. The auto-winder on his camera whirred efficiently; then he grunted in self-satisfaction, checking the numbers on the camera as the rest of the crowd watched the clock for the athlete's time. When all heads were up except for Jean-Pierre's, Brian grasped her hand and didn't let go.

At first she felt strange about holding hands with another man in front of Jean-Pierre, but then she realized she didn't care. She had already decided that Jean-Pierre was not the man with whom she wanted to spend the rest of her life. Yes, Jean-Pierre was available, and she knew he liked her. She probably should have been flattered that Jean-Pierre wanted to spend his time with her instead of with other women. She would have been blind, deaf, and mute if she couldn't see how other women envied every minute she spent with Jean-Pierre. He was intelligent and witty, he had a good job, and he was the most handsome man she'd ever met.

Yet as much as she liked Jean-Pierre, she couldn't see herself spending the rest of her life with him. She didn't love him.

But neither would she be spending her life with Brian. Regardless of what happened during the remaining days of the Olympics, they lived half a world apart. She knew opening up her heart would make the pain of parting worse, but she couldn't help herself. He couldn't be her eventual Mr. Right, but he certainly wasn't Mr. Wrong.

It wasn't wise, but she wanted to spend every moment she could with Brian. He had come early to the hotel that morning and waited patiently while Jean-Pierre fretted and changed his mind a hundred times about which lenses to carry.

After considerable time had passed, Brian made a few suggestions that helped Jean-Pierre decide what to bring, then helped Jean-Pierre pack. As he had been from the first time they'd met, Brian was gracious and kind, both with her and with Jean-Pierre. They arrived at the Olympic Park with only minutes to spare before the gates closed, and Brian wasn't even angry.

When she looked up the ice run to see if the next athlete was ready, she involuntarily shivered.

Brian pulled her closer, then released her hand, making her feel doubly cold. But then his arm wrapped around her, warming her from the inside out. "I heard on the radio that it's going to warm up, and it won't be so bad in the next few days. Are you okay?"

She opened her mouth to say she was fine but hesitated. Jean-Pierre's attention had finally strayed from his camera, and he was watching them so intently, she felt like an extra layer of cold had descended on her.

She stiffened to give herself more strength. "I can hardly wait for us to be able to buy some coffee. I think for tomorrow, I have a ticket for the skating. That will still be cold to watch but not as cold as outside."

Brian patted his pocket with his free hand. "I brought all my tickets today. I think when we go back to your hotel, it would be a good idea to compare my tickets to yours and see what we can do to be together for as many of them as possible." He gave her a gentle squeeze, then turned to Jean-Pierre. "While phoning around yesterday, I found a network of people who have tickets to trade. I don't want to associate with scalpers, but this group is 'traders' only. Sometimes, if there's a big difference in the price of the tickets, there will be money involved to pay for the balance, but only up to the actual cost of the ticket. If you're interested, we might be able to change some of your tickets, too."

At Brian's words, Sophie stiffened. Brian was a good man trying to help both her and Jean-Pierre with the monumental job of reporting back to their committee with enough material for their promotion. But as helpful as Brian was, part of her wondered if his offer might also be to send Jean-Pierre to other events so they wouldn't always be a threesome.

Jean-Pierre silently turned his eyes to Sophie. Sophie forced herself not to squirm and to remain unmoving as he openly studied her.

She watched the interplay of thoughts flitter through Jean-Pierre's expressions, varying from surprise to disbelief, then from anger to resignation.

"Yes, I will do that, for there are a few events I would like to take pictures that I did not get tickets."

Sophie tried not to sag with relief at Jean-Pierre's decision. "Then let's enjoy the rest of the luge together. Then we should go back to the hotel for lunch, and we may start making decisions on our tickets. I have a feeling these Olympics are going to go very fast," Brian said.

Chapter 6

Sophie turned her head to the scoreboard to see the score the skier from Germany had earned.

"Look at that woman over there," Brian whispered in her ear. "Look at what she's wearing."

Even without being told, Sophie knew exactly which woman he meant. A lady not far from them was dressed in a beautiful fur coat, a mohair scarf so fluffy it was decadent, and the most gorgeous leather boots Sophie had ever seen. The woman pushed back at her long, wavy hair flowing in the wind, with slim gloves that were an exact match to the scarf, adding a touch of mystique to her elegant appearance.

Sophie looked down at her flat-soled, double-lined snow boots, which were a size too big so she could wear an extra pair of wool socks. She stuffed her mittened hands into the pockets of her padded, shapeless acrylic parka.

"The woman, she is beautiful," she muttered. In addition to beauty, the fur coat showed the woman's class and dignity, with a touch of aloofness despite being at a crowded outdoor event. Even the woman's boots were lovely. They were slim and accented the feminine shape of the woman's legs, hinting that she would also be spectacular once the coat was removed.

Brian shook his head. "Don't you think that's the dumbest thing you've ever seen? I wonder how she walks in those boots, especially here. Look at the heels. Just wait for when she has to walk down the hill over there. She won't look quite so put together when someone has to dig her up out of the snowbank. It's a good thing you're wearing something sensible."

Sensible.

Sophie sagged. For once in her life, she wanted a man to find her attractive. To ignore that she was three inches too short. To overlook the fact that her nose was too big. To not notice her straight, ugly hair. She wanted to be told that she was pretty and appealing. Feminine. Refined.

She was none of that. She was sensible.

Maybe her clothing was sensible, but nothing in her life was sensible right now. Today was day fifteen of the Olympics. Tomorrow was the last day of the games, and every day the most nonsensible thing happened. Every day, she felt herself falling a little more in love with a man whom she would soon have to leave behind.

If she had been truly sensible, she would have contacted the ticket-trading people and obtained tickets to go to events with Jean-Pierre or traded to go to events alone.

But she couldn't do it. Every minute of every day, she only wanted to be with Brian.

Since tomorrow was the last day of the 1988 Winter

Olympic Games, she would have to say good-bye to the first man she had ever loved—in just one more day.

So she wouldn't cry, Sophie pulled her camera out of her bright Calgary Flames carryall to give herself something to think about that didn't involve Brian. "This scenery here at Nakiska is beautiful. Yet your mountains are different from our French Alps. I cannot explain how this is."

"I guess. I wonder how Jean-Pierre is doing at the bobsledding this morning."

"I do not know. It is too bad the weather has warmed enough to make the ice begin to melt."

Brian sighed. "That's one thing that's so appealing about living in Calgary. There are times when it's not so cold, but for those who like to ski, the mountains are close by and always full of good snow. Of course, when the Olympics are over, the ski jumps will stay. They're hoping it will boost tourism in the area."

"It will. That is always a big benefit to any city that hosts the games."

"I was thinking. Tomorrow is the last day of the games. After we all go to the freestyle skiing together, since we couldn't get tickets to the closing ceremonies, I'd like to invite both you and Jean-Pierre to my house for dinner for a closing ceremony of our own. I'm not a great cook, but I think it would be nice to be able to relax at my place for a good, home-cooked meal. It won't be fancy, but I think we've had enough fancy to last a lifetime." His voice lowered in both pitch and volume. "Besides, I think it would be nice to have some time together away from the rush of the crowd."

Sophie's foolish heart fluttered. "I would like that very much." She liked it except that Jean-Pierre would be there, but at this point, she would spend any time with Brian that she could.

Brian smiled, and all sensation of being cold left Sophie. Instead, she felt heat in her cheeks but attributed it to the effects of the wind.

"Great. The next skier is ready to go. We'd better start paying attention."

&

"Welcome to my humble home."

Sophie followed Brian inside the front door of his house, and Jean-Pierre followed behind her.

"Your house is lovely." Without saying so, she thought his house was possibly too lovely and definitely too big for the home of a single man.

His ears reddened, which she thought odd, since they were finally in the warmth of indoors.

"Don't forget, I work in building construction. I did most of this myself. I got good discounts on all the materials, and some of my friends, like electricians and gas fitters, did specialty work for free in exchange for me doing work on their homes for free. It's been a lot of work, but it's been a labor of love. This is my home, and I plan to stay here for a long time."

Jean-Pierre immediately walked to the wood-burning fireplace in the living room, which was Brian's pride and joy. He'd had the rocks he used for the facing specially shipped in from Squamish, British Columbia. His fireplace was the envy of all his friends.

"I like this," Jean-Pierre said as he ran his fingers along the overlapping edges of the layered rock. "You have done a good job."

"Thanks." Brian rubbed his hands together. "Let me hang up your coats, and I'll go into the kitchen and make us some coffee."

Jean-Pierre continued to inspect the fireplace, and Sophie followed Brian into the kitchen. She suspected that the second Jean-Pierre was alone in the room, he would take a picture when he thought no one was looking.

"Is there something I can do to help?" she asked as Brian began to measure coffee beans into a grinder.

"Nope. You're my guest. Sit down."

As she started to turn around, Brian opened the freezer to put the bag of coffee beans back in, causing a rush of cold air to flow out.

"*Oh la la!* I am having chicken skin!"

Brian's movements stopped. One eyebrow quirked. "Chicken skin?"

She wrapped her arms around herself. "I need a sweater. I am having *la chair de poule*. *Chair* is *skin*, and *poule* would be called *chicken*. I am cold, and I have, as you say, chicken skin."

As he looked down at her arms, his lower lip began to quiver. He pressed his lips together and sucked in a deep breath, but all attempts at control failed. He broke out into huge gales of laughter. "You mean you have goose bumps!" he sputtered at the same time as he laughed.

Sophie's heart sank. She had been trying so hard to get the English words and expressions correct, and she thought she had been doing well. She had even remembered to switch the words around to say the adjective before the noun instead of after as she did in her own language. However, this time, she had not translated correctly, and now she looked foolish in Brian's eyes.

"I think I will go sit in the living room with Jean-Pierre," she mumbled as she turned around.

"No! Sophie! Wait!"

She hadn't gone more than two steps when Brian stepped in front of her, blocking her path.

"I'm sorry. I didn't mean to laugh. It's just that it came out sounding so. . .well. . .funny." He lifted one hand and touched a finger to her chin, tipping her head up so she had no choice but to look into his face. "I'm very impressed by the way you speak two languages so fluently. I think it's great, and I really admire you for that."

Her throat clogged. It shouldn't have mattered because she'd been laughed at before. But it did matter today because she was with Brian. "Really?" she squeaked out.

His voice lowered to a rough mumble. "I didn't mean to hurt your feelings. I'm very sorry." His other hand came up, and he rested two fingers against the skin of her cheek and moved closer until they were only inches apart. "I like you a lot, and I hope you feel the same way."

Before she had a chance to answer, his lips covered hers. At first, all that registered in her brain was surprise, but it took only a fraction of a second for the surprise to turn to joy as Brian kissed her ever so gently and very tenderly.

Sophie tipped up her chin a little more to kiss him better.

At her movement, Brian dropped his hands, then wrapped his arms around her in a full embrace and kissed her so fully and so thoroughly that it took her breath away.

"I think I would like for you to light a fire in your. . ." Jean-Pierre's voice trailed off from the direction of the doorway.

Sophie and Brian bolted apart.

"Qu'est que ce? What is going on in here?"

Sophie wanted to tell Jean-Pierre that what was happening was none of his business, but no words would form. It wasn't like she was a young girl and had never been kissed. She was almost thirty years old, and she certainly had been kissed before. She'd just never been kissed like that, and she needed time to recover.

Brian spoke first. "I think it's pretty obvious, my friend. Maybe we should get a fire started while you figure it out." He turned to Sophie. "Sitting next to a roaring fire would be a good way to warm up."

She wanted to tell him that even though she had gotten a chill from being inside the arena for the length of the final women's speed skating competition, she was plenty warm now without any help from the fire. However, she didn't want to say anything like that in front of Jean-Pierre. Therefore, she remained silent and followed the men into the living room. Brian lit the fire, then stood. "If you want to stay here, I'm going to throw supper in the oven and get a few things ready. I'll only be a few minutes."

The second Brian disappeared from the room, Jean-Pierre turned to her. "Do not think that I have not seen this coming. Are you sure this is the right thing to do?"

Sophie gulped. Jean-Pierre had been her friend for years. Often they'd thought they could be more than friends, but it never happened. She was beginning to wonder if there was something wrong with her, if she couldn't fall in love with Jean-Pierre. He was so right for her in so many ways. But instead of falling in love with Jean-Pierre, she had fallen in love with a man with whom she could have no future. It didn't feel right, but Brian was too good a man for it to be wrong to fall in love with him.

She'd been praying about Brian every night since they'd met. The problem was, she hadn't received an answer. At least not one that she recognized as an answer.

She needed time, but time was the one thing she didn't have.

Tomorrow she was going home.

Sophie couldn't speak. All she could do was stare into the flames dancing in Brian's prized fireplace and wait for the right words to come.

Jean-Pierre rose. "That you cannot answer says much. I will also be right back."

Before she could stop him, Jean-Pierre was gone.

Sophie squeezed her eyes shut and prayed like she'd never prayed before.

Chapter 7

B rian had just managed to run the knife through the center of the sourdough bread when Jean-Pierre strode into his kitchen.

Brian set the big knife down and began to spread the butter, waiting for Jean-Pierre to speak.

"I would like for to talk to you about something."

"I'm listening."

"Sophie has been my good friend for many years, and I would not like for you to damage her heart."

Brian halted his swiping motion, then resumed when he figured out what Jean-Pierre meant.

The trouble was, he knew where the relationship between him and Sophie was going. He'd never met anyone like her, and he knew he never would again. Tomorrow she was going home, and Sophie wasn't going to be the only one to have a "damaged" heart.

He wanted to ask her to stay, but he had nothing to offer. Not only did she have a good job to go back to, but she was under contractual obligation to finish what she had started—a project that was a great expense to her company.

He had a steady job, but it wasn't the best-paying job in the world. Brian had no doubt that Jean-Pierre's job earned more money, to say nothing of the status of being a world-class photographer.

All he had to offer Sophie was a house in suburbia with his fence of white.

Brian stared down at the butter that certainly didn't need any more spreading.

Even though they hadn't had much time together, he truly had fallen in love with her. He'd prayed about it, asking God what he should do, but no specific answers had come.

"She does love you; you know of this?"

Brian's throat constricted. He wasn't sure of the depth of her feelings for him. For the entire time of the 1988 Winter Olympic Games, they had only been apart for a few hours each night to sleep. Aside from that, they had talked about everything and anything.

Anything except that. They were both too afraid, knowing their time was quickly running out.

But now he knew, even if he had received the information secondhand. As for himself, he hadn't said the words to Sophie yet, either. With her going home, there didn't seem to be any point. But now, talking to Jean-Pierre, it seemed not only safe, but it was also a relief to say it to someone.

"I love her, too."

Jean-Pierre sank down into one of the chairs. "You may

have been having some wonder about me being with Sophie."

"I did at first but not for very long."

Jean-Pierre smiled. "At times, I would have liked for it to become more, but we are friends, and we will be friends to stay. As a man, I know you can understand me when I say that many times, I have had different women who want me to become married to them."

Brian couldn't say he'd ever had the experience or the honor. He merely shrugged his shoulders.

"Do you think that Sophie is *Mademoiselle* Correct for you?"

Despite the serious nature of their conversation, Brian had to force himself not to laugh. "The correct term in English is 'Miss Right.' I know not much time has passed since we met, but, yes; I do think she is my Miss Right, if only she didn't live so far away."

"I do not know much about your God, but I know that Sophie says many prayers about this. Have you said your prayers about this issue?"

"More than you'll ever know."

Jean-Pierre stood. "Then I have nothing more to say about this."

Jean-Pierre left the room.

Brian couldn't move. All he could do was stare at the doorway, knowing that Sophie wasn't far away.

He hadn't thought that God was listening, but He obviously was. Now Brian had to respond.

He smiled as he slid the bread into the oven to warm.

For now, he would continue with his plans for dinner; then he would take Sophie and Jean-Pierre back to the hotel.

But after that, he had a lot of work to do.

If God was willing.

Chapter 8

Sophie stood at the airport, staring through glazed eyes at the opening to the gate leading to the boarding area.

This was the farthest point to which Brian was allowed to go.

She clutched the two stuffed bears he had given her as a parting souvenir: two white bears, a male and a female, dressed in Western hats and vests. They were called Hidy and Howdy, and she had seen larger, live versions of these bears many times as the official mascots of the 1988 Winter Olympics.

The Olympics that were now over.

It was time to go home.

She stepped away from Jean-Pierre and turned to Brian. "Are you sure you will not be in trouble for bringing us to the airport instead of going to your job?"

Not for the first time, Brian glanced over his shoulder. "No. I won't be in trouble. I've talked to my boss a few times, actually."

"Why do you keep looking backward? We only have a few more minutes before I must leave through the passenger gate."

He turned toward her. "I'm sorry. I'm expecting someone. He should have been here half an hour ago, and I'm worried that he's not going to—"

"Brian! Brian!" a man's voice called out from the crowd.

A balding man with glasses hurried toward them. "Sorry I'm late. I had a few phone calls to make first. About what we talked about."

Above her head, the speakers called for all passengers for her flight to make their way to the boarding area.

Beside her, Jean-Pierre didn't say anything, but he lifted his wrist to make a very obvious show of checking his wristwatch.

"I must go," Sophie said.

Brian rested his hand on her arm. "No. Wait. I know this doesn't give you much time, but this is my boss, Hank, and he has something to ask you."

Sophie's eyes burned. She didn't want to talk to Brian's boss. She wanted to talk to Brian, to kiss the man she loved for the last time, knowing that there was a big possibility she wouldn't see him again until the day they met in heaven.

Hank glanced up at the clock, then turned back to Sophie. "I know this doesn't give you a lot of time to think about it, but I just spoke to your boss on the phone."

"You have called Dominique? For why?"

"Yes. Actually, we talked about marketing and advertising and your work. He spoke very highly of you, and you have the skills I need. You do know that Canada is a bilingual country and that our second language is French?"

"Yes, I did know this."

"I've needed someone who is bilingual for years, but I could never find anyone with the right marketing skills. You have the skills and experience I need. Dominique says that if you want the job here, that's fine. All he needs is your promise that you will finish up your work for the upcoming 1992 Winter Olympics that you've started."

"You are offering me work? Here? In Canada?"

"Right here in Calgary."

Sophie's head spun. "How did this happen? Brian?"

Brian stepped forward and cupped her chin in both hands. "I want you to stay, Sophie, but I had nothing to offer. I couldn't ask you to give up your friends, your family, your job, everything you know just for me. I talked to Hank, and now, if you want, you've got a job here. And if you want, you can also have a family here in Canada."

"I do not understand."

"Forgive me for my bad accent." Brian cleared his throat. *"Je t'aime*, Sophie."

The tears that had threatened to spill earlier could no longer be contained. Her eyes overflowed, and she had to strain to speak clearly. "I love you, too, Brian."

"I know we haven't known each other very long, and I know you'll need more time to think about it, but I would like to ask if you would think about marrying me; then we can be husband and wife and raise a family of our own in my house with the fence of white."

Her heart pounded. "I think you mean a house with a fence made of pickets."

Brian smiled, and his eyes became glassy for a few seconds. "Yeah. That's exactly what I mean."

She shuffled the bears until she could hold them with one hand, then reached forward to rest her fingers on Brian's arm. "I do not need time to think about this thing. *Mon mémé* Sophia and *mon pépé* Henri, they met at the Olympics in 1896, and they were married and happy for many years until they went to be with God. Yes, I will marry you, and yes, I will accept this new job."

In an instant, Brian's arms were around her, and he kissed her soundly.

She pushed herself away much too soon. "But I must go to catch my flight. I will return as soon as I can."

She turned, ready to run for the opening, but Jean-Pierre blocked her path. "I do not believe you must go. Your visa is good for a long time, and if you get married, you may stay without getting a new passport. I think this is the best thing for you to stay."

Sophie's head swam. "But what about you?"

Jean-Pierre laughed. "I will do the same thing I always do on the plane. You only will be asleep in the seat, so I would not have anyone to speak with in the flight anyway. There will be no difference to me if you are not there. I must go now. I will write you letters. When I land in Paris, I will take your suitcases and send them back to you on the next plane."

Jean-Pierre waved quickly and dashed into the boarding area.

Her new boss, the man who was also her future husband's boss, turned to her. "I'd like Brian at work by noon. He's already had two weeks off, and I need him back. If you want to come to the office after then, we'll sit and talk."

"I would like that."

Hank turned and walked away, leaving her as alone with Brian as they could be in the middle of the busy airport.

"Come on, Sophie," Brian said. "Let's go home."

He picked up her Calgary Flames carryall, and they walked to the exit door.

Sophie was so happy, all she could do was smile and hold tightly to Brian's hand.

The current Olympic Games were over, but like her great-grandmother, her grandmother, and her aunt before her, Sophie had an Olympic memory to cherish forever.

GAIL SATTLER

Gail Sattler has written many books over the years and has many books out with Barbour Publishing in novels, novellas, and works of nonfiction. She has been named as the Favorite Author of the **Heartsong Presents** line for many years in a row. She writes inspirational fiction because she loves happily-ever-afters and believes God has a place in those happy endings. Gail lives in Vancouver, British Columbia—where you don't have to shovel rain—with her husband, sons, and a host of pets, which aren't all mammals. Gail invites readers to visit her website at http://www.gailsattler.com

A Letter to Our Readers

Dear Readers:

In order that we might better contribute to your reading enjoyment, we would appreciate your taking a few minutes to respond to the following questions. When completed, please return to the following: Fiction Editor, Barbour Publishing, Inc., P.O. Box 719, Uhrichsville, OH 44683.

1. Did you enjoy reading *Olympic Memories*?
   ❑ Very much—I would like to see more books like this.
   ❑ Moderately—I would have enjoyed it more if _____
   _____
   _____

2. What influenced your decision to purchase this book?
   (Check those that apply.)
   ❑ Cover   ❑ Back cover copy   ❑ Title   ❑ Price
   ❑ Friends   ❑ Publicity   ❑ Other

3. Which story was your favorite?
   ❑ *Olympic Dreams*   ❑ *Olympic Goals*
   ❑ *Olympic Hopes*   ❑ *Olympic Cheers*

4. Please check your age range:
   ❑ Under 18   ❑ 18–24   ❑ 25–34
   ❑ 35–45   ❑ 46–55   ❑ Over 55

5. How many hours per week do you read? _____

Name _____

Occupation _____

Address _____

City _____ State _____ Zip _____

E-mail _____

HEARTSONG ♥ PRESENTS

Love Stories Are Rated G!

That's for godly, gratifying, and of course, great! If you love a thrilling love story but don't appreciate the sordidness of some popular paperback romances, **Heartsong Presents** is for you. In fact, **Heartsong Presents** is the premiere inspirational romance book club featuring love stories where Christian faith is the primary ingredient in a marriage relationship.

Sign up today to receive your first set of four, never-before-published Christian romances. Send no money now; you will receive a bill with the first shipment. You may cancel at any time without obligation, and if you aren't completely satisfied with any selection, you may return the books for an immediate refund!

Imagine. . .four new romances every four weeks—two historical, two contemporary—with men and women like you who long to meet the one God has chosen as the love of their lives. . .all for the low price of $10.99 postpaid.

To join, simply complete the coupon below and mail to the address provided. **Heartsong Presents** romances are rated G for another reason: They'll arrive Godspeed!

YES! Sign me up for Hearts♥ng!

NEW MEMBERSHIPS WILL BE SHIPPED IMMEDIATELY!
Send no money now. We'll bill you only $10.99 postpaid with your first shipment of four books. Or for faster action, call toll free 1-800-847-8270.

NAME _____

ADDRESS_____

CITY_____ STATE_____ ZIP_____

MAIL TO: HEARTSONG PRESENTS, P.O. Box 721, Uhrichsville, Ohio 44683
or visit www.heartsongpresents.com